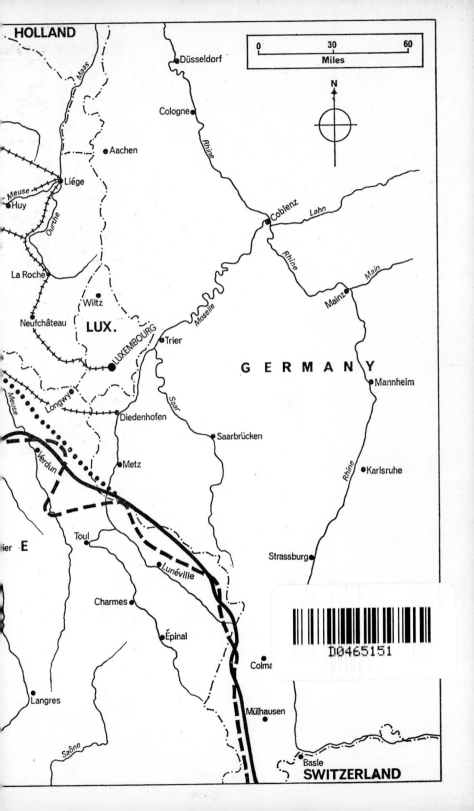

HOLLAND

Düsseldorf

Cologne

Aachen

Maas

Liége

Meuse
Huy

Ourthe

La Roche

Wiltz

LUX.

Neufchâteau

LUXEMBOURG

LUXEMBOURG

Trier

Meuse

Longwy

Diedenhofen

Saar

Verdun

Metz

Saarbrücken

E

Toul

Lunéville

Charmes

Épinal

Langres

Saône

Coblenz

Lahn

Rhine

Rhine

Main

Mainz

GERMANY

Mannheim

Rhine

Karlsruhe

Strassburg

Colm

Mülhausen

Basle

SWITZERLAND

0   30   60
Miles

N

THE BATTLE FOR EUROPE 1918

'During the first four years of the last war the Allies experienced nothing but disaster and disappointment. That was our constant fear; one blow after another, terrible losses, frightful dangers. Everything miscarried. And yet at the end of those four years the morale of the Allies was higher than that of the Germans who had moved from one aggressive triumph to another, and who stood everywhere triumphant invaders of the lands into which they had broken. During that war we repeatedly asked ourselves the question—How are we going to win? And no one was ever able to answer it with much precision, until in the end, quite suddenly, quite unexpectedly, our terrible foe collapsed before us and we were so glutted with victory that in our folly we threw it away.'

Churchill's broadcast of 18 June 1940
at the time of the fall of France

H. ESSAME

THE BATTLE FOR EUROPE 1918

CHARLES SCRIBNER'S SONS
NEW YORK

Printed in Great Britain

Library of Congress Catalog Card Number 72–643

SBN 684–12946–9 (Trade cloth)

A–6.72 (I)

CONTENTS

ACKNOWLEDGEMENTS

The Author would like to express his heartfelt thanks to Mr. D. W. King, OBE, FLA, Chief Librarian, Ministry of Defence Library (Central and Army) for his valuable and knowledgable assistance.

Acknowledgement is due to the following for quoted material appearing in this book: R. Blake (ed.) *The Private Papers of Sir Douglas Haig 1914–18* (Eyre and Spottiswoode, 1952) for page 34; J. H. Boraston *The Eighth Division in War 1914–18* (Medici Society, 1926) for pp. 41 and 109; Sir Frank Fox *G.H.Q.* (Philip Allan & Co, 1920) for page 113; *History of the East Lancashire Regiment in the Great War 1914–18* (Littlebury Brothers, 1936) for page 40; Sir T. Maurice *The Life of General Lord Rawlinson of Trent* (Cassell, 1928) for pp. 103, 115 and 136; Sir J. Monash *The Australian Victories in France in 1918* (Cassell, 1928) for pp. 26–7 and 184; J. J. Pershing *My Experiences in the World War* (Hodder and Stoughton, 1931) for pp. 106 and 154.

The Author and Publishers also wish to thank the following for permission to reproduce the photographs appearing in this book: Australian War Memorial for figs 24–6, 28–9 and 34; E.C.P.–Armeés for fig 2; Imperial War Museum for figs 4, 5, 9, 14, 15, 17, 22–3, 31–2 and 36–8; Radio Times Hulton Picture Library for figs 13, 19, 30, 33, 35, and 39; Roger-Viollet for figs 1, 10, 16, 18 and 27; Süddeutscher Verlag, Munich for figs 3, 8 and 21; Verlag Ullstein, Berlin for figs 6, 7 and 20; US Army for figs 11 and 12.

ILLUSTRATIONS

THE MAPS

Preface

To write with detachment of a war in which one has been personally involved at the rough end and on a low level, even after the lapse of half a century, is not easy. It is therefore my duty at the outset to place my cards face upwards on the table and outline the personal experience which must inevitably colour this attempt to describe the operations of the Allied and German Armies in North-West Europe in 1918. The effects of battle experience in youth like those of early poverty are seldom completely overcome.

I joined my battalion as a second lieutenant early in 1916 and survived the Somme battles in both July and October. In 1917 I was present at the Third Battle of Ypres, generally known as the Passchendaele Offensive, in the attacks of 31 July, 16 August and late October. After a winter spent in the line in front of Ypres the battalion with which I was serving as part of the 8th Division fought with the Fifth and Fourth Armies in Ludendorff's Spring Offensive. I was wounded on 24 April in the night counter-attack on Villers Brettoneux by the 13th and 15th Australian Brigades, the 2nd Northamptonshire Regiment and the 22nd Durham Light Infantry, and evacuated to hospital in England. I managed to get back to my battalion in France in July and served with it till the end of the war in the advances described in this book. The 8th Division's casualties in 1918 exceeded 20,000.

These extenuating circumstances I hope will explain why I cannot go all the way with the late Sir Basil Liddell Hart, an old and generous friend of many years standing, or bask in the sunlight alleged to have been cast on the art of war by the late Major-General Fuller and other protagonists of the tank. All only too often fought their own private war within World War One and after. Neither has the British Official Historian, the late Brigadier-General Sir James E. Edmonds, in his attempt to be scrupulously fair in three monumental volumes of de-humanised English, filled me with awe nor carried me off my feet. When I am asked about the War Poets, now apparently obligatory reading for a university degree in English, I am compelled to reply that I never met any and that their point of view was neither mine nor that of the majority of my generation with whom I came in contact. In general too, my own experience has often led me to doubt the judgments of the many talented writers who have dealt with the battles of the First War with a cock-sure self-assurance which often betrays their lack of battle experience and their ignorance of the mentality of the rank and file of the armies of the period.

Although I found my experience in the First War most useful in fighting the Germans in the Second, my object in writing this book has not been to help others to fight bigger and better wars. Professional interest, however, never fades; the approach of my seventy-fifth year in fact has concentrated my mind wonderfully. I have therefore been unable to resist the temptation to study the operations of 1918 once again, with a view to testing the validity of some of the mythology concerning this war which already clouds the vision of posterity. For example, I have had to ask myself whether the tanks alone were the panacea for victory in 1918 Liddell Hart and Fuller claimed. If so, how, without their help, did the Germans succeed in making deeper penetrations of the front than the Allies when the tables were turned? Popular writers too have gained wide circulations by claiming that the British Generals were callous mediocrities driving men to their death like sheep to the slaughter, that the soldiers in fact were 'lions led by donkeys'. Is this a true picture? Having served under some of them during this particular war and after, I have always found this hard to believe. They at least had dignity, were honourable men and could command obedience. Now that I have had the chance to see something of their private letters and diaries I realise they they were men wracked with anxiety, carrying at times an almost intolerable burden, many of them with their own sons in the forefront of the battle, themselves under pressure from above almost as heavy as that which they had to impose on those below them. In particular, have critics and commentators, so far as the operations of 1918 are concerned, given Haig, who in 1918 fought and won battle after battle on the largest scale in the whole history of the British Army, a raw deal? If not, where in this last year of the war did he put a foot wrong?

I have often been told in those interchanges of clichés which only too frequently masquerade as civilised conversation that the British won the war and the Americans claimed the credit. This sortie therefore into the actual American contribution in particular and into the records as a whole has been for me an illuminating experience. So too have been my attempts to explain how it was that the German Army and the German people, after so many successes and so much self-confidence, came to accept defeat with apparent suddenness. Was there an element of truth in the legend of the 'stab in the back', in the claim that the German armies were not defeated in the field which helped Hitler to power and made the Second War inevitable?

In the past few years high-power academic acrobatics have obscured a vital factor in both orthodox and impure war: if the troops won't fight then no matter what the advantages in wealth, advanced technology, exalted intellectual advice and professional expertise, the war cannot be won. Consideration therefore of the fluctuations in morale recorded in this book may be of some relevance today. I personally still remain a disciple of Field-Marshall Wavell under whom I served who said that past wars should be studied as flesh and blood affairs not as a matter of diagrams, formulae and concepts, not a conflict of technicians, computers and ideologists but of men. Hence perhaps an element of over-emphasis on personalities in this book and in particular on the personal ascendancy of the Australian soldier on the battle-field which made him the best infantryman of the war and perhaps of all time.

I

New Year's Day 1918

Where dawn with silver-sandalled feet crept like a frightened girl.
Oscar Wilde

A silver streak in the eastern sky somewhere over Roulers herald-
ed the coming of the winter dawn. The men of the infantry
battalion in the front line immediately north of the rubble of the
village of Passchendaele faced another day and another year of
war. It was the first of January and the year was 1918. Mercifully
it was freezing hard and there was no wind. Behind them the darkness still brooded over the ruins of Ypres. Slowly the light
strengthened. A flurry of snow during the night had cast a veil of
decency over the vast morass. Shell hole intersected shell hole,
often containing the ghastly remains of a soldier fallen in the
attacks of late November and early December. Around here their
shoulder patches showed them to be mainly Royal Berkshires,
Lincolns and Rifle Brigade. Defiled with mud and slime they lay
huddled on their faces, their equipment still on their backs, their
rifles with bayonet fixed still in their hands, their faces almost as if
they were asleep. British and German steel helmets, petrol tins,
sandbags of jettisoned rations and coke, mingled with the abandoned equipment of the wounded, littered the landscape particularly along the dirty white tapes laid out to show the way to the
front line. Tangles of telephone wire tripped up the unwary.
Further back there were duckboard tracks over the huge tor-
mented bog: here the battery positions were dotted with little red
flags where guns had sunk from view. Before the frost came, one
step off the duckboards had meant sinking to the knees in mud
from which it was impossible to extricate oneself unaided. Men

slipped into it in the dark, and sometimes, after many hours of exposure, died of cold and exhaustion despite efforts made to trace and save them.

The men of the battalion stamped their feet, beat their arms in what they called the 'cabman's warm' and longed for a mug of tea. It had taken them seven hours during the night to cover the four miles between the bivouacs in the old front line of the previous July and these forward posts at the apex of the Passchendaele Salient. They were no strangers to the sector: they had attacked east of Ypres on 31 July and again on 16 August. They had come back again in October and fought there till early December. Their experience differed little from that of others fed into the hopper of Haig's 1917 Offensive at Ypres. Their division had lost in the process 502 officers and 9,073 men—a figure well above its total infantry fighting strength. Now after a fortnight's rest near St Omer they were back again. This time their luck was in: the hard frost had made the going easier and there had been sufficient moonlight to see the half-frozen pools formed by the larger shell holes. Admittedly a burst of machine gun fire had caught the captain and headquarters of one of the companies as they moved into the forward posts—for that is all they were. There was no continuous front line; there were no communication trenches. The capture of the Passchendaele Ridge in October had been announced to the British public as a great victory and would be claimed as one by future historians of repute. The truth was that like so many battles in this muddled war it had unfortunately been incomplete. The northern end of the ridge stretching from Pass-chendaele to Westroosebeek had remained in German hands. Here there were two redoubts giving observation over the British salient. A costly attempt to take them in early December had expired in the liquid mud. Any movement therefore in daylight on this New Year's Day on this part of the front would almost inevitably bring down a storm of Germany artillery and machine gun fire.

It was nearly 8.00 a.m. 'Stand to' had now lasted for half an hour. From the headquarters trench, the adjutant who had just finished inspecting the rifles of the signallers and checking that each of them had a position from which, if need be, he could fire, could just see the reserve company about two hundred yards away on the right. They too were stamping their feet. Soon they would 'stand down' and the daily ritual of rubbing the feet with whale oil and changing socks would begin. Working in pairs they would massage each other's feet and rub them with whale oil: this was to prevent 'Trench foot', a form of inflammation due to prolonged exposure to cold and slush combined with lack of exercise. To incur this was a disciplinary offence. The rubbing and the dry socks certainly were effective and the whale oil provided a useful fuel. With a piece of the flannelette issued for cleaning rifles in a cigarette tin and soaked in it, a man could heat a mess tin full of tea. To attempt to use the normal method of cooking in the trenches—a coke brazier for heating water or frying bacon —would inevitably raise smoke and attract enemy fire. Before coming into the line, therefore, the bacon ration for three days had been drawn in advance, boiled and distributed in the vain hope that the men would spread out its consumption. The odds were that they would eat the lot on the first day. They had also brought in with them sandbags full of biscuits, cheese, tins of corned beef, jam and milk, tea and sugar mixed together sufficient for the next twenty-four hours. Given luck carrying parties would bring up a further supply, arriving in the early hours of the morning. When the weather was really bad in this sector they often failed to get through or lost their way in the dark. The hope that the brigadier would certify that the weather was inclement and send forward a rum ration with the carrying parties sustained many.

To the adjutant it seemed strange that this flat expanse of misery should be called a ridge: in fact it was little more than a gentle rise. Two hundred yards ahead he could vaguely pick out some of the positions of the forward companies among the shell holes where the last attacks a month ago had finally fizzled out. All was quiet now and would remain so for an hour or two. The Germans like the British had their own domestic problems to which to attend: breakfast, weapon inspection, answering the questions of their masters who were now getting down to the business of the day after a good night's sleep. Very little digging had been possible in the almost liquid mud of a mild December. The battalion headquarters itself was a mere shallow trench with bivouac sheets stretched over it and two six-foot lengths of duck-board at the bottom. Thank God the frost was holding up the walls! Seated in his upturned steel helmet the commanding officer was still asleep, whacked to the wide. He had been on his feet all night groping his way in the darkness in the hope of finding his companies. There was just enough room for him, the adjutant, a couple of signallers with the field telephone and a clerk. The regimental sergeant-major and the runners were in another trench about twenty yards away. Someone had brought in the personal effects of the officer killed during the night. The watch apparently was missing and the regimental sergeant-major was insisting on knowing why. The signals officer was out somewhere in the waste trying to find the break in the cable to the headquarters of the brigade. They were all virtually cut off from the rest of the world until the fall of night once more made movement possible without inevitably bringing down enemy fire.

This was the end product of the Third Battle of Ypres—this vast obscene excrescence swallowing up men in the mud. It had ended on ground incapable of being drained or of being approached in daylight. To secure this abomination of desolation the British had in 1917 written off nearly a quarter of a million men.

The soldiers of this Army who now faced the final year of the war were unique. There had never been a British Army quite like them before and there never would be again. They were mainly infantry. Haig had very nearly 800 infantry battalions like this one in the front line east of Ypres. They in no way resembled the professional soldiers of the 1914 Regular Army, of whom few now survived in the front-line units. They lacked the enthusiasm of the pre-war Territorials. They had none of the sense of dedication of Kitchener's New Armies who were volunteers to a man, the very cream of their generation. These were the disillusioned survivors of the Somme and the big battles of 1917, many of them back at duty once more after being wounded, together with conscripts called up under the Act of 1916.

Haig had 60 divisions of them, each about 17,000 strong and organised as three brigades, each of four battalions. In a month's time the number of battalions in the brigade would be reduced to three, each theoretically of 30 officers and 977 other ranks of whom at most some 800 were ever present with the unit: the balance staffed the vast administrative set-up in the rear of the trenches. Within each division there was also a pioneer battalion primarily designed to provide labour for the engineers but also available and frequently used as a normal infantry battalion.

There was a machine gun battalion too with 48 Vickers guns. In the divisional artillery there were eight batteries of six guns of which three-quarters were 18 pounders and the rest 4.5 howitzers. Medium and heavy artillery came under corps control. Each infantry brigade had a battery of six so-called light Stokes mortars. These consisted of a heavy plain steel barrel with a spike at the bottom, a cumbrous bipod and a base plate like, and at least as heavy as, a manhole cover. A ballastite cartridge was attached to the base of the shell which was slid down on to the spike thus exploding the propellant. The arrival of these primitive pieces in the front line was usually greeted with marked coolness on the part of the permanent residents, as every available German gun invariably opened up on them the moment they fired. It was some consolation to the infantry on this frosty New Year morning that their own battery had lost its way in the dark: that was one nuisance less at any rate.

Within the division there were two companies of Royal Engineers—a surprisingly low number in view of the vast engineering problems presented by position warfare. They were, most unjustly, heartily disliked by the infantry who when out of the line were called upon to provide almost nightly a never-ending succession of working parties. Unlike his German opposite number, the British infantryman was not remarkable for his industry: it was surprising how little digging he would do under cover of night when supervision was impossible. When in the line the German soldier burrowed like a mole: the British soldier did what he was told to do and no more, firmly convinced that it was better to live at slightly increased risk and personal discomfort than to perform an uncongenial task. Signals were represented by one company only, primarily providing primitive line telegraphy by D3 cable. Over 1,000 yards voice telephony in the forward area was often barely audible.

In the infantry battalion there were a small headquarters, a signal section, a pioneer section (mainly carpenters) and four companies each able to produce in the front line what was called a 'bayonet strength' of about 120 men organised in four platoons. The regimental transport was entirely horse-drawn and based on the GS limbered wagon, a curious vehicle originally designed to meet the conditions of the South African veldt. Each company had its own brace of mules for carrying ammunition. These

B

animals normally lived in transport lines well out of artillery range, tenderly groomed and regularly fed. Visiting generals never failed to pay them a call.

The soldier's individual weapon was the short Lee-Enfield rifle. This was a well-balanced, accurate weapon easily handled and capable of delivering 15 rounds a minute in skilled hands. Many had now forgotten what a good weapon it was. There was also the Mills grenade still in use fifty years later: this by means of an attachment and with special cartridges could be fired as a rifle grenade, but seldom was. Finally each platoon had a Lewis gun, a primitive light automatic with a revolving magazine, rather like a frying pan with spikes. This speedily became useless in mud. It also had a wide range and to the mechanically minded an intriguing range of stoppages.

By this stage of the war the infantryman had descended almost to the level of a beast of burden: his load was formidable for, apart from his weapons, he had to carry a pick or a shovel, wire cutters, a Very pistol and cartridges, flares for signalling to the air, a square anti-gas box respirator, and, if he was a rifleman, 170 rounds of small arms ammunition. Add to these his personal necessities, a heavy greatcoat which soaked up the wet like a sponge, a rubber groundsheet, three pairs of thick socks, a spare woollen undervest and long pants of impressive thickness, an iron ration of a three-quarter pound tin of bully beef, two packets of cement-hard biscuits and tea and sugar. The ammunition boot was torture to wear till broken in. Each man also had a heavy mess tin, a knife, fork and spoon and his washing and shaving kit. In winter, leather jerkins were added for good measure. The lot weighed 64 lb.

There was one cooker for each company which for obvious reasons could only be used when not in action. This was a horse-drawn coke-fired boiler on wheels resembling an old-fashioned type of tar engine which could produce, according to choice, either stew or tea. Behind it when on the move marched the two company cooks, their uniforms black from head to foot with grease. Sometimes with macabre wit they would hang an enamel chamber pot on the cooker. This they would use for ladling out the tea or stew. There were always tea leaves in the stew and the tea had a strong suggestion of onions with an undertone of stewed jute from the sandbag in which it had reached its destination. On rare occasions the cook sergeant would construct a mud oven and there would be the luxury of roast meat. In the villages behind the lines the French and Belgian peasants carried on a thriving trade in *pommes frites*, omelettes, the bread of the country, slightly sour and glutinous, and salted butter sometimes faintly rancid.

The mood of these men in the forward posts on this bitter New Year's Day could be summed up as one of stoical endurance combined with an element of bewilderment. Any desire they had ever had to attack the Germans had long since vanished: now they counted the minutes and hours still to be endured before relief came. Of hatred for their enemies there was no apparent evidence. The majority, fortunately for themselves, were of limited imagination and their horizon seldom extended beyond the confines of their own battalion. Fifty years later the impression which remained of them was above all one of immense mutual loyalty and good nature. Order them to go forward and they would stolidly advance, however intense the fire; order them to stand fast and they would stay till told to go or to the end. For the most part they were sociable and kind-hearted men who sang sentimental songs when on the march out of the line. They went to sleep on the slightest provocation. They were unselfish and generous, as quick to go to the aid of a wounded enemy as of a wounded friend. They had one supreme quality, a capacity to endure without flinching prolonged bombardment and exposure greater than that of many soldiers of World War Two. The link with their regimental officers was very close; common exposure to hardship and danger had welded them into an association, an alliance from which were excluded the Higher Command and the civilians at home. In a dim way they felt that they were a race apart, morally superior to other men who lacked their experience, as indeed they were, and that henceforth, if they survived, they would continue to be.

There were now many married men in the ranks and the effect of news from home on them was bad. Wives in their letters complained of shortage of food; eggs they said were eightpence each on the Black Market. Milk was scarce. People were being told to go to bed early and save the coal. Men returning from leave told of notices in the public houses with the words 'No Beer'; some of the women filling shells had turned yellow and were nicknamed 'canaries'; all working on munitions were earning money beyond their wildest dreams and spending it without thought for the morrow. Anxiety for the well-being of his wife and family haunted many a sentry as he peered into the darkness of No-Man's-Land during the interminable nights in the front line.

Within their ranks the process of natural selection under fire had thrown up a magnificent breed of warrant and non-commissioned officers, often men in civil life accustomed to take the lead in the rough work of the world, ex-foremen in quarries and factories, in brickfields and the building trade, in the steel mills and in the docks. Sometimes the harsh life of the trenches had set alight the spark of leadership in unexpected quarters; in shop assistants, in hotel staffs and ill-paid clerks from obscure and dreary jobs. These non-commissioned officers, often illiterate and usually inarticulate, bristled with practical sense. They were the men who took charge when a shell burst caused a trench to collapse and buried some of their comrades, when a mule or a man got stuck in a flooded shell hole or when the wounded fell thick and fast. Those who before the war had been in the Regular Army and now had risen to warrant rank had immense prestige and carried their authority with ease and dignity despite their illiteracy and inability to express themselves except in the crudest terms.

In the circles which dealt with officer supply in Whitehall and at higher headquarters the Staff spoke of scraping the bottom of the barrel. The battles of 1914 and 1915 had virtually eliminated the younger Regular Officers and many of the pre-war Territorial Officers as well. Those who now survived were either on the Staff or in their mid-twenties commanding battalions. The commanders of companies and platoons in the front line were almost without exception wartime second lieutenants with appropriate temporary ranks. Indeed the casualty lists in the newspapers were now headed 'Second Lieutenants unless otherwise stated'. No longer could it be said, as had been possible before the Battle of the Somme, that they came from one class. The Public and Grammar School boys were now a drop in the bucket; they had been amongst the first to volunteer and had paid the highest price in the holocausts of 1916 and 1917 for the chances of being killed for a junior officer were far greater than for a private soldier. Now with boys of this class fresh from school there were Englishmen from all parts of the world who had felt it to be their duty to return home to fight in the war, men of enterprise, men who had found irksome the stuffiness and stagnation of pre-1914 British society; sometimes they were 'ne'er do wells' and remittance men who had gone overseas, as they said, for their country's good. A wise provision enabled commanders to select men for commissioned rank on the basis of their services in the field alone. These men were towers of strength, sometimes from the ranks of the pre-war Army, sometimes men of very humble social origin but all had the quality of leadership inborn and tested under fire. These young officers formed a society of their own based on mutual loyalty and trust from which distinctions of class had long since vanished. Their creed met the need of the hour; for them courage was the highest of the virtues; it was better to die than to betray fear; as officers they must set the example, their duty to their men overrode all other considerations, suffering must be endured in silence. It was as simple as that. The majority were in their twenties: in fact so severe was the physical strain that men over thirty were regarded as past their prime. With their men they formed a cross section of the tougher elements in the British people. They were magnificent potential fighting material but they had one defect—a defect which would soon bring them and their country close to almost irretrievable disaster. Although they had seen much fighting, they and their brigade and divisional commanders and staff were nonetheless, in comparison with the Germans, virtually untrained for any form of mobile war.

The Commander-in-Chief, Haig, probably had faced greater difficulties than any other British general in any British war. It has never been convincingly demonstrated that any other of the senior officers available would have done better than he did or shown more imagination. Nevertheless ultimate responsibility for the state of training of the Army four years after the outbreak of war must rest mainly on his shoulders. In extenuation it can be said that by origin he was a cavalryman who saw battles as the early stages of a process which would enable the arm nearest to his heart to clinch the victory. He could not bring himself to face the fact that the day of horsed cavalry had long since passed away. Unfortunately for him and his men it had turned out to be an infantry war. On the Somme he had hoped to blast his way through by means of overwhelming artillery fire, with his infantry attacking in wave after wave almost as they had done in the Crimea: he had failed and he had gone on far too long. In 1917 once again he had gone on too long. As a result he had written off well over half a million of his countrymen and almost broken the hearts of some at least of the survivors in two years of apparently futile war. It is not surprising that Lloyd George, with his lively mind, lack of scruple and vivid imagination, had lost confidence in his judgment. Lip service indeed had been paid by him and his faithful subordinate generals to the need for training but little had been done. The Germans held their defences in very great depth with a thin screen, mainly of machine guns in the front line, behind which they had constructed reserve lines covered by forests of barbed wire and well provided with shelter not only from fire but from the weather. Life therefore for the German soldier had been far more comfortable and less exhausting than for his British counterpart. When brought out of the line Haig's men were only too often too tired to treat training seriously: the mere struggle to survive had stifled any tendency towards creative thought. When it was proposed to the French farmers that their land should be used for training purposes they raised dramatic protests. In consequence many commanders were glad to have an excuse for doing nothing. It was not until late 1917 that Haig appointed Maxse with a special staff to evolve in the light of the vast experience now at their disposal a technique and tactics suitable for the conditions of battle they would obviously have to face in 1918. By the end of 1917 the problem of how to end the stalemate on the Western Front with the arms and equipment available and of getting the armies at long last on the move was baffling to a degree, but it was not insoluble. Indeed on the other side of the lines was a commander who would soon show how it could be done.

In the north about Nieuport the Belgians held the trenches in the sand dunes and behind the inundations up to a few miles north of the sinister city of Ypres. Here about Houthulst Forest they linked up with the base of the great British salient running out to Passchendaele: thence the flimsy line of shell-hole defences swung south-west to the area of the great crater on the Messines Ridge captured the previous June. Roughly south from here the line for 30 miles or more ran through the mining villages and pit head works and slag heaps of the Lille coalfield. Here it had been virtually stationary since 1915. The trenches in this strip, although trivial in comparison with those of the Germans, did at least include some deep dugouts, moderately effective communication trenches and drains. Then came the great bastion of Vimy Ridge commanding the approaches from Lille. Due south of Arras it then continued across the devastated area of the old Somme battlefield towards St Quentin where, under protest, the British were in the process of taking over a further 25 miles from the French. Altogether the British front line was 125 miles long. Judged as a defensive system it was a poor advertisement for years of effort. Haig and his commanders had always regarded it as the jumping-off area for their next offensives rather than as a defensive system in which men could fight and live. It was only too often badly sited: it embodied much ground, the 'sacred soil of France' held for its own sake and no valid military reason. Very little work had been done on the rear defences. In comparison with the German system opposite it was slipshod, squalid and amateur.

The French defensive system running east and south to the Swiss border was little better. Within it Pétain was slowly reviving the morale of the French Armies, now convalescent after the mutinies of the previous summer, the seriousness of which he had skilfully concealed both from his allies and his enemy. In Lorraine in the tiny hamlets opposite the St Mihiel Salient there had now arrived four large American divisions, each 28,000 strong and consisting of one field artillery brigade and two infantry brigades. To the war-weary French they seemed a race apart—for the most part young, physically fit and bursting with enthusiasm only equalled by that of the British New Armies before the holocaust of the Somme. Pershing, their Commander-in-Chief was proving a hard taskmaster: their standards of discipline and turnout were as strict as those of the British Brigade of Guards. He had set up his headquarters in barracks in the little town of Chaumont on the Upper Marne 60 miles south of the St Mihiel Salient. Already under pressure from the French and British to solve their man-power problems by feeding his men into their divisions at battalion strength, Pershing's mind was clear on three vital issues: he would not commit his troops to battle until they were trained, he would not allow them to fight piecemeal under foreign command and that finally he would build up an army of three millions so that his political masters in America would have a decisive voice in the settlement of the Peace Treaty at the end of the war.

Under his ruthless supervision his four divisions, the vanguard of the mighty army, were now training in open warfare varied by periods in the line during which hand-picked French officers acted as instructors. All would soon become famous. The 1st was a regular division; the 2nd consisted mainly of Marines; the 26th came for the most part from Massachussetts. It was a National Guard division and had brought with it a tradition stretching back to the War of Independence. The 42nd Rainbow Division came from every state in the Union. Its Chief-of-Staff was Douglas MacArthur. Already their patrols had achieved a reputation for offensive eagerness in No-Man's-Land. By 1 April they would be ready for combat. Meanwhile when not training they bore with good humour the all-pervading mud, the smell of the manure heaps outside the barns and cottages in which they rested, and the rapacity of the local peasants.

It was on the fresh impetus which these comrades from beyond the Atlantic would give to the struggle and their own efforts that the British troops in the north based their hopes of victory on this dark January day. Meanwhile they faced the stark reality of the world of the trenches—a world with its own ethos, its own values and indeed its own mythology, a world which its inhabitants loathed but to which, paradoxically, they were proud to belong. An invisible but nonetheless sharply defined barrier cut them off mentally and emotionally from those manning the elaborate command system and vast logistic backing of Haig's huge army, the largest ever commanded by any British general. To this complex organisation on this frosty New Year's Day of 1918 we must now turn.

2

The Sinews of War

Administration (logistics) is the real crux of Generalship.
Field-Marshal Wavell

Behind the devastation of the forward battle zone night and day the flow of traffic never ceased. In the wan daylight of this New Year's Day over 200 trains slowly steamed their way at little more than walking speed between the base ports at Calais and Boulogne and the railheads at St Omer, Hazebrouck, Poperinghe, Doullens and St Pol and the vast sidings at Longeau near Amiens where the railways from Le Havre, Rouen and Abbeville all linked up. So slow and fitful were the trains that men would jump out of the covered wagons, marked 'Hommes 40, Chevaux 8', to get hot water from the engine driver to brew tea: they were standard trains, all of one sort, equally adapted to the transport of men, animals, ammunition, supplies and forage. Sometimes there was a single passenger coach for officers, by this stage of the war often minus doors and window glass. Sometimes it took ten hours and more to travel the 60 miles or so from the Bases to the Front. On the straight paved roads endless marching columns of men sweated their way to the front or back to rest in the barns of the villages behind the lines. At ten minutes to every clock hour they halted, took off their heavy packs and en masse relieved their bladders. Punctually at the hour on the blast of a whistle they fell in in their fours and marched on. The steel tyres of horse-drawn transport rattled on the paving stones. At the goods yards at Hazebrouck, St Pol, Doullens and Poperinghe the solid-tyred lorries of the corps motor transport columns lined up to collect supplies, forage and ammunition and ferry them forward in due course to refilling points in the areas of the forward divisions where the quartermasters awaited them. The roads were battered to bits: on them amongst the ceaseless traffic pioneers in muddy jerkins fought a never-ending fight to keep them open.

Along the coast from Calais to Boulogne, Étaples and Le Touquet, amongst the dunes stretched a vast belt of tented camps with a few Nissen huts here and there: these were the base depots, the transit centres for troops arriving from England. Here the fusty smell from a hundred smouldering incinerators rose to the heavens. Huge dumps of stores fringed the by-roads. In this belt too, were the big Base Hospitals including No. 9 General for sufferers from VD and reputed, quite unjustly, to be crowded out by the Army Service Corps and the Royal Army Chaplains' Department. Seemingly endless queues of men were moving on and off the boats in the harbours of Boulogne and Calais, those on their way home for ten days leave bursting with high spirits and good humoured badinage: those returning to the Front sullen and silent. Flanking the course of the ships as they crossed the Channel flew the silver balloons of the Royal Naval Air Service known to the troops on account of their suggestive shape as 'Virgin's Dreams' (the German soldiers' nickname for their own sausage balloons was virtually the same: soldiers' minds whatever their nationality run on similar lines and levels). To land at Folkestone and Dover, where the leave trains waited, was for some heaven itself. To them, as they sped towards London, even the washing on the clothes' lines breathed romance and every girl who waved seemed a princess. Very soon they were running into the great vault of Victoria Station: the doors of the carriages burst open and a great crowd surged towards the exits and the Underground. Kindly old men in grey cotton uniforms of sorts with 'GR' armbands, which inevitably had won them the title of 'Georgeous Wrecks', came forward to guide them on their way across London. There were mobile canteens at which ladies of what had been the world of Beauty and Fashion dispensed overdrawn tea. Outside the station there were still taxis to be had, some with gas bags on the roof to save petrol.

The light of the raw afternoon faded over Grosvenor Gardens and Buckingham Palace Road. Now the traffic was the other way: sad little family parties centring round a heavily laden soldier going back to the Front, fathers in later middle age fighting hard to hide the thought that this might be the last time they ever saw their sons, wives and mothers openly weeping; young officers determined at all costs to look cheerful as they passed what they knew might well be their last few minutes with some golden girl. Near the cloakrooms a dense crowd of soldiers milled around the RTO's office; some red-hatted military policemen were propelling a couple of drunks through the khaki-clad crowd.

Outside night had now come down on darkened streets. Within the station Rembrandtesque dark shadows, wisps of smoke and steam suggested a sinister dream by a great artist. There was a hiss of steam and the noise of many metalled feet. The returning leave trains waited. There were six of them side by side at the departure platforms. Into five of them piled a great crowd of men with bulging packs on their backs to sit five a side in badly lit compartments: these were the regimental officers and men return-ing to the trenches—silent, each preoccupied with his own thoughts. In sharp contrast the sixth train was brightly lit: it had two dining cars and all the carriages were first class. Obsequious myrmidons of the RTO guided red-hatted and red-tabbed officers to their reserved seats. It was nearly 6.30 and the waiters in the dining cars were already taking orders for drinks. There was frantic whistling; a tall figure in a uniform fitting so perfectly that he seemed to have been poured into it, resplendent with buttons and leather shining with a glow only attainable by a batman of genius determined at all costs to keep his job, attended by the RTO himself, stepped into his reserved compartment. Slowly with a whistle and a shudder or so the Staff Train drew out into the winter night.

The irony of this nightly demonstration at Victoria Station of the great gap between the leaders and the led, this blatant display of privilege was to rankle in the minds of the soldiers in the front line and to survive in the national memory for the next half century. There were too many of these red-hatted and red-tabbed officers. In the Second World War only colonels and above wore red; in the First War even such lowly members of the Staff hierarchy as staff captains were thus arrayed. Armbands of many colours adorned their sleeves, some of them chromatic outrages such as the red and blue of GHQ—and were blatantly flaunted in the restaurants and theatres of London. Popular opinion, quite wrongly, lumped both commanders and staff officers into one category. The legend that they led lives of luxury in châteaux behind the lines whilst the soldiers wallowed in the mud, fostered by hypersensitive intellectuals and poets, was already born. The story went the rounds of the corps commander at the dinner table talking to his ADC. Outside the wind howled and the rain and sleet came down in torrents. Said the ADC to the General: 'The men must be cold in the trenches tonight, Sir.' 'Nonsense,' came the reply, 'they've got their greatcoats. Pass the port.'

When the British are faced by adversity, usually as a result of their persistent refusal throughout their history to exercise foresight, look facts in the face and make proper provision for their own defence, there arises a demand for equal sharing of equal misery. In this war Lloyd George when Minister of Munitions, and Haig and Robertson, the CIGS, had by 1918 built up a better logistic system than their countrymen deserved. The senior staff officers of the British Army had never in peace had the opportunity of practising the movement and maintenance of troops on a large scale. They were now like men trained to run a small shop in a provincial town suddenly called upon to manage a mammoth London store. Inevitably with the expansion of the Army many were now filling jobs far above their ceiling. This included elderly officers recalled from the reserve; officers passed over in peace-time filled key appointments and held ranks which even they sometimes recognised as beyond their capacity and deserts. There was no justification, however, for the fable, widely current at the time, that there was a mutual agreement between the British and the Germans that their respective General Headquarters should be spared from air raids. This, the narrators would remark, was a classic instance of British stupidity: the Germans scored both ways. Their staff was spared which was valuable to them. The British Staff was spared: this was even more valuable to the Germans. The truth is far different. By 1918, on the administrative side, the teething troubles were over and there now existed at Montreuil an organisation on the grand scale which in the coming year would stand up to unprecedented stress.

In 1914 and 1915 St Omer had served well enough for the BEF fighting on the extreme left flank of an Allied Army predominantly French. By March 1916, however, the British Army had expanded tenfold from five to some 50 divisions. In this war for every rifleman in the trenches or gunner in the gun pits there was a need for at least three other men to keep him supplied with food, clothing, ammunition and all his other necessities, simple though they were in comparison with those of the wars of a later day. St Omer was now ill situated to control the vast logistic build-up which had come into being. GHQ had therefore moved to Montreuil.

The choice of this little town justified itself by its obviousness. It stood on the main road from London to Paris though not on the main railway line which would have been an inconvenience. It was a little country market town with only about 3,000 inhabitants and those of a character unlikely to cause security complications. Furthermore it was centrally situated to serve the needs of a force based primarily on Calais, Boulogne, Dieppe and Le Havre with a front stretching from the Somme to the Belgian Frontier. A celebrated military pundit asked to define what is wanted for a great headquarters once said: 'A central remoteness or, to put it another way. a remote centrality.' Montreuil provided both the central position and the isolation from the distractions of traffic and a large population whether civil or military. The barracks of the huge 'École Militaire Preparatoire D'Infanterie' offered ample office accommodation. Within the little town and in the neighbouring châteaux, which seemed almost to have been designed to accommodate headquarters, there were adequate billets. Although by 1918 a number of Nissen huts had had to be put up, Haig's headquarters was on a far less pretentious scale than some of the great headquarters of the Second War. Its total population never exceeded 5,000 including the troops needed for its local protection. At first the garrison was provided by the Artists Rifles, then by the Honourable Artillery Company, then by the Newfoundland Regiment and finally by the Guernsey Regiment.

Montreuil itself had a long history: from it had sailed the Roman fleet which invaded Britain. In the sixteenth century its harbour had silted up and its importance had declined. A century later Vauban had built the fortifications surrounding the town and the citadel. Before 1914 its old-world charm had attracted English and American artists hoping to capture inexpensively in paint the ever-changing prospect from the ramparts. To the south gently undulating fields stretched towards the Forest of Crècy; westward, close cultivation extended almost to the sea: to the north lay the woods and the marshes along the Canche and to the east the valley of the river and the hills on its banks. Soon, with the coming of spring the wallflowers in the old walls would burst into bloom; in high summer the purple of great masses of valerian would vie with the brilliant red of the poppies in the green fields below stretching as far as the eye could reach.

For the 300 officers at Montreuil there was neither time nor leisure to enjoy the ever-changing beauties of their surroundings. All were at their desks by 8.30 a.m. and none left earlier than 10.30 p.m. Theoretically they were allowed an hour for exercise but few were ever able to take more than a walk on the ramparts. In times of stress, hours of work often extended to midnight and beyond: half-an-hour was allowed for meals. Staff officers occasionally fainted from sheer pressure of work: men fresh from duty with their regiments sometimes wilted away under the unaccustomed strain. All led a monastic life: the only women they ever saw were the waitresses in the Officers' Club. This institution was run by the Expeditionary Force Canteens, the ancestors of NAAFI and here originated that peculiar cuisine with which later generations would always associate it. Old Contemptibles over half a century later could still recollect the flavour of the plaice— invariably slightly off in spite of the nearness of the sea—and the odd taste of the tea. No smoking was allowed before 8.20 p.m. The waitresses were all members of Queen Mary's Army Auxiliary Corps, the predecessors of the ATS of the Second War, and the elegantly dressed WRAC of today. They were the only women, apart from the local housewives usually shuffling along in carpet slippers or sabots and clad in dingy black, ever seen in the neighbourhood. The QMAAC dressed from neck to ankle in grim utilitarian khaki, jealously shielded night and day from contact with men, maintained, at least in the public eye, those standards of propriety personified by their Colonel-in-Chief, Queen Mary. All cafés and private houses were out of bounds to them: they were never allowed to 'walk out' with a soldier except by permission of one of their officers.

Although most of the senior appointments at GHQ were held by regular officers, the Staff now included a considerable element of civilian ability. At least half came from the New Armies: very many had been seriously wounded in action and were unfit for front line duty. There was no room for the sychophant and the playboy: if there had been, the headquarters would not have been able to shoulder its gigantic task and stand the immense strain which would soon be placed upon it.

Much of the literature of this and other wars has been written by men with little personal experience of what actually goes on at the sharp end of an Army and even less comprehension of what its day-to-day management involves, especially at the higher levels. A brief examination here of the functions of GHQ in this war is therefore necessary if what lies ahead is to be understood.

Firstly, it was the link between the BEF and the Government with whom the Commander-in-Chief communicated via the Secretary of State for War. It was also the link between the Army and the Allied Armies—the French, the American, Belgian and Portuguese each of whom maintained a mission at GHQ just as the British maintained their missions at the various Allied head- quarters. Quite apart from operations, discussion of which was confined to the Chief of the General Staff and the heads of the foreign missions, there was an immense amount of technical, supply and financial business between the Allies. There was hardly an officer at GHQ who did not in some detail come into contact with these foreign missions all equally anxious to get what they considered was their legitimate share of British war production now in full spate.

The Commander-in-Chief's responsibility for the strategy of the campaign, for planning and for the direct control of operations inevitably involved almost every branch of the headquarters. GHQ had to arrange the supply from home and from its own workshops of all the Army's insatiable and multifarious needs, from a tank or a 15-inch howitzer to a tin of dubbin, of all the ammunition and all the food supplies for man and beast. Every month there arrived at the Base ports no less than 800,000 tons of stores. There were two-and-a-quarter million men to be fed and half a million animals. War production in England had now reached its peak. Between March 1915 and March 1917 ammunition output had increased twenty-eightfold. By 1 January 1918 it had in- creased a further fourfold. In response to the drive imparted to it by the Ministers of Munitions, first Lloyd George and then Winston Churchill, a further great acceleration not only in am- munition production but also in output of tanks, guns and every type of war equipment was imminent. The problem now had

become one of movement rather than supply. A month's require-
ment of ammunition alone weighed over a quarter of a million
tons. The headquarters managed a transport system which used
half-a-million horses and mules, 20,000 motor lorries running
nine million miles a month, light railways carrying more than
half-a-million tons a month, and ran every day 250 trains on the
broad gauge lines of the British Zone. It was constantly building
new railways and new roads and developing harbour facilities.
It ran big canal and sea services, forestry and agricultural under-
takings, repair shops, laundries and many other installations on a
large scale. The medical services alone, field ambulances, the
casualty clearing stations, the motor ambulance columns and
trains and the base hospitals were a vast commitment. There were
big veterinary hospitals and remount depots, huge reinforcement
camps, immense depots of engineer and other stores at the base
and in what was called the zone of the Lines of Communication.

In the year which lay ahead this gigantic logistic set-up would
have to be capable of adjusting itself to conditions varying almost
from day to day. So long as the front was static, the problem was
comparatively simple. Wastage of men, horses and materials could
be calculated with some certainty and replaced by a routine process. If however it should be decided to mount a large-scale attack,
then there would inevitably be a great strain on transport and
supply. The need for secrecy in particular would raise infinite
complications and difficulties. New roads and new railways would
probably have to be made: traffic in the area of the attack would
at least be doubled. The big problem however would be the
build-up of ammunition. In a quiet sector two divisions could get
along with about three trains daily. For a big attack ten divisions
might be concentrated in the sector: in this case in the preparatory
stage of the attack they would need 33 trains a day and during the
offensive 27 trains a day—in other words the rail traffic to and in
the sector would be multiplied fifteen times. The immediate
prospect however was not a continuation of the ponderous offensives of 1916 and 1917 but of a gigantic all-out attack by the
Germans. To meet this the Staff had calculated that the require-
ment would be 25 per cent less for rail transport and had built up
reserves of food, ammunition and stores in the forward area. They
had also tied up scarce rolling stock by keeping ammunition
loaded on trains held near the major railway junctions. The

Foch, Haig and Clemenceau (left to right) at their momentous meeting on Amiens railway station

2 Pétain, the French Commander-in-Chief

3 Ludendorff

4 Travers Clarke—the Quartermaster General who fed and moved Haig's huge armies

5 Von Hutier, Commander of the Eighteenth Army in the Spring Offensive

6 German transport pressing forward over the Old Somme battlefield, late March 191

difficulty here was that no one knew where the blow would fall. There were grave doubts on the part of some members of the Staff whether the system had the flexibility a fluid battle in which the enemy had the initiative would inevitably demand. Their anxiety would soon prove well founded. The great forward dumps in particular were hostages to fortune. Finally the Staff had to peer into what seemed the far distant future and plan for that general offensive the prospect of which seemed remote on this bleak New Year's Day of 1918.

Of the branches of the Staff, the quartermaster-general's was by far the largest. In its complexity it vied with the great industrial organisations of a later age such as ICI, Shell and General Motors. Travers Clarke, the QMG had two major-generals as deputies. Under them were no less than seventeen directorates and five inspector-generals. Agricultural production, postal services, canteens, engineer stores, hirings and requisitions, labour, pay, remounts, salvage, supplies, transport, transportation, veterinary services, war graves and works all came within their sphere. Under the director-general of transportation there were a further six directorates controlling construction, docks, inland water transport, light railways, rail traffic and roads. A thousand locomotives had to be kept running. The system would soon have to move half-a-million men in a week and one-and-a-half million in a month on an overstrained rail system sometimes near the verge of breakdown.

Plato placed the ability 'to get his men their rations and every kind of stores needed for war' first, in order of priority of the qualities essential in a good general. Ever since all front-line soldiers, although for the most part unaware that the great Greek philosopher ever existed, have held the same view. In his new quartermaster-general, Travers Clarke, Haig at this crucial moment had at last found a man with the courage, drive and knowledge to handle this vast administrative machine. His substantive rank was only that of major. At 47 he was at the height of his powers. He carried his authority with ease but no general ever made sterner demands on his officers and men or overrode more obstacles. He had one rule to which he never permitted an exception—that it was 'the fighting man who must be considered first and last'. He was quite willing that his staff should labour to the extreme point of endurance to take any load off the man in the

C

trenches. He did not like about him men, however clever, who had not seen fighting. 'Bad staff work arises mostly from not knowing the difference between an office and a trench' was one of his aphorisms.

For his selection and for the fact that the logistic system of the Army was soundly based and ably manned, Haig could at least take a good deal of the credit. Until 1907 there never had been a firm British doctrine on the subject. Except in the days of Marlborough and Wellington, muddle, waste and improvisation had characterised the war administration of the Army. Haig, at this time Haldane's right-hand man in carrying through the most drastic and thorough reforms in all the Army's chequered history, had forced through a hostile conference at the Staff College at Camberley the manual *Field Service Regulations, Part II* which laid down the system actually implemented in World War One. Having chosen Travers Clarke, despite the opposition his ruthless methods were likely to arouse, he would now stand by him and his adjutant-general Fowke through thick and thin. This at least was an aspect of the handling of armies of which he had a thorough grasp.

Only a man of almost incredible insensitivity could look back on the costly battles of 1916 and 1917 with even a suggestion of complacency or view the future without intense anxiety. In the light of the huge casualties incurred there was some justification for Lloyd George's loss of faith in the Commander-in-Chief himself and for the purge of the General Staff just completed at his instigation. Under pressure from him, Haig had had reluctantly to sack Kiggell, his Chief of Staff, Butler his deputy, Charteris his Chief Intelligence Officer, his Engineer-in-Chief and his Director-General of Medical Services. The evidence is strong that Haig was a bad judge of men who allowed loyalty to his fellow cavalrymen and close associates to influence his judgment. Kiggell's reputation was that of a 'nit picker' and a super head clerk utterly lacking in initiative and power of decision: nobody other than Haig himself apparently had a good word to say for Butler. Charteris in 1916 and 1917 had persistently presented Haig with ridiculously optimistic estimates of German powers of offence and resistance and these, unfortunately, Haig had passed on to Lloyd George. Robertson, the CIGS and a close ally of Haig, would soon follow in the footsteps of the rest. Haig himself was fully aware of the fact that he stood on none too firm a wicket. Every commander in every war faces a battle on two fronts. Menaced in the rear by Lloyd George and in front by Ludendorff, Haig's personal prospects had reached an all-time low. There was worse to come. In a week or two Smuts would provide that element of comedy without which even the greatest tragedy is incomplete. In 1901 in Cape Colony Haig had not only failed to catch Smuts but had had one of his columns cut up by him in circumstances which in any other war would have damaged not only his own self-esteem but also his reputation. Now, with a mandate from the Prime Minister himself, Smuts was about to tour the Armies in the hope of being able to find and recommend to the War Cabinet a more inspiring, flexible and tactically less expensive Commander-in-Chief than Haig.

Haig personally seldom appeared at the École Militaire at Montreuil. When he did so, all the staff felt entitled to stop work for a few minutes to go to a window to catch a glimpse of him as he passed from one side to the other or stopped in the courtyard to speak to an officer. Since 1916 he had lived with his immediate staff at the Château Beaurepaire, described as a commodious and comfortable residence two-and-a-quarter miles south-east of Montreuil. There was also a bungalow reserved for him at Le Touquet in case he ever wanted a game of golf.

Every Sunday at 9.30 a.m. he attended the Church of Scotland service conducted by the Reverend George Duncan 'in the old Covenanting style' in the barracks at Montreuil. Nightly he prayed for Divine Help from the God of John Knox whom his countrymen worship in cold temples of granite.

He would need it only too soon.

3

The Wrath to Come

The English have a notion that generalship is not wanted; that War is an Art, as playing chess, as finding the longitude and doing the Differential Calculus are (and a much deeper art than any of these); that War is taught by Nature as eating is.

Carlyle

Few books on the First War omit to include a photograph of Haig and his Army Commanders. Their boots are obviously masterpieces of the great shoemakers of the Haymarket and St James's Street and the cut of their jackets and breeches proclaim the artistry of the heyday of the military tailors of Savile Row. Their leather and buttons shine to high heaven. The shape of a man's jaw and the height of his brow provide no clue to his character but expression does. The faces of Haig and his generals are as inert as if they were carved in stone. They give nothing away. Smuts and Hankey, the Secretary of the War Cabinet, on their tour of the BEF in their role of talent scouts for Lloyd George had an unenviable assignment.

There seemed to be too many of Haig's own arm, the cavalry, in a war which for the past three-and-a-half years had been virtually an infantry and artillery affair. First there was Horne, a close associate of Haig ever since the days of French's Cavalry Division in South Africa at the time of the Black Week and Roberts' relief of Kimberley. No one questioned his loyalty to his chief: he was in the Haig mould, a man 'neither unduly elated by success nor unduly depressed by failure'. He could be relied on to obey without criticism and to the letter any order given him. He had dignity and could give clear if uninspiring orders. No original contribution or comment on his part to the Art of War can be traced; few junior officers and soldiers in his Army knew of his existence. Clearly he had reached his ceiling as the very apotheosis of the 'bon general ordinaire'. Byng of the Third Army, another cavalryman, was in the same class, but his stock was low as a result of the failure to exploit the breakout by the tanks at Cambrai the previous November and of the subsequent loss of all their gains. Gough, the remaining cavalryman amongst the Army Commanders, had greater charm and was better known if only for the high casualties sustained by his army in the Third Battle of Ypres the previous summer and autumn. His staff too were notoriously inefficient: the infantry dreaded the prospect of being posted to his army. Lloyd George in any case was known to be gunning for him: only Haig's loyalty to his fellow horsemen had so far kept him in the saddle. With Rawlinson away on Foch's Committee of the Supreme Allied War Council at Versailles there was for the moment only one infantryman amongst the Army Commanders—Plumer, over 60 but known to the men of Second Army as 'Old Plum'—competent, patient and methodical, a commander in fact who gained his objectives with the minimum expenditure of his men's lives, according to Montgomery, who served under him, 'a soldier's soldier if ever there was one'. Forthright, honest as the day and outspoken, his sphere was the front line rather than the mephitic atmosphere of intrigue and distrust of inter-Allied relations in which Lloyd George, Foch, Wilson and Rawlinson moved with comparative ease and in which Haig so far had managed to survive. Smuts and Hankey returned with an unhelpful report. Outside the framework of Haig's Armies there was Henry Wilson whose only experience in command had been a year with a provisional battalion long ago and a month or two marred by a minor reverse as a corps commander in a quiet sector. Anyhow Lloyd George wanted him to replace Robertson as CIGS. Robertson himself was a non-starter: he had risen from private to field-marshal without commanding anything bigger than a corporal's guard. Lloyd George had already decided that he would be more conveniently employed defending the east coast of Great Britain against invasion. After the war critics thought that the Australian General Monash should have been considered at this stage. In fact his abilities at this time were not generally realised. Furthermore to have promoted a man, who before the war had been a civilian engineer, over the heads of the whole Regular Army hierarchy would have been no more politically possible than allowing Montgomery complete control

over the British and American Armies would have been at the
time of the breakout at Falaise in August 1944.

The year 1917 had been a turning point in the history of the
world for two main reasons and all the world for once realised it.
First there had been the Russian Revolution leading after months
of virtual quiescence on the Eastern Front to the cease fire on 2
December. Secondly in April the United States had entered the
war. By 1 March there would be six American divisions, admittedly
only partially trained and incompletely equipped, in France, each
twice as big as their British counterparts. Thereafter there would
be an ever-increasing American build-up which must inevitably,
in view of her vast manpower, industrial potential and national
sense of destiny, tip the scale in favour of the Allies. The end of
the fighting in Russia had released some 44 German divisions
which could be rested and trained in Germany during the winter
ready for an all-out offensive in the West when the March winds
dried the battlefields. The British press and public had no illusions
that this was what the Germans intended to do, a view for once
shared by the authors of the British GHQ Intelligence Summaries,
cynically known to the fighting troops as 'Old Moore's Almanack'
or sometimes 'Comic Cuts'. The German people too were known
to be feeling the strain of war; the Allied naval blockade was
having its effect; the supply of industrial materials was running
dangerously low; there was hunger and smouldering discontent
in the big cities. Austria had become a liability and was on the verge
of collapse. The U-boat campaign was obviously failing either
to starve the British or to stop the arrival of American troops.

Following the disastrous Nivelle Offensive the previous spring
there had been widespread mutinies in the French Army which
was now being slowly nursed back to health by Pétain. How
serious and extensive these had been had been well concealed by
the French; indeed the whole truth, or most of it, would not be
generally known for many years (although Pershing at the time
had few illusions in this respect). Miraculously the Germans in
1917 had failed to realise that in the second half of 1917 the will
of the French to fight, even in their own defence, had virtually
ceased to exist. All they knew in the first months of 1918 was that
they had no reason to fear a French offensive or, for that matter,
an attack by the Italians still only convalescent after the débâcle
of Caporetto. If ever there was a clear-cut, unarguable situation

in World War One it was now: the Germans must stake all on early victory; the Allies must hold them at bay, till, to use the words of the Minister of Munitions of 1918 (Churchill) of a situation in a later war 'the forces of the New World restored the balance of the Old'.

Living conditions worse for the maintenance of the morale of the British Army and its build-up for the coming struggle than those which they had to endure in the trenches in January and February 1918 would be hard to visualise. Alternate periods of extreme cold and sudden thaw, varied by heavy falls of snow and hail maintained a seesaw of intense discomfort. On 15 January came a warmer spell ushered in by a terrible gale accompanied by torrential rain. Plank roads and duckboards were washed away. Men sank deep into the ice-cold clinging mud and had to be dug out; many collapsed from exposure and exhaustion. It is not surprising that Smuts on his visit in January thought the men, especially the infantry, were tired and said so in his report to the War Cabinet. In sharp contrast the Germans opposite, in far smaller numbers and on higher ground, led a far less unhealthy and depressing existence in comparatively well-drained trenches and concrete pillboxes. February brought little improvement. Overhead, when the skies cleared, the German air force seemed to range at will virtually unimpeded and their guns seemed to have at their disposal plenty of ammunition. When Montgomery took over command of the Eighth Army before El Alamein, its morale was described as 'brave but baffled'. That of Haig's Army in early 1918 was not dissimilar: perhaps to describe it as cynically disillusioned, contemptuous of what they called the Staff but still belligerent, would be near the truth. The troops themselves defined their state of mind in three words—all unprintable and all beginning with the letter 'b'. There is little in his diaries to indicate that Haig so far ever had his finger on the pulse of the morale of his Army. The reports on morale which he received from his subordinates were inevitably a poor guide: no commander in war is likely to admit to his superiors that the morale of the troops for whom he is responsible is bad: to do so is obviously to invite and probably justify the sack. The troops themselves were allowed to send some of their letters home in special green envelopes which were not censored in the unit but at the Base. From the official point of view these seem to have been unrewarding literature being mainly concerned with such problems as those of the soldier who had not been home for twelve months and who had been informed that his wife was about to have a baby and the bachelor faced with the prospect of paternity and all the worry this problem inevitably raises in the mind of an unmarried man. In any case, the infantry of World War One were men of few words. 'Dear Mother, this war is no ordinary war. This war is a b—' represented in most cases the limit of their literary powers. Within units, the invidious job of censoring letters was usually passed to the padre, provided he could be bullied or persuaded to take it on, and he, very wisely, like the doctor kept his mouth shut.

There were 57 British, Australian, Canadian and Portuguese divisions on the Western Front on 1 January 1918. Although the number of men actually drawing rations in the BEF was higher than it had been a year before, the actual fighting strength, or 'bayonet strength' as it was called, was lower. The explanation was that there had been a big influx of units for labour purposes only. Haig estimated that the infantry would be 40 per cent below establishment by 1 March. Lloyd George, whose sense of responsibility had been understandably aroused by the terrible cost of the Somme and Passchendaele battles, was, against the advice of Robertson the CIGS, actually holding back in England some 449,000 Category A men over 19 years of age. To avoid reducing the number of divisions in the field, the War Office, on the recommendation of a sub-committee of the War Cabinet which apart from Smuts did not include a single soldier, ordered the reduction of infantry brigades from four battalions to three, thus enabling 141 battalions of the BEF to be disbanded in February and their men to be absorbed into the ranks of the remaining units. The results were bad: the re-grouping was not complete till early March; old associations were broken up; men were sent away from units they had come to regard as their temporary home to fight alongside strangers. The whole sorry business was badly publicised: to assure troops that a three battalion brigade would be as effective on the battlefield as one of four battalions, needed a flair for public relations not available on Haig's and his Army Commanders' staffs. The troops rightly concluded that the re-organisation would mean more time in the front line for them and less rest.

Equally badly publicised was the policy of defence in depth announced by Haig in December. To our cost the Germans had demonstrated its soundness the previous summer—a lightly held forward zone merely to delay the attacker and a main battle zone held in great strength and depth. With 48 Vickers guns and 192 Lewis guns distributed in depth, with interlocking arcs of fire, a division on a front of two miles or so could be expected to put up a protracted resistance, especially if these automatic weapons were sited in defended localities flanked by wire obstacles, which were designed to shepherd the attackers into the fields of fire of the machine guns. The system demanded the digging of a choice of alternative, but not necessarily elaborate, fire positions and considerable initiative on the part of junior commanders to enable an elastic defence to be put up. It is, and always has been a platitude, that it is not sufficient for a commander to make a plan and give his orders: he must sell his plan and furthermore see that it is carried out. The commanders of World War One were men of few words; they had no public address equipment; they said little and what they said was sometimes obscure. Such information of the new policy as filtered through to the front-line troops was half understood and received with scepticism. The infantry had always fought shoulder to shoulder: that was their tribal tradition; they would do so again: they had no use for fighting as they said in penny packets. Generally speaking such training directives as reached them in the mud of the forward area were read with sarcasm and treated, to use their own coarse word for it, as 'bumph'.

The First War generals faced a much more difficult problem than their successors in the second war. They had no radio and no reliable cross-country transport. The defence had unquestionably become the stronger form of war: wire, concrete, defence systems in depth and massed artillery, backed by shell production on a gigantic scale, had petrified the battlefield. The battles of the Somme and Passchendaele had shown that the infantry could be blasted forward to the limit of the range of the field artillery. Thereafter there was a hiatus: the guns had to be moved, communications between the infantry and the artillery broke down and complete paralysis lasting for hours on end descended on the attack during which the defenders sealed off the penetration and in due course counter-attacked. At least a partial solution to this impasse was now in sight: at Cambrai in November it had been demonstrated that, provided surprise could be secured, massed tanks closely working with the infantry and artillery could crush the wire and break out. What is surprising is that it was not until after this battle that Haig had set up a committee to study and develop battlefield technique.

Generals who wish to avoid the exposure of their doubts and errors after their death by war studies experts and scandalmongers and who wish to cut a respectable figure in the eyes of posterity should not keep diaries. This seems to be one of those lessons which is never learnt. On 2 March after a visit to the Third and Fifth Armies Haig recorded:

> 'I emphasised the necessity for being ready as soon as possible to meet a big hostile offensive of prolonged duration. I also told Army Commanders that I was very pleased at all I had seen in the fronts of the three Armies which I had recently visited. Plans were sound and thorough and much work had already been done. I WAS ONLY AFRAID THAT THE ENEMY WOULD FIND OUR FRONT SO VERY STRONG THAT HE WILL HESITATE TO COMMIT HIS ARMY TO THE ATTACK WITH THE ALMOST CERTAINTY OF LOSING VERY HEAVILY.'

Little more than a fortnight before the most spectacular German success of the whole war on the Western Front he seems at this time to have thought that as the Germans had no tanks their experience when they attacked would be the same as his own on the Somme and at Passchendaele.

In the late autumn on the Eastern Front von Hutier using predicted artillery fire (or silent registration), as the British had done at Cambrai, after a short preliminary bombardment including the liberal use of gas shells and smoke, had brought off a spectacular success in an attack on a strongly fortified Russian defensive system at Riga. The gas and smoke shells made only the smallest of craters and thus did little or no damage to the 'going'. This particular technique had also contributed greatly to the German victory at Caporetto about the same time on the Italian Front. Ludendorff therefore was quick to bring into his councils von Hutier's Chief Gunner, Bruchmüller, as his own artillery adviser. He too as a result of his own experience on the Eastern Front had brought a fresh mind to the problems of the West. With the end of active operations in Russia training on a large scale for the coming offensive was now possible in Germany (where incidentally the troops destined for the assault could be accommodated and well fed in comfortable quarters, during the worst months of the winter). For the initial break-in, dog-fight and break-out he organised hand-picked formations of Storm Troops, equipped with light machine guns carried on sledges, light mortars, flame-throwers and light infantry guns designed for close support when temporarily held up. In place of the traditional waves of men he substituted an advance in widely separated groups of between six to ten men and, with considerable effect, partially solved the problem of communication between the infantry and artillery by an elaborate system of light signals. Here the pyrotechnic industry of Germany came to his aid on the grand scale: there were golden rains, rockets with red stars, green stars and blue stars in great variety—soon the British on the rolling uplands of the Somme would be treated to what they would describe as a 'Brock's Benefit'. This system he arranged to back up with large numbers of observers in observation balloons operated from motor lorries pushed boldly forward. Behind the Storm Troops plodded the more heavily equipped German infantry. The training not only of the troops but of their commanders and staffs was strenuous and thorough. Above all, Ludendorff and his generals stressed the importance of the maximum possible exercise of initiative by the junior officers and NCOs. Once the infantry had advanced beyond the range of their supporting artillery they were expected to take charge. Centres of resistance were to be reported and by-passed, to be mopped up later by troops coming up from the rear. They were to go for what the British called the 'soft spots' and go while the going was good. At all costs they must press on relying where necessary on fire support from their own mortars, light machine guns and light infantry guns. Reserves must be used to exploit success not reinforce failure: in other words they must not throw good money after bad. The training was realistic: much of it was done by night: where possible it was done with live ammunition and no fuss was made if a few men got hurt in the process. To ensure that this doctrine was understood at all levels no effort was spared to ensure that all senior officers attended the intensive courses held at Special Battle Schools and the indoor exercises on models run by formation staffs. In short, it was the anticipation in spirit of the Blitzkrieg doctrine of 1940 with the equipment and weapons of 1918, put over by front line soldiers many of whom had known a war of movement and victory on the Russian and Balkan Fronts.

The great strength of the German Army, however, in comparison with the Allies lay in the command and staff system it had inherited from the elder von Moltke. The General Staff were a brotherhood equalled only in professional efficiency, industry and dedication by the Jesuits. In some respects they anticipated the modern vocational man who does not work merely to live but who finds his whole *raison d'être* in meeting the demands of the organisation he serves. Many were of aristocratic but far from affluent origin: to them with their Spartan outlook the Army offered all they asked of life: the prospect of high command, great social prestige, close association with the Kaiser, the security and companionship of a strictly disciplined life. From them the inefficient were ruthlessly eliminated. Officers of middle class origin but of outstanding ability were freely admitted to their caste. Typical of the German Army in this, its heyday, were the three Army commanders selected to execute the coming offensive. Von Hutier with the Eighteenth Army faced Gough on the St Quentin front. Von der Marwitz, well known to the British since 1914, commanded the Second Army opposite Byng. Von Below and the Seventeenth Army confronted Horne about Arras. All were dominating personalities at the height of their powers, all had behind them long and successful fighting records and all had the capacity to impart immense and merciless drive to their troops. All were good trainers. Beneath them were highly professional and carefully selected staffs, smaller than their British counterparts and perhaps partly for that reason, more efficient. Confidence that the dynamic leadership of these three generals would ensure tactical success ran high throughout their armies. None doubted that Hindenburg and Ludendorff, the victors of Tannenberg and the saviours of their country on the Eastern Front, would provide the right strategic direction in the coming offensive and that the summer would see final victory for Germany and the end of the war.

The Allied dispositions were well known to the Germans. They knew that Haig had the bulk of his strength in the north. Here three Armies, the Third, First and Second, covered the northerly two-thirds of the British line from Cambrai to the sea with a total of 46 divisions. On the right the Fifth Army, which had just reluctantly taken over from the French a further 25 miles, had only 14 divisions. The Germans fully realised that Haig could not afford to give ground in the north. Wetzell, the head of Ludendorff's Operations Section, therefore advised that the main effort should be made in the north just south of Ypres in the general direction of Hazebrouck and that it should be preceded initially by an attack in the south on both sides of Peronne on the British Fifth Army Front designed to throw the British off balance and draw their reserves in that direction. Wetzell's advice was that this offensive should pause on reaching the area of the old Somme battlefield. This limitation, fortunately in the long run for the Allies, Ludendorff did not accept—with dramatic results as will be seen. Finally the British were to be misled by continual movements of troop trains behind the lines and the moving in of the attacking troops and their artillery at the last possible moment and by night.

Haig was a better strategist than a tactician. He, like Wetzell, had appreciated that the north was the vital area where his Armies must fight to a finish where they stood and where the Germans' final decisive blow must almost inevitably come. In the south on Gough's Fifth Army front he decided that he could afford to give ground provided he covered the key rail centre of Amiens and provided the French came to his aid.

Throughout the winter he had resisted French efforts to get control of the British Army. When Pétain had pressed him to take over an additional 55 miles of front, he had insisted that at all costs he must cover the Channel ports, that in the North he had scarcely any room to manoeuvre and that, proportionally, there were more Germans on his front than on the French. In this controversy that very obstinacy which had caused him to go on too long with the attacks on the Somme and at Passchendaele had stood him and his army in good stead. Eventually in January a compromise had been reached by which the demand was reduced to 25. At the same time, in the teeth of pressure from Lloyd George (who in addition to being Prime Minister was one of the most persuasive men who ever lived), he had refused to contribute nine of his divisions to the Central Allied Reserve to be controlled by an executive board under Foch. Instead, he preferred, despite a warning from Wilson (who having had a French governess knew something about the French), to rely on a 'soldier to soldier' agreement with Pétain that they would come to each other's aid, if the need arose, with the equivalent of six divisions and after five days' notice. It was one of those 'gentlemen's agreements' so called, in the circles in which the term is used, because they are never made between gentlemen. It was unfortunate too, as would be seen only too soon, that he never made it crystal clear to Gough how he wanted him to fight the battle in the south. It is even more important in war than in civil life that anything in the nature of a contract, especially where Frenchmen and Irishmen are concerned, should be clearly and unequivocally expressed and recorded in writing. For once his normal Lowland Scottish shrewdness seems to have deserted him. Within a week the British Army would face the greatest crisis in its history since Waterloo and its greatest disaster since Yorktown.

4

The German Offensive

For the last time the goodness of God smiled on His ungrateful children.

Hitler, *Mein Kampf*

More than half-a-century later it is virtually impossible for anyone caught up in it as a front-line soldier to write of the great German Offensive on the Somme in March 1918 without emotion—a mixture of indignation, admiration for some of his fellow men and contempt for others, tempered by the feeling that he personally had more in common with his German counterpart than with those in high authority on either side, whether military or civilian. Much has been written and may well continue to be written, all concerned being well dead, of the failure of the Soldiers and the Statesmen to evolve a general strategy for the war which makes sense to posterity, of the unending friction between the British and the French, of nauseating intrigue amongst the politicians and higher commanders and staff officers, of the men who allowed their personal ambitions to warp their judgment and of the command crisis which led to the Doullens Conference of 26 March and the appointment of Foch to coordinate the French and British operations. By contrast, to give even an impression of what actually happened to the Fifth Army, so local was the experience of survivors and so inadequate are the regimental records, is a baffling task.

In comparison with the artillery bombardment which preceded the German assault on 21 March, the barrages of 1,000 guns at El Alamein, of 2,000 in Hitler's offensive of December 1944 and 2,000 at the Rhine Crossing in 1945, pale into insignificance. About 5 a.m. no less than 6,473 guns opened up on the 40-mile front of the Fifth Army and the southern end of the Third Army between the Sensée and the Oise. For four-and-a-half hours they saturated every trench, every battery position, every headquarters, every dump, with high explosive mingled with mustard gas and lachrimatory shells. Dawn came with the whole front blinded by the dense fog normally prevalent in north-east France at this season in the first hours of daylight, and with the garrisons of the Forward and Battle zones dazed and deafened by the shock waves of the most terrible and accurate concentration of fire of the whole war. At 9.35 a.m. some 3,500 mortars opened rapid fire on the front-line defences: five minutes later three German Armies, over a million strong, on a front of 32 divisions, a veritable avalanche of men, preceded by their Storm Troops, advanced to the assault, backed by a further 39 divisions. The experience of the 4th East Lancashire Regiment is typical. Second Lieutenant V. H. Johnston a few weeks later in a letter to the father of Captain Hopkins, with the understatement characteristic of his generation, wrote:

'The fighting in which your son and myself with my own platoon were engaged was very severe and very disastrous to ourselves. As far as I can recollect only three or at most four out of about thirty came through without being killed or severely wounded. We fought for two hours from 10 a.m. till noon. Captain Hopkins and I each took charge of a section of trench and carried on with rifles and Lewis gun fire till there was hardly a man left. About halfway through the fight, Captain Hopkins came down to me and said he feared he could not go on much longer as he was wounded in the back and the leg, presumably by machine gun bullets. Nevertheless with wonderful courage he insisted on carrying on, controlling, directing fire and urging the men like the splendid soldier he showed himself to be. At last when not a single man remained of his party, he himself took a Lewis gun. I was then by his side, getting the other gun into action and saw what happened. A bullet struck the gun he was firing and hit him in the lower part of the face. As he sank back he said to me, "Fire the gun, Mr Johnston, fire the gun."'

At the end of the day of this battalion a bare forty men survived.

Countless small battles such as this of which there were no British survivors raged in the fog of the morning and the utter

Vorwärts! Vorwärts!—German infantry press forward into the breach at St Quentin,
arch 1918

8 A German Infantry Regiment deployed to exploit the breakout at St Quentin, la[te] March 1918

9 British Infantry en route to the Front, 1 April 1918

confusion of the afternoon. Everywhere communications were shattered, battalion and brigade headquarters swamped. The dense white fog blinded the fire of the machine guns and field guns in the Forward Zone. By nightfall the Germans had gained ground all along the line and had penetrated the Battle Zone north and south of St Quentin. On the 22nd there was again thick morning mist which the Germans were quick to exploit with the skill and initiative which their training had encouraged. By nightfall on this second day the centre of the Fifth Army had been shattered and its northern flank was in grave danger of being cut off from the Third Army. All its reserves had been committed; the Third Army also was fighting for its life and had not a man to spare. Later that night Gough had the moral courage to face the fact that to continue the battle east of the Somme could only end in disastrous defeat. He therefore ordered the withdrawal of his surviving troops to the line of the Somme some ten miles back. This is the scene which confronted the troops of the 8th Division, who after detraining in the early dawn had been hastily thrust into position along the west bank of the river on the morning of the 23rd.

'Most of the Fifth Army's transport had already crossed. About one o'clock the remnants of the infantry appeared—little bodies of men about 30 strong, all that remained of battalions, without equipment for the most part but all carrying rifles and at least one cotton bandolier of ammunition. It was not a cheerful sight. Down on the river sappers were blowing up the bridges and very badly they were doing it. The charges were inadequate and most of the bridges remained passable to infantry at least. They did however successfully prevent a number of our own tanks from getting over. We watched their crews set them on fire. By four o'clock the last of the dreary procession had crossed and the Germans, hot on their heels, had closed with the river. The line of the Somme—at least ten miles of it—was ours with all our nine battalions in line on its west bank and only the Pioneer Battalion in reserve. Strange to relate morale rose.'

Somehow or other this line remained intact until the morning of the 25th, when once more the flimsy British defences were again swamped in the morning fog which persisted till midday.

D

Then the sun came out over a countryside as devoid of cover as
Salisbury Plain. An officer isolated with some 150 men on a railway embankment recorded:

'In the sky, roughly parallel with the Somme, was a row of
some twenty or thirty silver balloons observing for the German
artillery. Over the open plain as far as the eye could reach the
Germans were advancing with wide intervals between each
man and in great depth. The leading troops were putting up
masses of light signals to show how far they had got and to
call for fire support. They were all the colours of the rainbow.
Amongst the infantry there were men dragging sledges carrying
machine guns. What impressed me most was the vast depth of
their formations. Officers on horses kept this mass of men under
control. When the leading waves struck opposition, they went
to ground. When they struck a gap, they surged forward. In
front of our pathetic position they had come to a halt but on
our right and well behind us this human sea flowed on. Then
we were spotted. Machine guns started to clip the top of the
railway embankment and 5.9 inch howitzers to lob shells
behind us. About this time a runner from Brigade Headquarters
arrived with an almost indecipherable message ordering us back
to an old trench system of the 1916 Somme battle. We were in
a quandary. If we obeyed and pulled out in daylight we would
be shot to bits: if we held on till dark even though virtually
surrounded, we might get away. Anyhow that's what we did.'

In spirit and execution the battle which now developed in the
open fields on a line running roughly north and south of the
village of Rosières and astride the main road to Amiens seemed to
belong rather to the Peninsular War than to the twentieth
century. For three days men stood shoulder to shoulder in hastily
dug trenches and ditches in one single line. They felt happier that
way. The field artillery in small groups engaged the enemy over
open sights. Grim determination and discipline triumphed over
tactical first principles and, indeed sometimes, common sense.
From the rear the military police fed in a heterogeneous mass of
men combed out from transport lines, army schools, administrative
offices, canteens, bath units and field-punishment camps—even
some of the foul-mouthed bayonet-fighting instructors from the
Bull Ring at Le Touquet. By night they shivered in the bitter cold

of a battlefield destitute of shelter. All had lost or abandoned their greatcoats: there was no hot food or drink. It was now that the real leaders emerged, the men prepared to go on to the end: the commanding officers who placed their headquarters in the front line and at the slightest sign of wavering strolled along the top; quiet and unassuming men who suddenly discovered that they possessed the divine spark of courage and a clear head in a crisis and that other men would follow them. They came from every level of British society. There were men who had sold newspapers in the streets and walked barefoot in the gutter; the apparently feckless offspring of the very rich; men who had known the inside of His Majesty's gaols; shy scholars, ex-barrowboys and shop assistants, old regular soldiers who had so far incredibly survived. There were men of mortar batteries who had lost their mortars, clerks from headquarters which had been destroyed, the rumps of engineer field companies who now fought as riflemen. There were even single guns in the front line firing point-blank down the roads. The crazy line bent, but somehow or other it was never really broken. On 27 March on the southern flank the German tide reached Montdidier. In the three succeeding days the line of sleepless men, numb with cold but still belligerent, shrank slowly back to the river Avre at Moreuil and the eastern outskirts of Villers Brettoneux on the high ground commanding Amiens. Here at long last what remained of the Fifth Army after nine days of continuous fighting, the 2nd and 3rd Cavalry Divisions fighting on foot with magnificent courage and two good French divisions brought in at long last on the southern flank, finally brought the German advance to a halt. North of the Somme a supreme German effort against Arras struck obstinate and unbreakable resistance from the Third Army. A last despairing thrust towards Amiens collapsed in the ruins of the aircraft hangars east of Villers Brettoneux. By 3 April, Rawlinson who had taken over from Gough on the 27th was able to report to his close friend Henry Wilson, the CIGS, that he had been able 'to get some sort of order out of chaos' and that 'his troops in spite of their ghastly casualties had had some rest and were ready to fight again'. Within a few days he would receive in the Australian Corps a reinforcement of troops of the highest reputation and who would soon prove themselves to be the best infantry of World War One. The March Offensive was over.

Nothing could conceal from the world that the British Army, in terms of men killed, wounded and missing, guns and equipment captured and ground lost, had, if not been defeated, at least suffered a disaster of the first magnitude. In ten days it had lost 178,000 men and 1,000 guns and had been pushed back 40 miles. These casualties were three times as many as would be sustained in 1940 in the Dunkirk operations, more than twice as many as the British Army's casualties in the Battle of Normandy from June to late August in 1944, three times as many as the American losses in the Ardennes and 25 per cent more than the British Army's total casualties in the whole campaign in North-West Europe from Normandy to the Baltic. The 36th, 16th and 66th Divisions had over 7,000 casualties each. The 8th Division, brought into the battle on the third day, lost 4,943 officers and men, that is more than 50 per cent of its infantry, and yet remained a fighting entity to the very end. Posterity may well wonder why and how this happened, why Pétain so quickly concluded that the British had been decisively defeated, why Ludendorff, having broken out into the open, failed to finish the job, and above all why reeling back after such a blow the whole ponderous edifice of Haig's command did not collapse, as the French, in not entirely dissimilar circumstances, would do virtually in the same area in May 1940. Ironically Pétain, on this as on the later occasion, reached the wrong conclusion: the Fifth Army, now renamed the Fourth Army, though sorely smitten refused to die. There was probably more despondency in London than on the battlefield.

At 5 p.m. on 27 March the Military Secretary had arrived at Gough's headquarters to inform him that 'it had been decided that he and his staff needed rest'—decided not by Haig but by Lloyd George and Henry Wilson, the CIGS, 'because he had lost the confidence of the troops'. It is one of the facts of life that governments whose armed forces sustain a great disaster must, if they are to survive, find a scapegoat. The reasons given in this case for sacking a commander were as good as are likely to be found in the future. It is better to ruin one man's career than to saddle an army with a Jonah and professional soldiers must expect to be sacked if they fail, whether they personally are to blame or not. In the immortal words of Field-Marshal Montgomery: 'War is a dirty business but politics, BY GUM.' Both were involved in this instance. There is no doubt, however, as Lloyd George was to admit in his later years to Liddell Hart, that Gough was unjustly treated. He had only just taken over defences scarcely worthy of the name from the French: rear defences were non-existent; he had been given too few troops for the task; he had reported these facts and stressed the risks he ran. He had done what he could with what he had before the battle. Finally, in making a clean break on the 23rd, he had avoided the running fight which inevitably would have been fatal. Finally, it is impossible to exonerate Lloyd George, despite his denials to Liddell Hart in his old age, from responsibility for keeping back in England the reinforcements for which Haig had pressed.

It will be recollected that the German overall plan had originally envisaged an advance only as far as the line of the Somme south of Peronne designed to draw the British reserves in that direction: the major and decisive blow would then be delivered south of Ypres. On the night of the 23rd, when his troops had closed with the river and had opened a breach in the south, Ludendorff changed the plan and decided to exploit his success and turn the line of the Somme. It is now clear that having reached this decision he should have gone all out for Amiens: there was little to stop him except an ill-organised single line of tired but admittedly desperate men. Behind the grim, apparently ruthless façade of Ludendorff there lurked a man who took council of his fears—in this case of a counter-attack on his exposed flank from the south which, in fact, Pétain had no intention whatever of delivering. It may well be that he was a very competent staff officer: there is no evidence that he possessed the qualities which characterise a great commander capable of recognising the crucial moment and of inspiring his troops to supreme effort.

Responsibility for the reduction of divisions from twelve to nine battalions, with all the heart-burning and disorganisation this inevitably involved, at a singularly inappropriate time just before the battle, must in the end rest on the shoulders of the War Cabinet. So too must the dispersion of effort in Italy, Salonika and the Middle East at a time when, if ever, the strategic centre of gravity was unquestionably in France. Haig was thus left with virtually no power to counter-attack and dependent on the charity of Pétain.

The German system of defence in depth involving the distribution of the troops in a Forward Zone, a Battle Zone and a Rear Zone had baffled Haig in his 1917 offensives. In adopting it himself he failed to make his subordinates realise that the forward defences should be only lightly held and the bulk of the troops held back for offensive defence. In consequence, many isolated detachments who fought on bravely in the hope of rescue were overwhelmed. Furthermore, the defences taken over from the French were in poor order, included virtually no provision for shell-proof cover and characterised by the normal Gallic care-free attitude to sanitation. Incredibly in the fifth year of the war there was a shortage of barbed wire. Despite the fact that on 1 January Haig had had at his disposal a labour force of over 300,000 men, it is claimed that there were insufficient men available for the construction of reserve defensive positions in the Fifth Army area. In fact the Rear Zone defences had been scarcely started when the blow fell. In any case the complexity of the system of defence in depth was not fully understood: too many troops were disposed in the Forward Zone and, to quote the Official History, 'overrun in the first rush', and too few in the Battle Zone. Thus about a third of the Infantry were written off before the battle really began.

It was when the operations became fluid, however, that the lack of training of the troops and their immediate commanders became apparent. As Pershing, the American Commander-in-Chief, who had his ear close to the ground, put it: 'In this sort of warfare the British were seriously handicapped on account of their long adherence to stabilised warfare ... when the men had to leave the trenches they acted as though something were radic-ally wrong in that there was not another trench system somewhere to get into.' This mental constipation extended to many of the commanders and their staffs. They could control the machinery of their commands well enough in static conditions but when confronted by a war of movement they were as much at a loss as their men. Without communications and often too far back, such orders as they were able to issue were almost always based on stale information, always late, almost always impossible of execution. The majority of the junior staff officers too were hope-lessly undertrained and incapable of drafting concise and un-equivocal messages and orders. The unpleasant truth is this: up to this moment in the fifth year of the war there had been no coherent policy for the training of the commanders and staffs. In retrospect, it can be seen that this higher training should have been carried out in Great Britain and the minor training in the techniques peculiar to the theatre in France. The man who could have seen to all this did in fact exist. This was Ian Hamilton, who despite his failure at the Dardanelles had behind him wide experience of war, imagination and enthusiasm. For once responsibility for this neglect cannot be off-loaded onto the politicians: the bill had now come in.

Nevertheless these under-trained troops and their half-trained commanders had by the first days of April brought their professionally more competent opponents to a halt on the Somme. There is no blinking the fact that they had been out-manoeuvred and out-generalled, that they had never grasped the value of cross-fire in defence and persisted in firing straight ahead and that, at the outset, they were static-minded and often physically tired. When the battle started many were disillusioned men. What had really stopped the rot was the personal courage of the officers and men in the remnants of the units and the battle groups. Miraculously, faith in discipline at all costs, the Army's tradition since the days of Cromwell and pride of race had survived: without sleep, without hot food, frozen stiff by night, they fought on till they dropped. 'It is questionable whether any British soldier ever entertained a thought of ultimate defeat.' For once, the much criticised Official History has got to the heart of the problem. Incredibly survivors half-a-century later would tell their sons and grandsons that it was hell but they wouldn't have missed it.

The history of the British Army is studded with disasters although none so great or so spectacular as this. Fortunately for the national self-esteem historians and others have usually been able to claim them as blessings in disguise. 'Those whom the Lord loveth, he chasteneth.' It was so in this case. In striking at the point of junction of the British and French Armies, Ludendorff had precipitated the crisis which compelled the Allies at the Doullens Conference to appoint Foch to coordinate the operations of their respective armies. Ludendorff too, in deciding to change his original plan instead of halting along the line of the Somme south of Péronne, had saddled himself with the defence of a great salient and thus deprived himself of many of the divisions he needed for the final decisive blow he now proposed to stage south of Ypres.

For this he had planned to use 33 divisions; the offensive on the Somme however had swallowed up most of the available reserves and he could now produce only 11. Once more however his luck held: the general northward movement could not be concealed. Haig and Horne of the First Army wrongly interpreted it as aimed at Vimy Ridge. In fact it came on 9 April on an 11-mile front south of Armentières directed on the vital rail centre of Hazebrouck. Much of its weight fell on the 2nd Portuguese Division at a moment when the Army Commander was in the process of withdrawing them into reserve. The unfortunate Portuguese, caught in the hurricane preliminary bombardment, panicked: by the night of the 10th the breach was 30 miles wide but only five miles deep. The divisions on the flanks stood firm and reserves promptly brought up temporarily stabilised the front. Here the British could not afford to give ground and Ludendorff knew it. He therefore brought forward further divisions and thus sucked into the battle, in addition to the British First Army, Plumer's Second Army, the guardians of Ypres. Fighting as desperate as any in this bloody spring now developed. Unquestionably to Haig this was the crisis of the war: had he not thought so, he would not have issued an Order of the Day so utterly out of character as that which would be remembered as the 'Backs to the Wall' Order. This said:

> 'There is no other course open to us but to fight it out. Every position must be held to the last man. There must be no retirement. With our backs to the wall and believing in the justice of our cause each man must fight on to the end. The safety of our homes and the freedom of mankind alike depend upon the conduct of each one of us at this critical moment.'

Naturally these sentiments met with acclaim from the home press and the literary-minded not personally involved in the battle. In the front line only too often the men to whom it was read as ordered had only one comment and that a rude one. They did not expect from their commanders this sort of rabble-rouser's rant in which Welsh politicians and press lords of the day were wont to wallow. A lieutenant-colonel serving as a general staff officer in one of Haig's divisions would, 34 years later, in not dissimilar circumstances, put all this in words they could understand. 'They would fight on the ground they now held at

Alamein and if they couldn't stay there alive, they would stay there dead.'

Fortunately, in the north Plumer was in charge. His troops knew him and trusted him. He now took the bitter decision to shorten his line by abandoning not only all the gains east of Ypres of 1917, gains which had cost a quarter-of-a-million men but also the swampy fields east of the city for which so many men had died to hold since the autumn of 1914. The German front line now reached the moat and the ramparts of the city. With the reserves thus released Plumer retained his grip on the bastion of Kemmel Hill. It would be pleasant to record that at this time the attitude of Foch was helpful. When Haig pressed for the relief of some of his troops to enable them to rest, he met uncompromising resistance. At long last on 16 April, when the crisis seemed over, Foch at last allowed the French Corps he was holding in reserve in the north to be committed. Promptly on the 25th Ludendorff renewed the attack and chased the French off Kemmel Hill which commanded the approaches to the vital railway junction of Hazebrouck. The British divisions on the flanks, however, once more refused to budge and by the 29th the renewed offensive in the north had clearly shot its bolt.

In the south astride the main highway to Amiens, Von der Marwitz of the 2nd Army had, on 24 April, made one final desperate fling to seize the high ground commanding the city. In the early dawn guns standing axle to axle and firing gas and high explosive blasted forward the storm troops of some nine divisions, supported for the first time by 13 tanks. Virtually all the 18-year-old soldiers who had been brought in to swell the ranks of the 8th Division after the heavy losses in March were swamped. In the low ground south-west of the town tank for the first time fought tank: in mid-morning seven small Whippet tanks swept through and scattered two German battalions forming up. Nonetheless by the early afternoon Heneker, the 8th Divisional Commander, had to face the fact that only his two reserve battalions had survived. Help however was at hand for the 13th and 15th Australian Brigades now arrived. Counter-attacks just before midnight in an inferno of bursting shells and machine gun fire, these superb troops and the remnants of the 8th Division re-captured the town in one of the most sanguinary actions of the war. In the succeeding days with the advent of spring the comparative quiet of temporary exhaustion descended on the stinking battlefield from Ypres to south of Amiens.

German casualty figures for this war cannot be calculated with full accuracy, but it is certain that since 21 March they had lost over 50,000 dead and a quarter-of-a-million wounded. The British losses were 239,793, including 28,000 dead.

The British were dead tired: the laughter had gone out of the troops; time was needed to absorb the reinforcements—mere boys of 18, men over 35 combed out of factories, veterans who had been wounded three and more times—into the shattered battalions. The French pessimistically awaited the wrath they knew was still to come. To the men in the ranks of both armies it seemed high time for the Americans, who had now been their Allies for over a year, to shoulder their share of the burden of the battle.

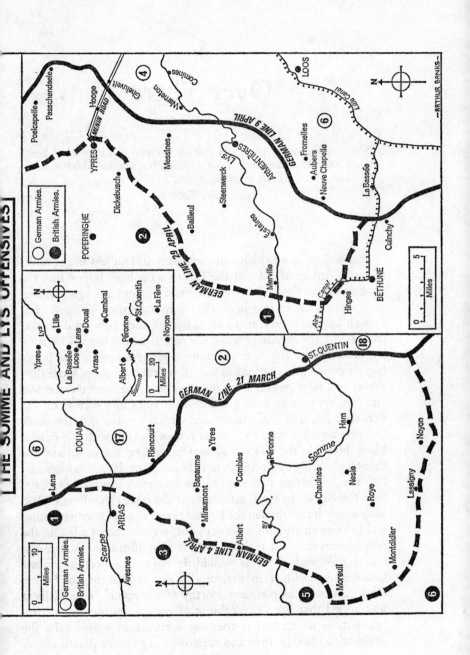

THE SOMME AND LYS OFFENSIVES

— ARTHUR BANKS —

5

Over There

'Sister Anne, sister Anne, can you see nothing coming?' And her
sister Anne answered her: 'I see nothing, but the sun which raises
the dust, and the grass growing green.'

Fairy Tale

A year before, the British and their sons and fathers in the ranks
of their Armies had faced the future with high hopes that the
autumn of 1917 would bring American soldiers in large numbers
to tip the scale in one final victorious campaign in 1918. The
French had convinced themselves that all they now need do was
to stand on the defensive while the new Ally and the British took
the strain of the last overwhelming decisive attack. These hopes
had sustained both nations in the grim ordeal of 1917. More than
a year had now passed since the Americans had entered the war
and yet, apart from four good divisions in quiet sectors on the
French front, they had contributed virtually nothing to the death
struggle now by early May in its seventh week, with the British
like a boxer in the last round beaten back to the ropes and the
French gloomily awaiting the next blow. They did not understand
that the Americans had entered the war even less well prepared
than the British in 1914; although, at the outset the decision had
very wisely been taken in the United States to impose conscription
and to raise an army of three millions, no one except a few in the
Armed services had realised what a vast industrial, social and
moral upheaval the war would involve. As Pershing, their
Commander-in-Chief in France, did not hesitate to emphasise,
there had been no planning worthy of the name. Industrially it
was hoped that the vast outburst of energy and genius for improvisation which had opened up a continent would take the
strain with ease. In 1917 and the following winter practically all

the mistakes the British had made in raising their New Armies were repeated, as in all things American, on the grand scale. The small Regular Army had had thrust upon it a burden it had never been designed to bear. As with the British there was no consistent policy for training the huge influx of eager young men pressing to be sent overseas. There were astonishing delays in building cantonments: there was friction between the authorities at home and Pershing in France. Pershing thought the situation called for cavalry: March, the Chief of Staff took the opposite view. Training did not really get going until the late autumn. The fact was that an American division, 28,000 strong and more than twice the size of the other Allied and German divisions, while it may have produced economies in commanders and staffs, raised many difficulties in training and administration and would in due course prove unwieldy and over-centralised. In the welter of inter-Allied conflicting demands, political pressures and intrigues one American at least was clear in his own mind as to what was wanted—an all-American Army independent of the other Allies. He took this view despite the fact that the sea transport needed to bring the armies to the war, most of the guns, nearly all the tanks and sometimes even the uniforms and gas masks would have to come from British and French sources. As early as May 1917 Pershing had already shown himself to be as tough a commander as the United States ever produced and that is saying a lot. At 56 he was in his prime; he had the will to fight, tenacity in negotiation, the ability to give a firm decision and skill in matching the right man to the right job. On first contact his natural dignity like that of Grant impressed Haig. From his earliest days at West Point his outstanding personality had been recognised. He had been a good regimental officer in the Spanish-American War and had gained national recognition in 1902 in the war with the Moros. He had been a shrewd observer of the Russo-Japanese War and in 1916 and 1917 had handled the expedition against Pancho Villa with conspicuous ability. He had in fact already shown that he could be relied on to safeguard what he considered to be the interests of his country and his Army. When therefore Lloyd George and Clemenceau in January 1918 started to put pressure on President Wilson to solve their manpower problems by incorporating American troops at company and battalion level in their armies his hostility was uncompromising. The aim must be an all-American Army and there must be no departure from this principle. He had a strong case on purely military grounds. National sentiment in the United States against service under a foreign flag was at least as strong as it would have been on the part of the British and French if called upon to fight in American battalions in this and the Second World War. The traditions and prejudices of all concerned were as the poles apart. In any case Pershing had no intention of allowing the morale of his men to suffer from close contact with either British disillusionment or French defeatism. All the British got that early spring was a vague promise that American divisions would in due course train in their area. In return for this apparent concession Pershing got the promise of more British shipping to transport his divisions to France. The French indeed got four Negro regiments which became organic parts of French divisions and incidentally relieved Pershing of an awkward political problem.

At the time of the March crisis, Pershing had declared with apparent magnanimity and to the acclaim of the Allied press that the 300,000 American troops in France were at Foch's disposal. All that came of this impressive gesture was the relief in a quiet sector of two French divisions by one American minus artillery and tanks.

By the end of April Lloyd George and Clemenceau were convinced that, if American aid in the form of troops did not arrive in the near future, collapse would be inevitable. At the Abbeville Conference on 1–2 May Foch went so far as to tell Pershing that the British looked like being pushed back into the sea and that, if this happened, the French would be forced to withdraw to the Loire. Pershing replied that he was ready to take the risk. Many writers have made emotional capital out of this apparently selfish attitude. Pershing's objections, however, can now be seen to have been militarily sound. To have thrust newly raised American infantry, unconditioned to the stress of battle, into the cauldron of one of Bruchmüller's bombardments, under the command of foreign officers who did not understand their mentality, would have been to risk panic comparable to that which occurred in World War Two at the Kasserine Pass and in the Marshes of Peer. Furthermore the American logistic system, which Pershing had built up, based on the five ports north and south of Bordeaux, was well adapted to support a front on the Loire. By now he had accurately sized up the climate of Anglo-

French relations; they did not trust each other: the French assumption of patronising omniscience on all military matters was not founded on achievement or existing fact; Haig, judged on his record so far, was no Napoleon. When Lloyd George, Clemenceau and Orlando, as plausible and persuasive a combination of politicians as ever ganged up together, united to impress upon him the urgent need to feed American troops into their battered divisions if the war was not irretrievably to be lost, Pershing thumped the table and said: 'Gentlemen, I have thought this matter over very deliberately and I will not be coerced.' He did, however, agree that for the next two months preference would be given to sending infantry and machine gunners to France to be carried in British ships. This left him free to transport artillery and technical troops in American shipping. In the event, the fears of Lloyd George, Clemenceau, Foch and Haig were not to be realised. Nevertheless in the coming weeks it would be as Wellington said of Waterloo a 'damned near thing', as will now be seen. At the very moment when the Allies were debating, Ludendorff was issuing orders for the re-grouping of his forces for a blow which would in three days carry his armies to the Marne and within 40 miles of Paris.

Despite the unexpected success of the March battles and the only too evident stalemate in the north now that his offensive on the Lys had attracted Foch's reserves in that direction, Ludendorff still adhered to his original broad strategic plan, that is, to strike his final decisive blow, known as 'Hagen', about Ypres and Hazebrouck, isolating the Belgians and driving the British into the sea. The immediate problem therefore was how to attract these reserves from this front. To this end he decided to stage a diversionary attack with some 44 divisions on the Aisne. This he designed in two parts: first an attack on the Chemin des Dames immediately west of Reims and second, as soon as possible afterwards, a thrust, later to be known as the Matz Offensive, towards Compiègne and Paris between Noyon and Montdidier. These threats, he thought and rightly thought, would result in panic in Paris which would compel Foch to move his reserves away from the British front to defend the capital. He would thus be left free to deliver the *coup de grâce* in the north with the certainty of success. Surprisingly his intentions were penetrated, not by the British and French Intelligence experts but by a junior officer on Pershing's staff, a Captain Hubbard. He argued that on their recent form the Germans would go all out to secure surprise: that the Chemin des Dames sector was the one which the French thought the least likely to be attacked: therefore the next blow must come here. Furthermore he produced evidence to support his theory: the concentration of 'Storm Divisions' behind the Ailette which runs parallel with the Chemin des Dames and movement towards this front in the latter half of May. Inevitably the French treated this prediction with polite disdain, having already with their celebrated logic and expertise in matters military reached the wrong conclusion—there was nothing to fear on the Chemin des Dames. Foch therefore in the process of building up his reserve decided to pull out four French divisions from this sector and replace them, with Haig's concurrence, by four British divisions who had suffered severely to the extent of 8,000 casualties each in the March and April battles and whose ranks had been refilled with 18-year-olds, Category 'B' men and troops from Palestine.

To the survivors of the fighting and of the exposure to the elements on the Somme and the Lys, the Champagne country basking in the May sunshine, to which they now moved, seemed another world. One wrote to another who had been wounded in the fighting of late April and was now in hospital:

'The battalion did exceedingly well, everything you would expect and more [they only lost about 55 per cent of their strength]. I have sad news for you. The Colonel died of wounds. Sergeant Smith was only slightly hit. Sheehan was wounded: a lot of small bits all over him. Vernon and Howard were both killed. . . . Well, we have not heard a shell for five days, nor a bomb for four days. We are now on virgin soil and in a beautiful part of the country. I think it is the best we have been in yet. When we go forward, I believe it is a comparative health resort —so look sharp old boy and return to enjoy the beautiful scenery and the wine of the country.'

The writer of the letter had in March and April survived two of the most costly battles in British history: it does not however seem to have occurred to him that his brother officer would not make every possible effort to get back to his battalion the very moment his wounds were sufficiently healed.

General John J. Persh-
g, Commander-in-Chief,
merican Expeditionary
rce

11 Pershing decorates
MacArthur of 42nd 'Rain-
bow' Division

12 Colonel George S.
Patton, Jr., Commander of
the 1st American Tank
Brigade

13 American Infantry attack at Cantigny, 28 May 1918

14 American Machine Gunners in action, late May 1918

15 Isolated soldiers of the Worceste‌r‌shire Regiment making a stand on th‌e Aisne at Maizy, 27 May 1918

16 British heavy artillery in action East of Amiens, spring 1918

The contrast was indeed striking between the drab monotony, mud and general squalor of the front they had just left and the rolling landscape not unlike the Sussex Downs of the Champagne country. Here and there were woods in full leaf with the first freshness of spring, neat vineyards, fields of corn two feet high and lush meadows along the banks of the streams. Forget-me-nots, larkspur and honeysuckle were in full bloom amongst the shattered tree stumps, shell holes and rusty barbed wire of the front-line trenches. Peasants were going about their business within a mile or so of the front line as if there were no war. The French had lost the plateau of the Chemin des Dames in 1914; in October 1917, Pétain, with a view to restoring his troops' morale, had staged a battle here with overwhelming artillery support and recaptured it with little loss. Since then both the French and Germans in this part of the line had followed a policy of live and let live and almost perfect peace had reigned. The Germans called it 'the sanatorium of the west'. The trenches were very deep and there were many concrete pill boxes like square forts and apparently of great strength.

The French Sixth Army, under whose command the British 9th Corps had now come, was responsible for a front of some 50 miles from Reims to Noyon. This it was holding with some 16 divisions, 11 forward and five in reserve. Lieutenant-General Hamilton Gordon, the Commander of 9th Corps, had hoped that he would now be given a chance to absorb and train his reinforcements. On arrival, however, Duchêne, the Army Commander, promptly ordered him to take over the front line from just west of Reims to Crâonne. This Hamilton Gordon proceeded to do with the 21st Division on the right, the 8th Division in the centre and the 50th Division on the left. The fronts allotted to each division were disconcertingly wide and disquietingly weak. The defences on the right lay beyond a canal; the centre was enfiladed from the north and the left lacked depth. In front a wide No-Man's-Land covered with high grass stretched down to the Ailette. In the left sector a French officer said to the staff to whom he handed over: 'You are rats in a trap. If you keep quiet all may be well.'

The silence of the front to troops accustomed to the round the clock shelling in the north seemed uncanny. When the 2nd East Lancashires reported seeing a train drawing up a siding inside the German lines and large fatigue parties engaged in unloading it in

E

broad daylight, they were ordered 'not to disturb the peace'. Even the rare shell when it came over seemed to explode with a tired and listless air. Soon a vague feeling of unease spread amongst the battalion, brigade and divisional commanders. They had, under French orders, taken over French dispositions, trench by trench and post by post. The more they thought about them in the light of their recent experience on the Somme and the Lys, the more it dawned on them that they were unsound.

The defences consisted of an Outpost Line some 1,000–1,500 yards in depth in touch with the enemy. Immediately in rear was a Battle Zone 1,500–2,000 yards in depth. Both were north of the Aisne. They thus fulfilled one of the classic prescriptions for defeat—to stand with one's back to a river. Duchêne laid down categorically that not a single yard of the sacred soil of France was to be given up. The Outpost Line must fight to the last; the Battle Zone must be held at all costs and all reserves must be thrown in to retake any part of this zone which might be lost to the enemy. This meant that the greater part of the three divisions was committed to the defence of these two zones. Furthermore, to support them most of the guns of the three divisional artilleries, as the range of the 18-pounders was less than that of the French 75s, had to be posted north of the Aisne. The infantry and the guns thus presented a compact target within easy range of an opening German bombardment. Apart from a few old trenches there was no organised rear zone in the British sector. All three divisional commanders forcibly pointed out to Hamilton Gordon that it was suicidal to ignore the lessons of the March and April battles and that the method of defence laid down by Duchêne would inevitably result, if the enemy attacked, in the bulk of the troops being wiped out by his mortar and artillery bombardment. It would, they said, be far better to make the heights immediately south of the Aisne the main line of resistance. Hamilton Gordon duly reported to Duchêne at his headquarters in Soissons that, in the light of his own experience a few weeks before, he considered the whole system to be unsound. Duchêne's reputation in his own army for bad temper and rudeness was well known. He wore pince-nez, a type of spectacles seen in England only on the noses of spinster school-mistresses and pacifist intellectuals. All Hamilton Gordon got was the rude reply 'J'ai dit'. With a small British contingent he stood among French troops, under a French commander, defending French soil: he could do no more than report the situation to Haig. It is hard to see what else he could have done: in the event the blow fell before he could be helped.

The four French and three British divisions holding the Chemin des Dames had in fact become the victims of a radical difference of view about the conduct of the defensive battle between Foch and Pétain. Pétain had prescribed elastic defence in depth, the Outpost Zone being merely regarded as a screen. On 4 May Foch had issued an instruction which said that every foot of the ground must be contested 'coute que coute' without thought of withdrawal. Duchêne had been Foch's Chief of Staff and still remained one of his disciples. When Pétain criticised his dispositions on the Chemin des Dames he stressed Foch's orders on the subject saying that in any case he was too close to Paris to consider giving up any ground, that his first line was very strong and that any withdrawal here would be bad for the morale of both the civil population and the troops. Pétain, unsure of his own position and against his better judgment, gave way. That Foch the so-called Generalissimo, Pétain the French Commander-in-Chief and Franchet d'Espérey the Army Group Commander, as well as Duchêne, should all now have been taken by surprise is one of the most astonishing features of World War One. The technique now to be demonstrated in its highest perfection by the Germans was to set the pattern for most of the coming offensives of this war and to continue to be employed in World War Two on the Russian Front and finally, with remarkable initial success, in the Ardennes in December 1944. The measures taken to conceal the assembly of some 30 divisions earmarked for the offensive and over a 1,000 additional batteries were elaborate and thorough. Command of the air over the battlefield was gained and held. By day movement was restricted to the March level. Troops marched by night and hid in the woods by day. There was wireless silence; telephone discipline of the strictest order was imposed. Daylight reconnaissance was restricted to a minimum and strictly controlled. Horses' hoofs were muffled by rags; the camouflage plan was elaborate and imaginative. Marking of vehicles, railway trucks, billets and headquarters was forbidden. The number of officers in the secret was kept to a minimum. Incredibly, each of the attacking corps succeeded in building up dumps of over 300,000 shells and a similarly astronomic tonnage of mortar ammunition close to the front line without the French having an inkling of what was in the wind until the day before the attack. As late as the morning of 26 May a communication from Duchêne's headquarters informed the British, whose suspicions had now been thoroughly aroused by the repulse of their patrols, that 'there is no indication that the enemy has made preparations which would enable him to attack the Chemin des Dames position tomorrow'.

Suddenly, in the bright sunshine of the early afternoon of 26 May all was changed. Early that morning one of the French divisions on the flank of the British had captured two prisoners, one a private soldier and the other a potential officer. The soldier said that all was now ready for an attack on the morrow. The potential officer at first refused to speak. According to a British survivor: 'The French are pretty tough: he talked in the end.' 9th Corps Headquarters sent out the message, 'The enemy will attack on a wide front at 0100 hours tomorrow', and ordered battle positions to be taken up. Night came with an awesome silence broken only by the croaking of the frogs in the valley of the Ailette. Soon after 10 p.m. the British artillery started to fire counter-preparation on the approaches to the front line. There was no reply. Midnight passed. As 1 a.m. approached the tension in the front line became almost unbearable. Then on the very stroke of one, the whole eastern sky burst into flame as nearly 4,000 guns and as many mortars opened rapid fire. The earth shuddered like a jelly under the avalanche of shells. The din was beyond description. Trenches were literally flattened and dug-outs smashed in. Over all hung the sickly smell of gas and the acrid fumes of cordite. Such men as survived staggered like punch-drunk boxers unable even to think. This bombardment was Bruchmüller's masterpiece. The barrage and target map has survived. Never, even on 21 March, had there been a bombardment as accurate and terrible as this. Not a single forward position, dug-out, communication trench, command post, headquarters, dump or battery position was missed. About 4 a.m. in the first rays of the rising sun some 14 German divisions advanced through the dust and smoke to deliver the *coup de grâce* to the dazed survivors of the appalling bombardment. At the Bois des Buttes, the 2nd Devons who had somehow survived the hurricane of fire fought it out to a finish, holding up a complete German division for three hours. By six o'clock the 50th and 8th Divisions and the two French divisions on their left had been virtually wiped out and the attacking Germans had swept across the unguarded bridges over the Aisne towards their goal—the high ground south of the Vesle. Duchêne's and Hamilton Gordon's pitiful attempts to stabilise the battle on the heights immediately south of the Aisne by flinging in their reserves, the French 39th and 157th Divisions and the British 25th Division, were ruthlessly swept aside. A two-mile gap opened up between the British and the French. By nightfall the Germans had reached the river Vesle on a nine-mile front. In one day, the German Seventh Army had crossed two, and in places three, rivers; they had driven a salient 25 miles wide at the base and extending nearly 12 miles into the Allied line. They had destroyed four of the divisions originally in the line and nearly wiped out four more sent up from the reserve. All this had been accomplished through the skilful exploitation of surprise, by overwhelming artillery and mortar bombardment, worked out according to a programme accurate even to the minutest detail and yet geared to meet the unexpected, and by infantry trained to use their initiative and go where the going was good. Here, twenty years before it became a household word, in spirit at any rate, was the essence of Blitzkrieg.

With the coming of daylight on the morning of the 28th some 20 German divisions surged forward across the Vesle sweeping before them five French divisions and the debris of eight British and French divisions. Instead of attacking their flanks, Duchêne fed his reserves frontally into the battle as they came up; inevitably they too were caught up in the rout. Fismes was lost: the fall of Soissons was imminent. By midday Ludendorff had accomplished what he had set out to do; he had captured the high ground immediately south of the Vesle, one of the very ramparts of the very heart of France, and enormous quantities of material. He seemed to have succeeded beyond his wildest dreams; his divisions were surging forward virtually unchecked and many Frenchmen with Gallic fervour were on the run. On the east flank the bewildered remnants of the British 9th Corps fought on with the courage of despair.

Ludendorff had not only surprised the Allies: he had surprised himself. If the results of the decision he now took to abandon his original intention and halt on the high ground south of the Vesle had been successful—and they came very near to doing so—he

would have been acclaimed as one of the greatest commanders
of all time. After Ramillies Marlborough had pressed on to
Brussels; after Jena Napoleon had gone all out for Berlin. Von
Rundstedt would take a very similar decision in May 1940 which
would ensure the decisive defeat of the French and British.
Montgomery too in August 1944 would find himself confronted
by unexpected success and be able to claim that if all British and
American resources had been placed under his command for a
single thrust he could have finished the war in 1944.

Throughout the 29th, the third day of the offensive, the
Germans, sometimes fortified by the vast quantities of Champagne
which had fallen into their hands, pressed forward in the centre
virtually unimpeded, their spearheads by the evening reaching a
point within three miles of the Marne. By the afternoon of the 30th
they looked down on the Marne itself on a six-mile front east of
Château Thierry and got a small bridgehead. They were now
within 40 miles of Paris. Supply was no problem: they could feed
from the vast French dumps and devote all their transport to
ammunition. They had captured over 50,000 prisoners and over
800 guns. All seemed to be going well, except at Reims where the
French held out and west of Soissons where a timely withdrawal
by the French had forestalled exploitation. So far they had advanced against the grain of the country. The only railway into the
salient ran along its western edge. Ludendorff therefore decided
to put forward in time the second part of his offensive—the attack
towards Compiègne from the front immediately to the north
between Noyon and Montdidier. At the very worst this would
flatten out the awkward French bastion between the two great
salients he had now created on the Somme and the Marne. Given
luck this might carry him through to Paris and a French capitulation. 'Hagen', the offensive in the north, could wait; it might
never be necessary.

Behind the French line conditions closely resembling panic now
reigned. Pathetic columns of refugees, their miserable possessions,
cooking pots, feather beds, even chickens piled on carts, mingled
with artillerymen who had lost their guns and infantry, sometimes
without arms, all fleeing from the Germans. In the Chamber
excited deputies clamoured for the blood not only of Duchêne
but of Pétain as well. The Government prepared to bolt to
Bordeaux; the American Embassy got ready to accompany them.

In all this confusion three men kept their heads—Clemenceau, Pétain and Pershing. There were ominous signs that another over-whelming blow was imminent, this time directed at Paris itself from the direction of Compiègne. Clemenceau, who had been to see for himself by car what was happening at the front on the preceding days, now, like Churchill in England in 1940, rose to the level of the event. To General Mordacq who had outlined the further horror to come he declared: 'Yes, the Germans may take Paris but that would not stop me from fighting. We will fight on the Loire, then on the Garonne, if we must, then even on the Pyrenees. If at last we are chased from the Pyrenees, we will continue the war on the sea; but as to making peace, never!' In sharp contrast to most of his countrymen, Pétain remained calm. Within twenty-four hours of the start of the breakthrough he had had 16 reserve divisions on the move towards the Marne. As has been seen the first few were swept aside. Thereafter he ordered the rest to dig in around the salient intending, when the situation stabilised, to attack its flanks. Addressing his staff, he assured them that the German attack could be contained and that the worst was now over. If they could hold out till the end of June, then in July the Allies would be able to go over to the offensive. Even in this darkest hour he saw two things clearly; the Germans were over-extending their line and eating up their reserves: the Americans and the tanks were on the way. He now turned to Pershing for help and he did not ask in vain. Promptly Pershing set the 3rd United States Division on the move to the point of the greatest danger, Château Thierry. The first troops in action were the motorised machine gun battalion of this division who reached the Marne just in time to stop the Germans crossing the river. There followed the 2nd United States Division in motor trucks. On reaching Meaux they too headed for Château Thierry and took up a position astride the main highway allowing the French to fall back through them. The sudden spectacle of American soldiers, all fresh, high-spirited and in the prime of life, eagerly pressing forward to fight the Germans electrified the tired French troops. Soldiers as eager as this to close with the enemy had not been seen in this part of France since 1914. German attempts to cross the Marne withered before their fire. In numbers alone they were the equivalent of six French divisions; morally they were the equivalent of an Army.

It was against this sombre background with Paris itself under bombardment by long-range German guns and ever-multiplying indications of a further German build-up north of Noyon obviously intended for a massive thrust via Compiègne on Paris along the good road and rail communications of the Oise valley, that the Allied Council on 1 June met at Versailles. At this meeting, after prolonged argument with Foch and Lord Milner, Pershing threw caution to the wind and agreed to demand that the United States should transport across the Atlantic in British ships 250,000 troops per month in June and July whether they were trained or not. Furthermore he undertook to move the American divisions training behind the British front to support the French. Accordingly the American 77th Division entrained for the Baccarat area and the 35th for Epinal, the 4th and 28th moved to Meaux, north-east of Paris and the 82nd to Lorraine.

All now turned on the ability of the French troops on the front immediately east and north-east of Paris to survive the next few weeks. The rumble of the guns could be heard on the Champs-Élysées. The Battle of the Matz was about to break.

6

Mangin

Anything may happen in France.
Duc de la Rochefoucauld

In these tense early days of June when trucks stood ready to evacuate the British and American Embassies to Bordeaux, no one saw more clearly than Pershing that the fall of Paris would also involve that of Clemenceau's Government and its replacement by another prepared to make peace, no matter what the British and Americans might think. Fortunately for the Alliance, despite their heated arguments, there had grown up between him and Clemenceau a strong feeling of sympathy and respect. He now called on him alone and said: 'Mr President, it may not look encouraging just now but we are bound to win in the end.' Clemenceau clung to his hand and 'in a tone that showed the utmost solicitude' replied: 'Do you really think that? I am glad to hear you say it.' 'This,' later recorded Pershing, 'was the first and only time I ever sensed any misgiving in his mind.'

It is in the light of the panic in Paris at this crisis that the wisdom of Pershing's decision to use the 2nd Marine Brigade to attack the death traps of Belleau Wood and Bourescues on 6 June must be judged. In twenty days of continuous battle the cost to the Marines rose to 5,200 and there was little to show for it. Skilfully publicised, the knowledge that American troops were fighting beside their own and near to Paris put new heart into the French. No longer could the defeatists say that the Americans would fight to the last Frenchman. No matter how well trained troops are, sooner or later they must get battle experience and this historically has seldom been cheap.

Since 30 May signs of another German offensive being prepared between Montdidier and Noyon had become so blatant that the French Intelligence seriously considered that they were deliberately designed to put the Allies off the scent of an attack elsewhere. Fortunately, they decided that they were due to inordinate haste to exploit their victory on the Marne. The 9th Brigade of the Royal Air Force, moved to Beauvais to operate under the French on this front, reported heavy traffic on all the roads and fresh troop concentrations. Prisoners taken on 7 and 8 June openly spoke of a big attack timed for 10 June. There was a marked increase in deserters claiming to be Alsatians, always an indication of an imminent attack. Air photographs confirmed the presence of fresh batteries and ammunition dumps. In any case it was obvious that to support their advance on Paris the Germans must get control of the railway running along the western edge of the Marne Salient and that they would make the line Montdidier–Compiègne their first bound. There could be little doubt that another great thrust was imminent, this time across the Matz and over the gently rolling country west of the Oise along the grain of the country to Paris.

The terrain of the battle about to break, now resplendent in the first glory of high summer, fell into three parts. The River Oise flowing south from Chauny towards Compiègne to join the Seine north of Paris provided the western boundary of the eastern sector: this was heavily wooded right up to the river. In the centre the great loop of the River Matz linked up with the Oise about eight miles south of Noyon and about the same distance from Compiègne. Here the French front line ran along the northern slopes of the Massif of Lassigny, as far as the upper reaches of the Matz. The hills were wooded and within the loop of the river were many small farms, copses and hedges. The Matz itself was an insignificant stream never, even in its lower reaches, exceeding ten feet in breadth and nowhere more than three feet deep. Throughout its course it was overgrown with reeds and rushes. The watermeadows sparkled with buttercups and the grass was knee-high. The western sector was much more open. Here gently rolling cornfields stretched northwards without a break save for the occasional small copse or clump of trees.

The Third French Army had held the front here since the last days of March when it had filled the gap between the British right and the French left. It had four corps in line on a front of twenty miles and a further eight divisions in immediate reserve. The defences consisted of a forward position of continuous trenches mainly on forward slopes: there were no deep dug-outs and few communication trenches. Immediately in rear a well-wired intermediate position had been partially dug. A further mile-and-a-half to the rear was another trench system similar in character. Finally two miles further back a third position had been traced out along the south bank of the Aronde stream which joins the Oise near Compiègne. The outer ring of the Paris defences was four miles further to the rear. The position thus had depth: it only remained to occupy it intelligently and to defend it with resolution. When Humbert had taken over responsibility for this part of the front in April Foch had told him to regard it primarily as a springboard for an offensive rather than a defensive position. When he next visited him in early May Foch instructed him to defend it 'foot by foot' if attacked. Humbert had therefore concentrated all his efforts on strengthening and manning the forward trenches and done little to the rear lines, despite the fact that the disaster on the Chemin des Dames had been due to Duchêne's insistence on piling up the majority of his infantry and field artillery where they would inevitably be swamped by the opening German bombardment. Incredibly Foch and his circle once again chose to ignore this experience. They also deliberately ignored the fact that they were acting in flagrant defiance of Pétain's policy of elastic defence in depth. To add to the confusion, Pétain on 4 June ordered Humbert drastically to cut down the numbers of the infantry likely to come under the hammer of the German mortars and to pull back the guns as far as their range allowed. A heated argument now developed between Humbert and his staff, and Fayolle, the Army Group Commander and his staff, as to where the line of resistance was to be, culminating in Fayolle insisting on its being sited outside the range of the enemy field artillery. Humbert therefore chose a position between 3,000 and 4,000 yards from the likely positions of the German trench mortars. This however was still in front of the Second Position. It would, he said, take eight days to move back the guns, lift the dumped ammunition and relay the communications. Thus it came about that it was on the rear line of the First Position and not on the Second Position that the battle would be fought. Late in the day Pétain insisted that the Line of Resistance must be the Second Position. Finally to cap the lot, on 6 June came a directive from Foch himself with instructions that it be given the widest possible circulation. With all the pomp and circumstance of high French military authority he proclaimed: 'The road to Paris must be denied; possession must be kept of the northern ports; there must be indissoluble liaison between the Allied Armies.' These ideals, the Generalissimo continued, could only be attained by 'a foot by foot defence of the ground'. There followed a stream of military platitudes: the need for close supervision of subordinates, for the utmost energy, for the defence of every yard of the sacred soil of France to the very end, for the spirit of sacrifice, for firm decisions at all levels and the radiation of confidence however black the outlook. In the circumstances it is surprising that the morale of the French did not take a further dive. Foch did however make it clear that in the coming battle he personally and not Pétain proposed to have the last word. All the key commanders, Humbert, Fayolle and Mangin, were his men. It was Humbert who, in 1914, had commanded the Moroccan Division in the Marshes of St Gond at the crisis of the Battle of the Marne and gained a victory on which Foch's own fighting reputation was based. Fayolle he had recalled from Italy and placed in command of the Reserve Army. Mangin was Clemenceau's choice and Foch and Clemenceau stood or fell together.

Fortunately, Foch was a better strategist than tactician. Pétain with only 12 fresh divisions was obviously underinsured. Foch therefore proceeded to assert his authority as Generalissimo and, having secured the approval of Clemenceau and Milner, ordered Haig to be ready to move his reserves, should it prove necessary, to cover Paris and to thin out his front line so as to create fresh reserves. Under protest, Haig unshakeably convinced that Ludendorff's main effort would come in the north, prepared to move the 22nd Corps, 19th Corps and the Canadian Corps south of the Somme. Further to strengthen Fayolle's Army Group Foch placed under his command 11 *groupes* of 15 tanks each organised as four *groupements*. These were heavy tanks, Schneiders and Saint Chamonds. Fayolle stationed them behind the westernmost Corps of Humbert's Army where the country resembled the easy rolling slopes of Cambrai and the going was as good.

In the threatened sector Foch had already achieved an impressive build-up of his air forces on the airfields around Beauvais. These included the 9th Brigade of the RAF, 200 aircraft strong. Altogether some 1,200 aircraft were available of which 600 were bombers. By the 6th the struggle for the mastery of the air over Roye, Montdidier and Noyon approached parity.

Like Hannibal at Cannae, Foch proposed when the Germans had shown their hand to counter-attack with the maximum possible weight, dash and ferocity. The actual execution of this blow he proposed to entrust to the most ruthless and dynamic general in the French Army, Mangin, whom he had brought forward to wait at the headquarters of the First Army near Amiens until he was required. It was Mangin who in the shambles of Verdun had re-captured Forts Douaumont and Vaux. Like Patton in a later war, battle for him meant all-out violence, brutality and, above all, speed. In Nivelle's disastrous offensive of April 1917 he had written off over 60 per cent of his infantry and, in the witch hunt which followed, had been sacked, to appease the politicians and journalists hysterically demanding a scapegoat. Thanks to Clemenceau, he had been unobtrusively reinstated as a corps commander, in December 1917. From the day when he passed out of St Cyr at the bottom Mangin's career had been un-orthodox: not for him the dialectics, lobbying and paper battles which have enabled so many in all Armies in the twentieth century to rise to high rank without any experience of actual fighting. His record before 1914 had been one of almost continuous active service in the French Congo, Cochin China and Morocco. Not for him the sloppy trousers and bulging bellies of some of his fellow generals which scandalised the British; his turnout was impec-cable. At all times he had the air of a bird of prey. Like Ney and Murat he lived in the grand manner accompanied always by his orderly, a gigantic coal-black Senegalese of terrifying aspect. A troop of captured horses and looted motor cars made his head-quarters conspicuous from 1914. An incident during the retreat in 1914 well illustrates the difference in style between him and Pétain. Both were commanding divisions at the time and their respective headquarters had halted side-by-side about noon. Pétain pulled out of his haversack a piece of cold meat wrapped in a newspaper, a chunk of stale bread and a lump of cheese. Mangin's orderly, wearing a red tarboosh, then appeared, placed a small camp table in front of his master, and spread a clean cloth on it. On this he placed a large well-grilled steak, fried potatoes and a well-dressed salad plus a bottle of good wine, glasses and the appropriate cutlery. 'Do you realise we are at war?' said Pétain with that icy sarcasm in which his race excel. 'Yes, indeed,' came the prompt reply, 'that is precisely why I must be well fed. I have been at war all my life and I have never felt better than I do now. You have been at war for a fortnight and you look half dead.' Every night, no matter what the circumstances, he wrote a letter to his wife and asked for news of their eight charming and intelligent children. Pétain, even when Commander-in-Chief, was addicted to low-grade intrigues in dubious premises. Mangin's sphere was the battlefield itself and the front end of it, no matter what the cost in terms of human life and suffering, including his own. He would be well matched in the battle now imminent by no less a maestro than von Hutier himself, the Commander of the Eighteenth Army who at Riga in November 1917 had first tried out the technique which since March had carried the Germans to the gates of Amiens and now to the Marne, a bare 40 miles from Paris.

It will be recollected that the purpose of the German offensive which opened on 27 May and which had now carried the German armies to the Marne was diversionary; so far, only the first part of it had been executed; the second stage was now due—the thrust on the Noyon–Montdidier front towards Compiègne. For this originally no definite date had been fixed or final objective prescribed. In the event the success of the attack on the Chemin des Dames had surprised Ludendorff almost as much as it had the French. The original intention had been to halt on reaching the high ground above the Vesle after an advance of about 12 miles. When, however, the French collapsed, Ludendorff had been unable to resist the temptation to chase them back to the Marne. As a result he now found himself committed to the defence of a deep and awkward salient, the long western flank of which ran along the edge of a large belt of forest offering ideal cover for an Allied counter-offensive. Along this flank too ran the railway he needed to sustain his troops on the Marne and the main Soissons–Château Thierry highway. The need therefore to mount von Hutier's attack on the Matz, known as 'Gneisenau', had become urgent. He therefore ordered him to thrust forward on a front of 15 divisions to the lower course of the Matz; he was then on a front of 11 divisions, supported by a further seven, to drive forward to reach at least the line Montdidier–Compiègne. Thereafter anything might happen; the French might be forced to face the prospect of the likely loss of Paris; perhaps it might not be necessary to mount the final blow with the Crown Prince Rupprecht's Army Group against Haig's Armies in the north at all.

Ludendorff had originally intended to stage the new attack on 7 June. In fixing this date, however, he had presented his staff with a movement problem of the greatest difficulty and complexity. To blast in the new offensive it was necessary to move a vast number of batteries from the Marne front; at the same time the possibility of a counter-attack on the Marne had to be faced. Horses and men were tired; staff officers showed signs of excessive strain; troops moving southwards towards the Marne crossed columns of artillery and mortars moving west. Inevitably normal security precautions went by the board. The ammunition build-up fell behind schedule. It was not surprising that the arrival of hundreds of new batteries on the 20-mile front between Montdidier and Noyon was observed by the French from the end of May onwards and indeed headlined in the Paris press. Inevitably von Hutier had to postpone the date to 9 June.

On 7 and 8 June there was a sudden increase in the number of German deserters all surprisingly well informed. On the night of the 8–9 June one of these men prepared to betray his country came over and stated that the preliminary bombardment would start at midnight on the following night and that the infantry advance was fixed for 3.20 a.m. The French artillery were thus able to get their blow in first, opening up on known German battery positions, communications and likely forming-up places at 11.50 p.m. Consequently some of the attacking troops were caught in the process of deployment; others got off to a ragged start. Nonetheless the hurricane of fire which descended on the Third Army had all the characteristics of the Bruchmüller technique which had already thrice since March blasted a way through the Allied defences. For the first ten minutes all the infantry, gun and mortar positions were saturated with gas shells, thus forcing their occupants to put on their gas masks. Then von Hutier's 600 batteries switched their fire of gas and high explosive mixed on to the French batteries. Meanwhile the mortars concentrated on the destruction of the forward defences. The majority of the

French batteries were soon smothered and simultaneously all headquarters, telephone exchanges and reserve positions were subjected to continuous shelling. For the next hour-and-a-half the French defences quivered under concentrated fire sweeping forward like a red-hot rake. Within them such men as survived, deafened and often wounded by the shells, staggered as if drunk, incapable of rational action. All communications were cut; all the forward trenches were obliterated; many men were buried.

As a result of the debate, order, counter-order and disorder before the battle, the four French corps commanders, in flagrant defiance of both experience and common sense, had placed nearly half their infantry within 2,000 yards of their front line and thus well within the zone of the opening bombardment. In consequence the covering position was overrun with ease; the few men who survived to resist were ignored by the leading troops and left to be mopped up by reserves. By midday the Germans had reached the position of resistance prescribed by Humbert and passed beyond it. In the centre their advance was particularly rapid. By the evening they were over the Matz on a wide front south of Ressons, had carried two-thirds of the Second Position and were pressing on in force three miles beyond it. Here by last light Humbert's reserve of five divisions and two cavalry divisions temporarily brought them to a halt. In one day von Hutier had advanced six miles, taken over 8,000 prisoners and virtually wiped out three French divisions. He now ordered his victorious troops, both infantry and artillery, to press on throughout the short summer night. All seemed to be going as well as it had done a fortnight previously on the Chemin des Dames.

This time, however, there had been no loss of nerve on the part of the French Higher Command. Their Air Division and the 9th Brigade RAF had intervened in the battle with great courage and conspicuous success with low flying attacks on transport columns, batteries and reserves moving up to the front. Furthermore, except among the unfortunate infantry caught in the forward zone, there had been little panic. On the whole control had been maintained. When troops had fallen back they had, on the whole, done so in an orderly manner. Fayolle had been quick to move three further divisions from his eastern flank towards the breach. When, however, Pétain at 7.30 p.m. demanded the immediate despatch of the British 22nd Corps from Amiens to Estrées St

17 Mangin—'the Paladin of Africa'   18 Gouraud—'the Lion of the Argonne'

French Colonial troops, with machine guns, on their way to the Front, summer 1918

20 Close-support German artillery in the breakout towards the Marne, late May 1

21 German transport column moving up to support the forward troops in the bre
through near Reims, late May 1918

Denis behind the threatened front, Foch demurred and pointed out that the general situation did not justify depriving the British of the reserves behind their front. But he did move one division of this corps into his own reserve at Conty as he had every right to do. Meanwhile Fayolle, Humbert and their staffs had gone ahead with planning a two-pronged counter-attack on either side of the bulge in the centre of the Third Army front. Obviously before it could be delivered some sort of stability had to be achieved.

In the face of intense French artillery fire the Germans resumed their advance at dawn and despite vigorous resistance and even local counter-attacks managed by the early afternoon to get forward a further two miles on Humbert's western flank and south of Ressons on the Matz. The 53rd Division of the 2nd Corps suddenly stampeded, dragging back with it the 72nd Division and thus exposed the right wing of Humbert's Army immediately west of the Oise. Here his 18th Corps which up to this time had not been involved in the battle now stood in a dangerous salient. Humbert's reaction was prompt and effective. Without more ado he ordered the whole corps to fall back for six miles to the northern edge of the Forest of Laigue. Inevitably the plan for a counter-attack on both sides of the German penetration must now go by the board: its whole weight must be thrown in on the western flank alone.

Fayolle, the Army Group Commander, had available in reserve three fresh infantry divisions and the four *groupements* of Schneider and Saint Chamond tanks facing the open country in the western sector of Humbert's front. To these Pétain added a further two infantry divisions brought forward in trucks. At 4 p.m. Fayolle placed all these troops, and the 35th Corps which was actually holding the line on the western flank of Humbert's front, under the command of Mangin and ordered him to restore the situation by attacking the Germans in the flank in the general direction of Ressons. At this very moment Foch arrived and volubly and vehemently insisted that the counter-attack must be delivered like a thunderbolt. Wisely he left the details to Mangin.

In both World Wars the mounting of a large-scale counter-attack demanded military ability of the highest order comparable to that displayed by Montgomery in the Ardennes battle. The first essential was to stabilise the situation to enable the attack to

F

take off from a firm base; the second consideration was accurate
timing: the attacking infantry must have time to reconnoitre,
issue orders and deploy, the artillery to work out their fire plans
and get their ammunition forward and the tanks to marry with
their infantry. Above all the blow must be delivered at the earliest
possible moment and come as a surprise. When Foch appeared
upon the scene only one of Mangin's divisions was in its assembly
area; the second was on its way closely followed by the third; the
fourth could not arrive before midnight and the fifth till the early
hours of the next morning. Their commanders had, however,
come forward, so Mangin without further ado, in the presence of
Foch, Fayolle and Humbert, proceeded to give them his orders.
The attack, he said, in a calm but nonetheless emphatic voice,
would take place on the morrow. To each he gave his assignment
in unequivocal clarity and concise form. Some protested that they
were being given a task beyond their means; others asked for
more time. Mangin listened patiently: then in a low voice not
without a hint of menace he addressed them all:

> 'You will do exactly what I have ordered you to do. We will
> attack at 1100 hours. There will be no preliminary bombard-
> ment. The attack will be ruthlessly pressed to the limit. This
> will be the last of the defensive battles we have been fighting
> since the Spring. From now on we attack. We must succeed.
> Go back to your soldiers and tell them just that.'

Fayolle would have liked to postpone Mangin's attack for
forty-eight hours to enable the artillery to locate the new positions
of the German batteries and silence them with a preliminary
bombardment pre-planned in minute detail. Foch, however,
backed Mangin: the attack must go in at the time and in the
manner he had laid down.

At long last fortune favoured the French. At dawn a thick mist
concealed the deployment of Mangin's troops. The Germans who
had already advanced beyond their objectives on this part of the
front were quiescent and uninquisitive. Not until 11 o'clock did
the mist begin to lift. At 11.30 the French guns opened up and
Mangin's four attacking divisions stepped forward behind a
barrage of shells lifting a hundred metres every two minutes.
Above their heads fighter aircraft flying low fired ahead of them
as they advanced against the German flank south-west of Ressons

sur Matz. Other aircraft shot down the long line of German observation balloons above Montdidier one after another and scattered long columns of reserves moving up to the threatened front. Mangin had prescribed that 'the infantry should advance as if there were no tanks'. He had in fact placed one *groupement* (36 tanks) under command of each division, echelonned in depth behind the infantry and given the same objectives. They were to remained concealed till the attack got under way; they were then to catch up with the infantry, pass through them and run over any machine guns holding them up. The Germans had had no time to dig in: caught in the open they were no match for the infantry and tanks. The villages of Mery, Belloy and Fretoy were carried at the point of the bayonet; such machine guns as continued to fire were squashed by the tanks. Over 1,000 prisoners were taken and 19 guns. But now came a check. As Fayolle had feared, the Germans had massed their batteries in the woods on the high ground north of Belloy. From here they had excellent observation over the whole of Mangin's front. Unfortunately he had given too little attention to these woods in his fire plan. The German guns now opened up. By the early afternoon they had halted the infantry and, firing in many cases directly over their sights, knocked out about half of the tanks. On the French right wing the 18th Corps, profiting from Mangin's counter-attack, not only stopped all German attempts to advance east of the Oise, but actually gained ground in two places. At long last the short summer night came down on both sides at death grips.

At first light next morning both sides resumed the attack, the French on Mangin's front and the Germans on the old battlefield south of the Aisne. This was Operation 'Hammerschlag', the second half of Ludendorff's plan, a thrust by two corps of the Seventh Army on a five divisional front due westwards from Soissons with the right directed on Compiègne. If it had been delivered on the previous day it might well have hamstrung Mangin's attack. There had, however, been delays and when it eventually went in after an hour-and-a-half's preliminary bombardment, the advancing infantry met withering artillery fire from the batteries Pétain and Fayolle had now fed into the battle in large numbers; this, and the infantry encouraged by Mangin's success, soon brought it to a standstill. By the late afternoon the survivors of the attacking divisions were back on their start lines.

That night Ludendorff had to face the fact that his offensive on the Matz had shot its bolt. He therefore ordered it to be closed down.

On this day too, Mangin had resumed the attack at first light, after a preliminary bombardment of thirty minutes. But so severe had the tank losses been on the previous day that none were available, and the infantry, without the benefit of surprise, got nowhere. Undeterred, Mangin ordered the attack to be resumed at 1700 hours. During the afternoon, however, Fayolle reached the conclusion that further operations would merely result in unjustifiable loss of life. This the French, with their reserves down to rock bottom, could not afford. Fayolle therefore cancelled the attack Mangin had ordered. At least it could be claimed that, even if they had an advance of only two or three kilometres to their credit, they had halted the German advance on Paris. Mangin had shown that the French soldier despite his war weariness was still capable, if well led, of advancing to the attack with at least a trace of his traditional offensive spirit. His victory had unquestionably saved Clemenceau's government and soothed the supersensitive nerves of the politicians of Paris.

It had been a costly battle. During the four days, 9–13 June, the French had lost 35,000 men and about 50 per cent of the 144 tanks engaged. Accurate German figures for the same period are not available. Despite French claims to the contrary, it is reasonable to assume, in view of the large concentrations of artillery achieved by both sides, that their losses were at least as great.

Gouraud, no mean judge, would later describe Mangin's counter-attack as one of the greatest feats of arms of the war. In terms of morale this may well be true. He personally had dominated the battlefield. Whether some of the other French generals, even after this experience, had fully grasped the implications of Pétain's system of defence in depth, had still to be seen. It should by now have been clear to all that never again must the bulk of the infantry be caught in the forward zone, that the line of resistance must be out of range of the enemy's guns and mortars used in the opening bombardment; that the enemy must be forced to move his field artillery before tackling the main line of resistance and that reserves must be close to the places where they would be most probably be called upon to intervene. Mangin had shown too that a large-scale counter-attack, delivered with surprise and without preliminary bombardment, was a feasible, and not necessarily unduly costly operation, especially if delivered with the support of tanks and low-flying aircraft.

In the actual fighting the contribution of the tanks had been mainly moral. The Saint Chamond and Schneider tanks were slow, under-armoured and of low cross-country capacity: their losses had been heavy. How many had fallen victims to direct artillery fire and how many had been caught in the German barrages was never accurately ascertained. They did, however, point a way to the future. Some of the French generals at any rate and a certain Major Patton who had watched the battle realised that what the British tanks had accomplished at Cambrai the previous November was no mere flash in the pan and that their potential was great, provided they were supported by the infantry and the artillery as well.

In the air it had been an intense and confused battle marred by unfortunate incidents in which pilots, both British and French, bombed their own troops. Sometimes inadvertently they fought each other. One British pilot complained that a French two-seater not only shot him down but continued firing at him when he was on the ground, a thing no gentleman would do. A British bomber, thinking he had spotted a German concentration, wounded seven French staff officers and killed 75 horses. It did, however, seem that provided the war went on long enough the possibilities of close cooperation between the ground and the air forces were great.

The Matz battle, outside French circles, has received less attention than it deserves in the literature of World War One. It was in fact a turning-point. Foch had found at least one general who could inspire the French soldier to attack. The morale of the French nation as a whole, already stimulated by the news in the first week of June of the American attack at Belleau Wood and the presence of American troops barring the way to Paris at Château Thierry, took a further upward turn when the news of Mangin's victory became known. The victory, for strategically victory it was, also strengthened the hand of Foch in his dealings with both Pétain and Haig. When Pétain had demanded that the reserves behind the British Front be moved to cover Paris, he had refused to comply. When Haig had insisted, rightly as it turned out, that the existing reserves on his front should remain there, Foch, while agreeing with his diagnosis of Ludendorff's intentions, had made it clear that the last word in this vital matter must be with him.

Ludendorff now faced a situation approaching stalemate. Once again he had failed to attract the major Allied reserves away from Haig's front and had lost many irreplaceable men in the process. If he did not stage his major effort soon with the Crown Prince Rupprecht's Army Group in Flanders, the military balance of power, both material and moral, which had been with him since the spring, would soon swing against him.

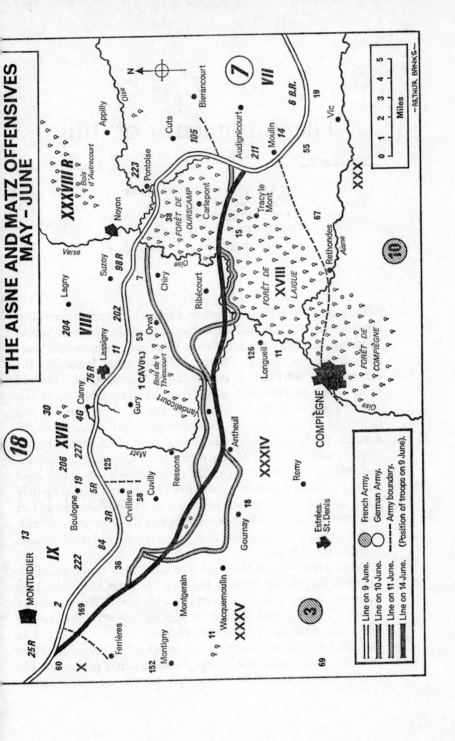

THE AISNE AND MATZ OFFENSIVES
MAY – JUNE

~ARTHUR BANKS~

N

Miles
0 1 2 3 4 5

Legend:
— Line on 9 June.
▬ Line on 10 June.
▨ Line on 11 June.
▰ Line on 14 June.

◉ French Army.
⊗ German Army.
--- Army boundary.
(Position of troops on 9 June).

Place names and units:

18 MONTDIDIER 13 IX 222 2 169 25R 60 X Ferrières 152 Montigny

30 XVII 206 227 4G Canny 75R Lassigny 204 VIII Lagny Appilly Oise

XXXVIII R Bois d'Autrecourt Noyon Verse 223 Pontoise Cuts Bierancourt

N 7 VII 6 B.R. 19 Vic 55 Moulin 14 211 Audignicourt 105

Boulogne 19 5R 3R 84 36 Orvillers 58 Cuvilly Ressons 125

Suzoy 98R Chiry Oise 38 FORÊT DE OURSCAMP Carlepont Tracy le Mont 15

11 202 53 Orval Bois de Thiescourt Gury 1 CAV (Ft.) Vandelicourt Matz

Ribécourt Longueil 126 11 7 FORÊT DE LAIGUE XVIII 67 Rethondes Aisne

XXXIV Antheuil Remy Estrées. St. Denis FORÊT DE COMPIÈGNE Oise COMPIÈGNE

XXXV Wacquemoulin Montgerain Gournay 18 11 69 3 XXX 10

7

The Eighteenth of July

Far and near and low and louder
On the roads of earth go by,
Dear to friends and food for powder,
Soldiers marching all to die.

A. E. Housman, *A Shropshire Lad*

It was a battered and tired German Army which had now recoiled for what all in it, Ludendorff included, profoundly hoped would be its last decisive offensive. Before this could be mounted, however, it needed time to fill its depleted ranks. Inevitably the bravest men had fallen in the battles of March, April, May and June. Their places were now taken by men often with less stomach for the fight, combed out from the rear services and staffs, the offices and factories and ex-prisoners of war from the Russian Front resentfully re-enrolled and often infected with revolutionary ideas. Soldiers, particularly Germans, Americans and British, if they are to retain their fighting efficiency, need meat. Prisoners captured by the British reported that they only got it on nine days a month when not in action. Poor diet in fact may well explain their lack of resistance to the influenza epidemic at this time. At its height as many as 2,000 men in each division were on the sick list.

On 28 June Mangin, who had now taken over command of the Tenth Army on the western flank of the great bulge south of Soissons, staged a minor operation with two divisions east of Villers Cotterets with a view to getting a good start line for operations later on. To his astonishment he found a decline in German opposition: no continuous trenches had been dug. There was very little wire. Altogether he took 1,200 prisoners. The British too from their front reported that the Germans, usually meticulous in field sanitation, had apparently ceased to bother about burying their dead or constructing latrines.

Ludendorff was not only running out of men: he was running out of ideas as well. In essence, his broad strategic plan remained what it had been since March: a blow by the Crown Prince's Army Group in the south to draw the Allied reserves in that direction and a final decisive stroke in the north against the British. Accordingly, he now planned to attack on both sides of the fortified area of Reims with 49 divisions in three armies. West of the city the Seventh Army was to force the crossing of the Marne on either side of Dormans and then, having gained adequate depth, link up with the First and Third Armies on the other flank thrusting on Chalons. Reims, thus isolated like Sedan in 1870, he thought, must inevitably attract Foch's reserves like a magnet. Once again the Allied defences would be saturated with another overwhelming Bruchmüller-type bombardment. This completed, the heavy artillery would start to move north for the grand climax provisionally fixed for early August. Unwisely, he named the operation 'Friedensturm' ('Peace Offensive'), thus giving his troops the impression that this would be the last major battle of the war.

Much of the success of the Germans in March, April and May had been due to the skill and discipline with which they had enforced strict security before the battle and thus achieved surprise. Now, partly as a result of lassitude and relaxed discipline, all indications from the last days of June onwards added daily to the growing French conviction that the next big attack would be in Champagne. On 28 June prisoners captured on Gouraud's front stated that reconnaissances were being carried out and bridging material being accumulated for a crossing of the Marne between Épernay and Château Thierry. Others spoke of a double attack, one part west of Reims against the Marne sector of the line and the other east of the city. From the first days of July onwards French air observers reported a great increase in traffic behind the German lines on both these fronts. Air photographs revealed badly-camouflaged new dumps, fresh cross-country tracks and signs of troop concentrations. The area north of the Marne, it seemed, was a veritable ants' nest.

The French Fourth Army held the line immediately east of the fortified area of Reims; on the east side of the salient stood the

Fifth Army; the Sixth Army held the line along the Marne and the Tenth the west flank. These Armies, which on 1 July amounted to 17 divisions in the line and nine in reserve, Foch now proceeded to build up to 20 in line and 15 in reserve. Of these, three divisions and a cavalry corps belonged to the Ninth Army which Foch stationed behind the Sixth Army opposite Dormans. Furthermore on 10 July he arranged with Haig for the intervention of the nine squadrons of bombers and fighters of the 9th Brigade RAF on the Marne front. Under pressure from Pétain to make the British 'bear a greater share of the burden of the war', he requested him to be ready to move two corps, a total of eight divisions, to the Marne Front.

At long last the experience of the British in March and April, and their own in May and June on the Aisne and the Matz, had more or less convinced the French generals that the answer to the overwhelming Bruchmüller opening bombardment, followed by a breakthrough, lay in reducing the number of troops in the first position to a few heroic machine-gunners and in fighting the main defensive battle on a second position about three miles or more in rear. The Germans would thus be taken by surprise and forced to bring their field artillery forward and make a fresh fire plan in the face of unbroken defences held by troops unshaken by their opening bombardment—in other words, they would be 'false-fronted' so that their initial blow fell on thin air.

East of Reims, Gouraud, the commander of the Fourth Army, established in a well-developed trench system, found little difficulty in applying this technique. Thanks to his personal magnetism the morale of his Army, which included the 42nd United States Division, was high. Its Chief of Staff, MacArthur, described him as 'a heroic figure; with one arm gone and half a leg missing, with his flaming red beard glittering in the sunlight, the jaunty rake of his cocked hat and the oratorical brilliance of his resonant voice, his impact was overwhelming'. His reputation for courage in battle in the French colonial wars, in 1914, in Gallipoli and afterwards, equalled that of Mangin. The Fifth Army west of Reims was less fortunate in its commander, Berthelot, much of whose service had been spent in higher staff appointments. In the Chemin des Dames battle his Army had been pushed back: its defences were flimsier than those of the Fourth. The Second Position was little more than a trace and the

Third Position existed only in the imagination of his staff. Moreover he allowed himself to be fascinated by the Marne itself, 80 yards wide, flowing across his front at his western end; surely, he thought, this must be the real line of resistance. He also reached the conclusion that certain localities in between the First and Second Positions would be useful later on and should therefore be held even if outflanked or surrounded. Unfortunately, he succeeded in persuading Pétain, Fayolle the Army Group Commander and Degoutte of the Sixth Army that he was right—a decision they would all subsequently regret. As a result the attack when it came would find his First Position held in excessive strength and about a third of the effective infantry of the two right-hand corps of the Sixth Army, including the United States 3rd Division, in the First Position on the banks of the Marne.

Having thus, they hoped, led the Germans into a trap, Foch and Pétain planned to deliver a massive counter-stroke against the western shoulder of the salient with 24 divisions of the Tenth Army under Mangin and part of the Sixth Army on a 30-mile front, supported by over 2,000 guns, 500 tanks and 1,200 aircraft in a ground-attack rôle. Along this flank the Forest of Villers Cotterets gave ample scope for concealment before the attack. Six miles from the western edge of the salient ran the main highway from Soissons to Château Thierry. An advance across this main artery to be delivered about 18 July and directed on the plateau north-west of Fère en Tardenois, combined with an attack on the other shoulder of the salient by the Fifth Army must inevitably hamstring the German offensive. The Allied air forces therefore were ordered at all costs to prevent the enemy discovering the concentration in the Forest of Villers Cotterets. This they very efficiently proceeded to do.

Normally the French when not involved in active operations followed a policy of live and let live with the Germans in the belief that if they were not provoked they would be let alone. This was as anathema to Gouraud as to his Allies the British, who never missed a chance when in contact of being as aggressive as possible by day and night. Gouraud, hungry for information and determined not to be surprised, insisted that on his front at least one German should be captured every day. On 14 July he mounted a particularly deep raid and took 27 prisoners. Among these was a man who under interrogation betrayed the fact that the grand attack would open with a bombardment at 12.10 that very night and last for three hours. He went on to state that the name of the operation was 'Friedensturm'. He seemed particularly anxious not to be separated from his gas mask. The inference was obvious. At 11 p.m. all the French heavy batteries opened up with rapid fire on every likely forming-up place and battery position. Punctually at 12.10 a.m., as the prisoner had said, the blast of 2,000 field and heavy batteries deafened anyone within a mile of it. The noise woke the citizens of Paris: in the streets of Chalons by the light of the gun flashes it was as bright as day. For three hours the avalanche of shells descended on empty trenches and evacuated battery positions. Then as dawn broke at 4 a.m. the storm troops and about 20 tanks moved forward behind a curtain of fire and steel, advancing 100 metres every two minutes. In the dim light of the sultry dawn they looked for the crowds of prisoners and the piles of dead bodies they had encountered in previous offensives: there were none. Virtually unopposed they reached their first objectives within the hour. It was now full daylight under a lowering sky; the last 77 mm shell of the barrage expired on the final line. They looked ahead. There in front of them were the French and the 42nd United States Division strongly entrenched behind a forest of uncut wire. Then down upon them came the fire of 800 batteries and countless machine guns. All their tanks went up in smoke. Caught thus without shelter in the open the attack collapsed.

West of Reims it was a different story. Apart from the 3rd United States Division the troops holding the Marne were partly Italian and partly French divisions which had been badly mauled in the battles of May and June. Degoutte, in his anxiety to distribute his troops in depth and yet retain a grip on the river, had succeeded in being weak everywhere. Between the Marne and Reims, Berthelot now paid the penalty for a similar error. Their troops were no match for the German Seventh Army who less than seven weeks previously had chased them for over 35 miles and whose morale was high. At first light their guns opened up with an annihilating bombardment, including a high proportion of gas shells, on the French outpost position on either side of Dormans. Under cover of a dense smoke screen their storm troops swarmed across the river on rafts, in rowing boats and punts; simultaneously their engineers launched the pontoons destined to bear the bridges required for the field artillery, transport and reserves. Disquieting reports filtered through to Pétain's headquarters. Low cloud and smoke on the river blinded the French reconnaissance aircraft. Another breakthrough seemed imminent. Fearing the worst, at 9.50 a.m. Pétain raised the telephone and ordered Fayolle, the Army Group Commander, to halt the eight divisions and the tanks now en route to the west flank for Mangin's counter-stroke. Mangin was indignant. He too raised the telephone and managed to get through to Foch himself who had at that very moment called at Fayolle's headquarters on his way to a conference with Haig at Monchy le Chatel. According to Mangin's biographer, Commandant Bugnet, 'The fury of Mangin beggared description. "They" [Pétain and his Staff], said he, freely translated, "are a shower of stinking little grocers. Give me all the divisions of the French Army and I will show you what to do with them. Leave the battle to me." ' Meanwhile the sun had come out enabling the Allied air forces to intervene. The situation became clearer. The Germans in fact had succeeded in capturing a bridgehead on either side of Dormans three miles deep and seven to nine miles wide. At least six divisions were over the river. On the eastern shoulder of the salient between the Marne and Reims they had made a similar advance. Foch, unruffled, dictated a message for Pétain: 'Please understand that until you inform me of some fresh crisis there can be no question of slowing down in any way, still less of stopping Mangin's preparations.' He then went on his way to meet Haig at 1 p.m. He was in the best of spirits; a great weight, he told Haig, had been taken off his mind for he had feared that the attack would extend as far east as Verdun where he had no reserves. Haig replied that in his opinion Ludendorff still intended to make his major effort in the north. Foch agreed with this diagnosis, which indeed was the correct one. Nevertheless he insisted that he badly needed the four divisions of the British 22nd Corps on the Reims front. Haig loyally raised no objection.

All day the bloody struggle continued in the bridgehead south of the Marne. In clear skies the Allied aircraft swooping down on the footbridges over the Marne did immense execution; one after another they shot down the serried rows of observation balloons along the front. On the ground in intense heat the

United States 3rd Division pushed back the Germans into the river. On Gouraud's front the infantry, including those of the United States 42nd Division, infiltrated forward among the disorganised Germans. Both here and on the river confused and bitter close-quarter fighting continued throughout the 16th and 17th. German losses at the Marne crossings reached a terrifying height.

Despite the reverse east of Reims, Ludendorff succeeded in convincing himself that he had accomplished his purpose of attracting Foch's reserves away from the vital northern front On the 17th he started the move by rail of the heavy artillery and mortars to the north to prepare for the final blow and himself set off for the Crown Prince Rupprecht's headquarters at Tournai to make the final arrangements.

That very evening the weather broke and the rain came down in torrents over the battlefields. On this night of thunder and lightning seven men held the lives of some three million soldiers and the destinies of Europe in their hands: Ludendorff, the super German general staff officer par excellence, politically out of his depth, inwardly wracked by anxiety and frustration beneath a harsh and forbidding exterior; Foch, the exuberant military academic whose panacea for success was to attack at all times whatever the cost; he had gone on saying it ever since 1914; like the punter who always backs the second favourite in every race, he was bound to pick a winner sooner or later: Haig, the dour inarticulate Scot, with good reason, trusting none of his Allies 100 per cent and concerned above all with what he conceived to be his duty to his King, his Armies and himself; Pershing, coldly practical, equally without illusions concerning his Allies, unshakeable in maintaining what he considered to be the interests of his nation and his Army; Pétain still at heart a French peasant, cunning, obstinate, mean and selfish, ultimately concerned only for the survival of his own kind and the propertied classes of France; Mangin and Gouraud, veritable reincarnations of Napoleon's great fighting Marshals of France.

The essence of Mangin's plan was to secure surprise by assembling his assault troops under the cover of the Forest of Villers Cotterets and then, at the last possible moment, moving them forward to their start line to attack, without any preliminary bombardment, under an intense rolling barrage to come down at 4.35 a.m. on the 18th. Pétain's temporary loss of nerve on the

15th had put the concentration behind schedule. Some of Mangin's subordinate generals accordingly protested that it would be suicidal to attack without allowing proper time for reconnaissance and for arrangements to be made for liaison between the tanks and the infantry. They were overruled. The night was black as pitch. On the narrow roads and tracks within the dripping woods half-a-million soldiers, French, African and American, soaked to the skin, groped their way forward. The ditches were full to the brim; off the few metalled tracks the floor of the forest was bottomless; many lost direction. At 2 a.m. Mangin himself and his staff joined the dense flow of men moving forward in the darkness. He was en route for his Command Post on a commanding hill three miles north-east of Villers Cotterets. Here he had had constructed an observation platform 60 feet above the ground whence he proposed to survey the battlefield. Ahead within the German lines there was dead silence. Not even a flare went up.

The two *groupements*, equivalent to a battalion each, of Saint Chamond tanks which were to operate with the 1st United States Division were late. They were the best the French had, mounting a 75mm gun and four Hotchkiss guns. They had a crew of eight men each; their armour was thin. Over good going they could rise to five miles per hour. The country was strange to their officers; there was no time for liaison with the Americans. Nonetheless they somehow or other managed to link up with the American infantry, 48 of them at any rate. On the other flank of the 20th Corps 28 tanks succeeded in joining the 2nd United States Division similarly just in time. Twelve of the tanks moved with each leading battalion; the rest followed in depth. It was a near thing for the infantry of the 2nd United States Division who had to cover the last 500 yards to the start line at the run. They got there, breathless but full of fight, at the very moment when the barrage crashed down at 4.35 a.m. During the past forty-eight hours the Americans had had no food and little water. Nonetheless they pressed forward on either flank of the veteran Moroccans with equal ardour into the murk ahead behind the moving curtain of fire. Mangin's Tenth Army, on a front of seven corps, supported by 500 tanks and over 2,000 guns, in the thick mist and smoke of the early dawn was advancing to the kill. Surprise was complete.

Mangin had the Napoleonic touch. On his way to his Command Post he spotted a French soldier asleep under a tree. Pulling him by the ear, as Napoleon would have done, he said: 'Wake up you skunk, you don't know what you're missing. Today we knock the Boche to Hell. You'll never get a chance like this again.' Whereupon he pushed the soldier into his car and told the driver to deposit him with all speed in the front line.

In the wan light of the early dawn the Americans and Moroccans and the French tanks found the going good over a gently rolling plateau covered with knee-high corn. The tanks romped ahead crushing machine gun after machine gun. By 7.15 a.m. they had advanced over a mile-and-a-half. Now, if ever, was the time for the cavalry to break out. Mangin turned to Robillot, the Commander of the 2nd Cavalry Corps beside him and ordered him to thrust ahead for Fère en Tardenois. The cavalry were nowhere to be seen. They were in fact miles back trapped in the gigantic traffic jam which had built up in the forest. The mist began to lift; the fleeting moment had gone. The infantry and tanks had now reached a belt of close country interspersed with small woods and ravines choked with undergrowth. They were now amongst the enemy batteries and the slaughter of the tanks began. German reserves, hastily flung into the battle, faced with fanatical courage the savagery of the Moroccans and the ardour of the Americans. The smoke of burning tanks smothered the battlefield.

A truly terrifying situation confronted the Crown Prince and his staff. Simultaneously with Mangin's attack, Gouraud had opened up with every gun he had, leaving them in doubt till, ten o'clock as to which was the major blow. As the fog slowly thinned out and the clouds lifted, it at last became clear that the west flank of the Marne Salient between the Ourcq and the Aisne had been smashed on a front of 12 miles: the possibility of a gigantic débâcle loomed up. Planning must start at once for a possible withdrawal: Soissons must be held at all costs; two reserve lines must be reconnoitered and stiffened with machine guns. By 11.45 a.m. the situation of the divisions south of the Marne had become desperate. Orders went out for their immediate evacuation; their fantastic losses of the past three days had been in vain. Meanwhile the whole vast salient was surrounded by a circle of flame. Five hundred Allied aircraft swept the skies.

On Mangin's front the Americans and Moroccans by noon had advanced over three miles and the other corps were not far behind.

Meanwhile that very morning at Mons a very high-level conference had assembled presided over by Ludendorff himself. The Crown Prince Rupprecht, the Commanders of the Fourth and Sixth Armies and all the Chiefs of Staff down to corps level were there. They had come together to decide the final details of the artillery programme for 'Hagen', the grand attack by 32 specially trained divisions designed to carry the high ground west and south-west of Ypres and to drive the British into the sea, which had been in preparation ever since February. While the discussion was going on the news from the Marne front began to arrive. Ludendorff ordered two divisions to move to Soissons. The discussion continued. More bad news arrived. Ludendorff ordered a further two divisions to follow them and, abruptly dismissing the conference, left for Supreme Headquarters. Late that afternoon, by telegram, he stopped the northward move of all troops and guns destined for 'Hagen' and placed them at the disposal of the Crown Prince on the Marne front. At the same time he ordered the suspension of all attacks against the fortified area of Reims.

In the early afternoon there came a lull in the fighting south of Soissons: in the Forest of Villers Cotterets the traffic congestion had reached nightmare proportions. It seemed that Mangin's attack had lost its momentum. General von Eben, the Commander of the Seventh Army, with reviving confidence went ahead with his preparations for a counter-attack to be delivered with the maximum violence next day. He reckoned without Mangin. In the heat of the late afternoon the Tenth Army once more swept forward sucking into the mêlée to form a southern defensive flank the troops von Eben had destined for the counter-attack on the morrow. The Germans had lost the initiative for good. As night closed in the Marines and infantry of the United States 2nd Division, their flanks in the air, dug in on the plateau east of Vierzy. Since dawn they had made the deepest advance of the day—over five miles fighting all the way. On their northern flank the Moroccans and the United States 1st Division finally extinguished all resistance in the ravine and village of Missy aux Bois. From Mangin came peremptory orders to resume the attack at dawn.

G

Mangin's motives in choosing to direct his battle from his lofty platform were not entirely disingenuous. He was particularly anxious to avoid the embarrassment of having Pétain breathing down his neck all day. He had no intention of either being tied down to the telephone answering awkward questions or receiving suggestions he did not want. In these respects he had succeeded. When therefore, footsore and sweating, in the late evening Pétain and Fayolle managed to get through to him after struggling on foot through the enormous traffic jam and bottomless sloughs of the forest, their congratulations had a hollow ring. Mangin, said Pétain, must return to his Main Headquarters to coordinate the operations of his corps and to keep in touch with his superiors. 'Here,' he added 'you command nothing.' 'But I do,' replied Mangin with ill grace, 'I have all my staff with me ready to go forward on horseback with my orders.' Pétain was obdurate, making it quite clear that he did not approve of these colonial methods of command. Mangin must understand that the situation of the Army as a whole did not justify unlimited exploitation on the Tenth Army front. Mangin continued to press for all reinforcements to be sent to him. 'No,' replied Pétain, icily, 'return to your Main Headquarters.' The interview was at an end. No sooner had he departed than Mangin issued orders for all-out exploitation on his front at dawn and rang up Foch to tell him he had done so.

Next morning the Paris press, forbidden by the censorship to mention his name, praised to the skies 'this brilliant, dynamic and original general with the face of a bird of prey whose courage is already legendary'. Barrès, the arbiter of the intellectuals, wrote of 'a manoeuvre in the grand manner of the great French military tradition which shows what our generals can do when given the means'.

Duly at first light the Tenth Army resumed the attack. Surprise had now gone and the French and Americans found themselves faced by countless machine guns hidden in the standing crops and among the bushes. There were no tanks left: it was a purely infantry battle now. Nonetheless they added another two to three miles to the gains of the previous day. By nightfall the Marines and infantry of the 2nd United States Division had the main Château Thierry–Soissons road under their fire. In two days' continuous fighting they had captured

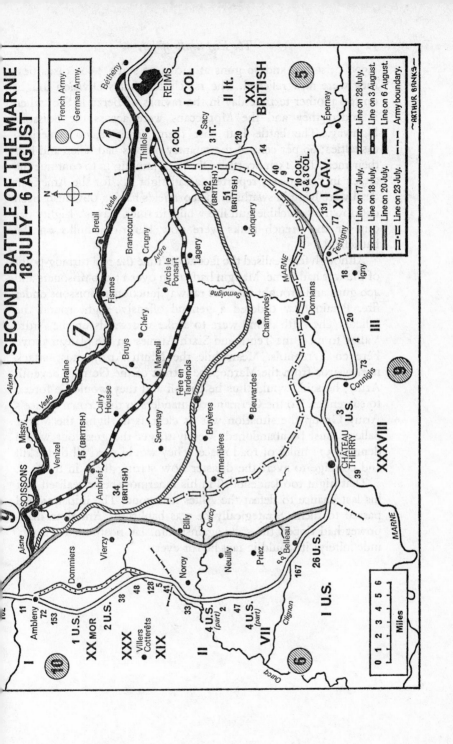

SECOND BATTLE OF THE MARNE
18 JULY – 6 AUGUST

French Army.
German Army.

Line on 17 July.
Line on 18 July.
Line on 20 July.
Line on 23 July.
Line on 28 July.
Line on 3 August.
Line on 6 August.
Army boundary.

~ARTHUR BANKS~

Miles
0 1 2 3 4 5 6

Aisne
Aisne
SOISSONS
Missy
Venizel
Ambrief
15 (BRITISH)
Braine
Vesle
Vesle
Breuil
Fismes
Branscourt
Crugny
Arcis le
Ponsart
Chéry
Bruys
Lagery
Semoigne
Arcire
Béthény
Thillois
REIMS
Sacy
Epernay
I COL
2 COL
3 IT.
II It.
XXI
BRITISH
120
14
40
9
7
10 COL
5 & 3 COL
131
77
I CAV.
XIV
18
Igny
Festigny
62
(BRITISH)
51
(BRITISH)
Jonquery
MARNE
III
20
4
73
Connigis
9
Dormans
Champvoisy
Beuvardes
Bruyères
Armentières
Billy
Ourcq
Noroy
Neuilly
Priez
Belleau
Clignon
Ourcq
26 U.S.
167
I U.S.
6
47
2
33
4 U.S.
(part)
4 U.S.
(part)
VII
II
XIX
5
128
41
48
38
Villers
Cotterêts
XXX
XX MOR
1 U.S.
2 U.S.
153
72
11
Ambleny
I
10
Dommiers
Vierzy
Cuiry
Housse
Servenay
Mareuil
Fère en
Tardenois
CHÂTEAU
THIERRY
39
MARNE
XXXVIII
3 U.S.
1
7
5
N

2,900 prisoners and 70 guns at a cost of some 4,000 casualties; they were now relieved. The 1st United States Division fought on for another terrible day in the ravines of Berzy le Sec: when it ended they and the Moroccans were across the Soissons highway. The battle had cost them nearly 8,000 American casualties; 60 per cent of the infantry officers had fallen and half their men. The 15th Scottish Division, moving in to continue the attack in their place, reported 'a sad sight . . . for the American dead were lying in swaths in the cornfields having obviously been cut down by machine gun fire whilst in thick waves'. Eighty per cent of the French tanks were now burnt-out hulks on the battlefield.

Although few realised the fact at the time the real turning-point of the war had come. Mangin had taken over 15,000 prisoners and 400 guns and brought the vital railway junction at Soissons under fire. Pétain now ordered a general offensive right round the salient. The Fifth Army were to strike westwards up the Ardre Valley to meet the Tenth and Sixth Armies on the plateau above Fère en Tardenois. Meanwhile the Ninth Army must attack northwards from the Marne; the retreat of the German Seventh Army, he said, would thus be cut off and they would be forced to surrender. To the German commanders in the Crown Prince's Army Group the situation was as clear as daylight: the Marne Salient must be abandoned. Merely to get the guns out would demand 375 miles of road space. They would need all their skill and courage to avert the disaster now staring them in the face.

That night too Ludendorff in his innermost heart realised that his last chance to defeat the Allies had gone. The initiative had passed to them. Strategically he was bankrupt; American man-power had tipped the scale against him. He postponed 'Hagen' indefinitely: it would in fact be for ever.

8

High Summer

Although strategically the First Quartermaster-General now
faced a dilemma beyond his ability to solve and partly of his
own creation, his subordinates from Colonel-General down to
Feld-Webel had the will and the skill to do tactically what needed
to be done. By 20 July the Crown Prince's Headquarters had
the situation once more under control. Obviously the aim of the
Allies was to cut off all their troops in the Marne Salient; its
shoulders therefore at Soissons and on the Ardre must be held
at all costs and the line shortened by pulling back that very night
the three corps on either side of Château Thierry for five miles.
Accordingly they manned the new line with reserves and set
about the preparation of a series of other defensive positions in
depth behind which to recoil later. Simultaneously they concentrated all their air effort on the Soissons flank where the
danger was greatest. Finally they made it clear to Ludendorff's
Staff at OHL that the whole salient must be gradually abandoned
and the front shortened by eventually pulling back to the line of
the Aisne and the Vesle: only thus could the initiative be regained.

In adopting this text book solution to their difficulties they
had in fact divined Pétain's aim almost to the letter. It was: 'not
merely a matter of driving the enemy from the Château Thierry
pocket but also of cutting off his retreat to the north and capturing
the bulk of his forces', by continuing to apply the maximum
possible pressure on the hinges of the salient. To this end, he
ordered the Tenth and Sixth Armies to continue the all-out

attack on the west flank and the Fifth Army to thrust up the valley of the Ardre in the general direction of Fismes. On Mangin's front fresh divisions were now resisting with character-istic German obstinacy. Tanks and attacks eight times repeated on the 20th failed to dislodge them. Pétain therefore diverted to his front two fresh French divisions, the United States 32nd Division and the British 15th Scottish and 34th Divisions. To the Sixth Army he gave the United States 42nd Division; on the Fifth Army front the British 22nd Corps was already in action astride the Ardre.

The two divisions of this Corps had been hurriedly moved from the British front and concentrated after an arduous night march in the southern part of the Forest of the Montagne with a view to relieving the 2nd Italian Corps reported to be 'in an exhausted and shaken condition'. This they found to be no overstatement: out of a fighting strength of 24,000 they had lost nearly 10,000 and all their guns except seven. Berthelot, the Fifth Army Commander on the morning of the 19th, elated by Mangin's success on the previous day, jumped to the conclusion that the Germans on his own front must withdraw. Accordingly, he cancelled the plan for the relief of the Italians and ordered Godley, the Commander of the British 22nd Corps, to pass through them and attack the eastern half of the salient on either side of the Ardre. Theoretically this would have been a sound course provided the Germans on this front had had the slightest inclination to withdraw, if the country had been less enclosed and if the British divisions, strangers in a strange land, had been given time to reconnoitre the ground, and to familiarise them-selves with French methods of command. All these conditions were absent. All English-speaking officers had apparently been sent to the Americans: few British officers had ever seen before the black and white hachured maps with the unfamiliar 1/80,000 scale. Nevertheless Godley and his divisional commanders, determined at all costs to avoid any suspicion that their hearts were not in the fight, accepted Berthelot's plan without criticism, little realising the ordeal to which their men would soon be subjected.

The very detailed Fifth Army Orders for the attack at 8 o'clock the following morning reached both divisions too late for any reconnaissance to be done that day. The barrage map did not arrive till 3 a.m. They envisaged an attack on the axis of the River Ardre on a four-divisional front with the two British divisions sandwiched between the 2nd French Colonial Division on the right and the 9th French Division on the left. The valley of the Ardre, 2,000–3,000 yards wide, was knee-deep in standing corn, affording perfect concealment to the enemy, and was bounded on each side by heavily wooded ridges with bastion-like spurs, from which the German machine-gunners could and did rake the valley. The line of advance of the 62nd West Riding Division lay along the northern ridge: the 51st Highland Division was allotted the southern. There were many sunken roads athwart both. Here and there, both on the ridges and in the valleys, strongly built villages provided ideal centres of resistance. The country in fact combined many of the unpleasant characteristics of the Normandy bocage plus some of those of the Falaise plain. The operation therefore, staged by the French Fifth Army Staff entirely off the map, mounted in haste, characterised by slipshod staff work and finally anticipated by the Germans, was inevitably doomed to near-disaster from the start. Everything went wrong. The attacking infantry, Highlanders, Yorkshiremen and Northumbrians, traditionally men as tough as any the British Isles produce, after a nightmare six-mile approach march in the dark, subjected to persistent delays owing to the complete absence of traffic control in the hopelessly congested rear areas, only just reached what they thought was their start line at 8 a.m. The barrage now came down a long way ahead and soon bounded out of sight. Many German machine guns, thus missed, opened up. Nevertheless the four British and French Divisions, now without artillery support, stepped off into the unknown. A day of utter confusion and bitterly contested little battles followed on all divisional fronts. On the 62nd (West Riding) Divisional Front the struggle was exceptionally bloody. Of it a German survivor of the 50th Division defending the villages of Cuitron and Marfaux wrote: 'From every bay window many rifle barrels faced the attacking enemy. Below in the cellars our heavy machine guns were mounted . . . every bullet found its mark. The attacking enemy fell in rows, doubled up and collapsed silently in the high grass of the parkland.' When night fell, the 62nd Division reorganised a bare half-a-mile in advance of their morning start line. The French 2nd Colonial Division had made no advance whatever. On the other side of the Ardre, the 51st Highland Division in a day of attack and counter-attack, despite many casualties resulting from the highly sensitive French shells bursting in the trees over their heads, had managed to advance a mile. The 9th Division, one of the best the French could produce, had been driven back. Similar attempts on the 21st to get forward proved equally costly and abortive, not surprisingly as the Germans had now fed four fresh divisions into the battle. When therefore the attack was resumed on the following day both British divisions encountered machine-gun fire on a fantastic scale: nevertheless they did succeed in advancing a further half mile.

Meanwhile on the western flank Mangin had found himself confronted by well-rested troops and many batteries which shot his tanks to bits and decimated his infantry. Overhead German aircraft dominated the air by day and bombed unchecked by night. Faced by stalemate, he decided to fling the 15th Scottish and 34th British into the cauldron with all speed. What his motives were in placing the 34th Division under command of his 30th Corps and the 15th Scottish under his 20th Corps in relief of the 1st United States Division are unknown. The result was that the two British divisions were not only under command of different corps commanders but separated from each other by two French divisions sandwiched in between them. Major-General Reed, commanding the 15th Scottish Division, got his orders to attack at 8 a.m. the following morning at 10.35 p.m. the previous night, the 22nd July. His artillery had not arrived. Major-General Summerall of the United States 1st Division, however, generously came to his aid and ordered his own artillery, despite the fact that they had been in continuous action for five days, to remain a further twenty-four hours in the line to support the British. Summerall also lent his motor ambulances and kept his hospitals open for four days after his own troops had gone out of the line. Without his help the heavy British casualties now to be sustained would have been exposed to the none too tender mercies of the French Medical Service, such as it was.

Not surprisingly in view of the haste with which it was mounted, the attack on the morrow on a front of eight divisions with about 100 tanks soon fizzled out in bloody and futile muddle.

On the 15th Divisional front the line taken over was not where the French staff said it was. The barrage therefore left many of the German machine guns untouched and the Scots, when they advanced, were soon halted by withering machine gun fire. The attack by the British 34th Division and the French 58th Division, largely owing to the fact that the British CRA spoke French well, had more success. Communications, however, soon broke down and at the end of the day only the British 102nd Brigade, which had advanced about three-quarters of a mile could claim any success on the whole Tenth Army Front. Short shooting by the French artillery had added to the general frustration and useless slaughter. The French signal lights designed to indicate the position of the infantry to the artillery unfortunately could not be fixed to the British rifle.

The only significant Allied advance on this day was made on the Ardre where the 62nd and 51st British divisions succeeded, in spite of resistance of the bitterest character, in capturing the village of Marfaux. Here they rescued some of their own wounded who had been captured three days previously: the Germans had dressed their wounds and given them water but no food: probably they had none themselves. By nightfall these divisions had advanced their front line by a further 1,200 yards. It was now abundantly clear that the Germans, although they were withdrawing gradually at the southern end of the salient, had no intention whatever of relinquishing their hold on its shoulders for the time being. In actual fact only the fear of a large-scale Allied counter-offensive on another part of the front prevented them from launching a massive counter-attack against Mangin's and Berthelot's Armies at this time.

The virtually complete ignorance, after four years of war, of the British and French of each other's language, mentality, organisation and methods, now glaringly apparent, almost surpasses belief. Surprisingly, far more British officers had a smattering of French than their opposite numbers of English. Hardly any, however, were capable of conducting a conversation on the telephone. Those French officers who could speak English were generally from the Reserve and lacked both prestige with their own superiors and military knowledge. Admittedly in the front line, despite the language barrier, understanding of a sort was achieved. Physical courage provides a bond between all

men no matter what their race, language and creed: elsewhere
frustration, misunderstanding and exasperation reigned. All
communications had to be in French. It was impossible to get a
message in English passed back either in Morse or plain language
over the field telephone. Written messages sent back or to a
flank in English were not understood: if given to French despatch-
riders the chances of their being delivered to the appropriate
address were remote. French abbreviations were unintelligible.
French operation orders when received went into detail which in
British eyes seemed absurd. They were not accompanied by a
distribution list so no one knew who else had got them and who
had not. Invariably they arrived late. Fear of loss of secrecy
apparently prohibited the despatch of warning or anticipatory
orders by the French staffs. Last-minute alterations were legion.
Almost without exception troops were committed to battle in a
hurry without being given time for reconnaissance or for ensuring that all concerned knew what they had to do. This would have
been excusable if the element of surprise had been present; now
that it had gone the wasteful expenditure of British life on the
orders of foreign generals was a bitter pill to swallow. For
British officers this will always be a difficult problem in view of
their personal responsibility to their King or Queen to ensure
that the lives of the men under their command are not thrown
unnecessarily away.

Immediately behind the front, traffic congestion anticipated
some of the great pile-ups of the Second War. Most of the roads
had collapsed under the heavy traffic. The need to move at night
without lights added to the chaos. British troops suddenly
moved to the French front by rail found themselves in cattle
trucks from which the horse dung had not been removed: no
provision was made for food or water. Only the threat of being
shot would induce the drivers of French troop-carrying vehicles
to deviate from their route. 'Information concerning latrines,'
solemnly records the British Official History, 'was vague and
untrustworthy.' In fact when found these installations beggared
description. British wounded unlucky enough to become involved
in the French evacuation system were liable to be reported
'missing'.

American experience of French staff and command methods
had been almost as exasperating and costly. They complained

particularly of repeated changes in orders, lack of advance warning and consideration for their logistic needs. Their troops had led the van of Mangin's great counter-stroke and had advanced further than any of the Allies at disproportionate cost, admittedly in some cases as a result of lack of experience. Only too often French troops had lagged behind leaving them exposed to German enfilade fire and counter-attacks. There had been a particularly irritating incident on 15 July. Several companies of the United States 28th Division had by mistake been assigned to French battalions in the front line. When the Germans attacked, the French withdrew leaving the Americans to fight their own way out. It was not easy for Pershing to explain to Washington and the American press why Mangin's 20th Corps which had struck the decisive blow on 18 July, although 80 per cent American and the rest Moroccan, had to be commanded by a French general. His worst fears had now been realised. He now had six divisions committed in the battle in the Marne Salient and would soon have eight. American troops had, at least in German eyes, shown dash equivalent to their own in 1914. He was sick to death of derogatory remarks by high officers of the Allies about 'our poorly trained staff and higher commanders which our men have stood as long as they can'. To save the French from collapse he had consented to allow his troops to be thrust piecemeal into battle under French commanders without due consideration for their logistic needs and to defer the formation of his own Army with its own sector of the front. He and his officers had been patronised to the limit of endurance and he wished 'to hear no more of that sort of nonsense'. He had now made it clear to Pétain that he proposed to send out orders at once for the formation of an all-American Army: how it would be formed and where it would be could be finally settled at the Allied Conference called for 24 July at Foch's headquarters. On the previous evening Haig was his guest. Mutual cordiality and expressions of esteem, tempered by caution on both sides, characterised what would be described half-a-century later as a 'working dinner'. Haig spoke of his proposals for taking the offensive but he did not, as Pershing feared he would, ask for American help. Pershing outlined his plans for uniting his army. He did not mention the fact that he had decided to withdraw the divisions training behind the British front.

When on the morrow Haig, Pétain and Pershing met at Foch's new headquarters at the château of Bombon near Melun, 25 miles south-east of Paris, Pershing at once sensed an atmosphere of pronounced optimism and bonhomie in sharp contrast with the gloom and suspicion which had characterised their conferences in May and June. Foch opened the proceedings, reading from notes, by summing up the general situation with which, in fact, all present were already familiar. There could be no doubt now that the fifth German offensive of the year had been checked by Gouraud and that the Allied counter-offensive under Mangin had transformed it into a defeat. Every effort, said Foch, must be made to retain the initiative—a sentiment in which all present heartily concurred. At last it seemed his doctrine of 'L'offensif à l'outrance' was the right answer to all their problems. They had as many divisions as the Germans and more aeroplanes and tanks. . . . The Americans were now arriving at the rate of a quarter-of-a-million a month and this would be maintained. There were indications that many of the German divisions were tired and under-strength. They must be attacked all along the line and given no respite. The immediate need, Foch went on to say, was to straighten out the great salients created by the German spring offensives and at St Mihiel, thus freeing the railways on which the logistic infrastructure of the Allies depended. He therefore gave to Pétain the task of continuing the counter-offensive on the Marne, the strategic aim of which was to free the Paris–Verdun railway. Haig he requested to go ahead as soon as possible with the attack east and south of Amiens with his Fourth and the First French Armies, the plans for which were already far advanced: this would remove the threat to the Paris–Amiens railway. Finally Foch accepted Pershing's plan for the reduction of the St Mihiel Salient so that the use of the railway from Paris to Nancy would be regained and placed under his command the 2nd Colonial Corps. On conclusion of these operations, Foch said, would come the second stage of his plans for the future—a series of offensives against parts of the German defences, where vulnerable, mounted at short notice and designed to keep the Germans guessing where the next blow would fall. As a result he hoped that eventually their whole front might crumble and make possible a general advance. The primary aim of these later attacks would be to liberate the coal mining area in the north and to drive the Germans back from the neighbourhood of Dunkirk and Calais. Apart from asking his Allies to supply him with statistics of the forces they would be able to put into the field on 1 January and 1 April 1919, Foch was not prepared to forecast the future. No one present suggested that the plans immediately envisaged and those to follow might be developed so as to end the war in 1918. The confirmatory memorandum issued at the end of the Conference makes this unequivocally clear. Nevertheless the three Commanders-in-Chief departed for their own headquarters in an optimistic mood; at last under Foch's direction they were at least fighting the same war. At last it was clearly understood that in future operations the Americans would constitute an independent Army on the same footing as the British.

In fact the balance of military power was far more in the Allies' favour than any of the belligerents realised at the time. Although in terms of divisions, always an unsatisfactory yard-stick, the Germans could field 201 against the Allies 194, many of these were under strength and 10 would soon be broken up. Furthermore 106 of them were fit for defensive duties only. British and American writers on both World Wars have adversely criticised this German practice, preferring a high general level of mediocrity to an Army consisting partly of cannon fodder and partly of a Corps d'Élite. It did, however, serve the Germans none too badly; expendable troops at least can be used to gain time and that, as Napoleon remarked, is everything. Counting heads, since March the British and French had lost half-a-million men each; by the end of July the German casualties for the same period would exceed a million. All three European powers had now scraped the bottom of the manpower barrel. The Americans, on the contrary, had well over a million men in France and were building up their forces to a planned total of 80 divisions, equivalent in manpower to 160 Allied divisions. Thus, in terms of riflemen, where in March the Germans had had a superiority of 300,000, the balance in favour of the Allies was now 200,000.

The mere sight of American troops training behind the British lines north of the Somme, raw though many of them were, acted as a stimulant. Some British survivors of the Somme and Passchendaele saw in their offensive eagerness a recollection of their own in 1914. Since the end of April only the British 9th

Corps on the Aisne and the 22nd Corps on the Marne had been
engaged in really heavy fighting. The huge losses of March and
April had been made good. Haig's conviction that the German
main effort would eventually come on his front about Bailleul
had resulted in the concentration of his reserves in the north.
Relieved of trench duty, they had at last a chance to train. Furthermore, with the advent of summer the physical discomfort of
life had greatly diminished. The divisions mauled on the Chemin
des Dames had been reconstituted and nursed back to health
on the Channel Coast. The effect of the purge of Haig's senior
staff officers six months previously was now apparent. Lawrence,
Kiggel's replacement as Chief of Staff, was an infinitely more
capable man. The influence of the new Quartermaster-General,
Travers Clarke, a man big in size and in many other respects, was
being felt throughout the vast administrative machine. Haig, his
evil genius Charteris having departed, was now receiving more
realistic intelligence. Officers whose inefficiency had been
demonstrated in the recent battles had been removed and their
places taken by others who had proved their capacity in action.
Higher authority now looked askance at battalion commanders
over 33 years of age. There had been a great increase in junior
officers promoted from the ranks for their services in the field
without regard to educational or social background. A new
spirit now permeated Haig's command system from top to bottom.

Since March the Germans had taught the British much: at long
last Haig had set up a special branch to study the problems raised
by a return to mobile warfare under an Inspector-General of
Training. This was Maxse, a man of imagination, originality and
drive with a wealth of battlefield experience behind him: from
him in fact Liddell Hart would in the future derive many of the
ideas he so widely and skilfully publicised in the twenties and
thirties, sad to relate, more to the advantage of his country's
enemies than his own or of the French. The influence of Maxse and
his staff, freed from responsibility for the daily conduct of
operations, with a roving commission to go where they wished,
was now felt throughout the Army. A new spirit seized the
Army and Divisional Schools. How rapidly the spirit of the new
doctrines had spread had already been revealed by two other very
able commanders, Rawlinson of the Fourth Army and Monash of
the Australian Corps in a minor battle at Hamel near Villers

Brettoneux on 4 July in which four companies of the United States 33rd Division, without Pershing's permission, took part. Of them Rawlinson wrote in a private letter at the time to his friend Colonel Clive Wigram, Assistant Private Secretary to the King:

'I selected the date of Independence Day as it was the first occasion on which American troops had taken part in an actual attack alongside our own fellows: and I was not a little put out when, at the very last moment, I got a direct order from Pershing that no American troops were to be employed. All went well and the Americans did not have many casualties; but if things had gone wrong I suppose I should have been sent home in disgrace. The American troops conducted themselves admirably, fought like tigers and have won the undying admiration and affection of the Australians, who were heard to remark: "We are damned glad they are on our side." '

As this little battle, the ostensible aim of which was to secure observation over the Somme valley, was to set the tone of greater operations for the rest of the year it is worth considering in some detail.

The new Mark V tank, thanks partly to the drive of Winston Churchill the Minister of Munitions, was now arriving in considerable numbers and it was necessary to convince the Army as a whole, and particularly the infantry, of its value. In his zeal for the promotion of the new arm its major advocate, Colonel Fuller, had missed no opportunity of being as offensive as possible to anyone reluctant to accept his point of view.

In April 1917 at Bullecourt the Australians had had a bad experience in working with tanks: they had been late in arriving and when they eventually turned up had fired on the Australians instead of the Germans. In fact Australian opinion had written them off as a nuisance which merely attracted shell fire on the battlefield. Before the Hamel battle therefore Monash rehearsed the parts his infantry and the tanks should play until he was satisfied that they understood each other's limitations and capabilities and had learnt to trust each other. In the actual attack there was no preliminary bombardment. Every possible step was taken to ensure surprise. Altogether some ten battalions and 60 tanks attacked on a frontage of 6,000 yards to a depth of

2,500 yards. The noise of the assembly of the tanks on their forming-up line was drowned by low-flying aircraft and routine harassing fire. At 3.02 a.m. the tanks moved forward towards the leading infantry: eight minutes later the supporting barrage fired by some 600 guns opened up and the tanks, under command of the infantry battalion commanders, advanced to their objectives. The tanks, supported by the infantry, crushed many machine guns and flushed the Germans out of Hamel village and Vaire wood into the arms of the Australians. They finally rallied, carrying cheering wounded on their backs. Supply tanks brought forward pickets and wire for consolidating the position and aircraft dropped 100,000 rounds of ammunition on the new front line. All was over by 5 a.m. The Australian losses were only 775, the American 133; of the 60 tanks 58 reached their objectives and only 13 of their crews were wounded; 1,500 prisoners were taken. A war-winning combination had been found: a corps commander of genius, the Australian infantry, the Tank Corps, the Royal Artillery and the RAF. The news spread: what the Australians could do, the 18-year-olds, the veterans with the golden wound stripes and the blue service chevrons, and even the middle-aged citizens combed out of offices and factories who made up the home-based British divisions, could at least attempt to emulate. One of the greatest stimulants to high morale is intelligent training; an even better stimulant is success. The first was at last forthcoming; the will to deserve the second was already there.

Ironically, at this very moment when Haig's house was at last in order, the brothers Lord Rothermere and Lord Northcliffe, both members of Lloyd George's government, were violently clamouring in the newspapers, the *Sunday Pictorial* and *The Times*, for greater civilian control over Haig and the War Office, for the despatch of a million coloured troops to the Western Front, and insisting that mercenaries should be employed wherever possible. The British public were being told to expect another seven years of war. Ironically too, *The Times* was giving full publicity to the hysterical campaign for the immediate internment of all aliens. The issue of 15 July contained a full and sympathetic account of the largest public demonstration of the war in Trafalgar Square demanding 'a clean sweep' and the internment of all members of the huge German spy network alleged to permeate every walk of

22 German Machine-gun section coming into action on the Matz, June 1918

23 The Marne at Dormans after withdrawal, late July 1918

24 Monash—the Commander of the formidable Australian Corps

25 Lt. L. D. McCarthy VC, 16th Australian Infantry Battalion

26 Private R. MacAti VC, 23rd Australian Infantry Battalion

27 Pilots of the RAF being briefed before take-off, summer 1918

British life. The truth in fact was the opposite. Ever since the outbreak of war the German Intelligence System had been almost incredibly inefficient; at no time was it able to obtain reliable information with regard to the strength and disposition of the Allies' reserves beyond the immediate areas of operations or to divine their long term strategic intentions. Mangin's offensive had in fact caught Ludendorff completely off balance; there had followed a fortnight of agonised indecision on his part, characterised by outbursts of bad temper and fiddling interference in minor matters which he should have left to his junior staff and culminating in the issue to the four Groups of Armies on the Western Front of an appreciation of the situation on 2 August which must go down to History as the all time low directive of the Great German General Staff. Like a Civil Servant anxious to evade personal responsibility, no matter what may happen, Ludendorff opened with the statement that 'the situation requires, first, that we stand on the defensive, and secondly, resume the offensive as soon as possible'. He went on to say that in view of the large forces engaged between the Marne and the Vesle, a large-scale Allied offensive elsewhere was unlikely in the near future. The Allies might however resume the attack on the Vesle. At a later date Allied attacks might be expected elsewhere: in the north about Kemmel, between the Somme and Soissons a distance of 70 miles, east of Reims, in the St Mihiel Salient or on the Lorraine front—in fact anywhere on the whole 600-mile front from Switzerland to the North Sea. Surprisingly, he failed specifically to mention the Amiens front. 'We must adhere to surprise attacks,' sententiously added the First Quartermaster-General. Foch and Haig had similar ideas, as he would soon learn.

H

9

The Army of the British Empire

Every man thinks meanly of himself for not having been a soldier, or not having been at sea.

Samuel Johnson

One of the most astonishing features of history is the persistent inability of the Continental Europeans to understand the British. Failure to appreciate their resilience in adversity and their determination to fight on to ultimate victory, no matter how black the outlook, has more than once been the eventual undoing of kings, emperors and dictators. Thus it had been ever since the days of Elizabeth I and Philip of Spain, of Louis XIV before Blenheim and Ramillies, and in Napoleon's time almost to the very end at Waterloo. In the future, Hitler after Dunkirk would fall into the same trap. Another constantly recurring factor in history seems to be the inability of anyone to learn anything from it. It is understandable therefore that Ludendorff, the super military technician and little else, who himself had laid so much stress on the importance of surprise in war, should now himself be on the point of becoming, at the hands of the British, the victim of surprise on a scale surpassing in its ultimate results anything he himself had achieved.

In underrating the British at this time Ludendorff was not alone. On 28 July Pershing in a letter to the Secretary of War, Newton D. Baker, wrote in explanation of his intention to do without French and British assistance in training:

'The additional fact, that training with these worn out French and British troops, if continued, is detrimental, is another reason for haste in forming our own units and conducting our own training. The morale of the Allies is low and association with them has a bad effect on our men. To counteract the talk our men have heard, we have to say to our troops, through their officers, that we have come over to brace up the Allies and help them win and that they must pay no attention along that line by their Allied comrades.'

Herein probably lies the explanation of the badinage at this time between the British rank and file coming out of the line for a brief rest and the American troops they found training in their rear areas, and incidentally buying up all the eggs at prices no Frenchman could resist. It was tactless on the part of some Americans with only a few months' service and no battle experience, to tell British veterans of the Somme and Passchendaele, often with several wound stripes, that they had crossed the Atlantic with a view to bracing them up. Repartee therefore on the lateness of their arrival on the scene was inevitable. Thus was born so far as the British were concerned the popular misunderstanding of the reasons why the Americans had entered the war which was to survive for the next half-century to nobody's advantage. These simple soldiers did not understand that the Americans had declared war against the Germans because their President could see no other way of protecting American lives and ships on the high seas and of ensuring that American influence would be decisive at the peace conference. They had not entered the war in support of British and French ideals and interests.

The literature of the period, some of it of high quality, represents for the most part the views of an educated, hypersensitive minority in the British Army: as an expression of the morale of the Army as a whole it is an unsatisfactory guide. The poets Edward Thomas, Wilfrid Gibson and Alan Seegar were introspective individuals obviously temperamentally unsuited for the leadership of men in battle and indeed for any form of service in the infantry. Siegfried Sassoon, at the time of his highest poetic output, was obviously suffering from what would later be described as combat fatigue or battle exhaustion which in the Second War would have been promptly detected and nipped in the bud. The play, *Journey's End*, which had a phenomenal success between the wars, represents a study of moral disintegration as seen through the eyes of a bank clerk. C. E. Montague would later advertise the sordid side in all its full horror. Paul Nash, Gilbert Rogers and William Orpen were honest artists: pictures of corpses in any case have a wide appeal, a fact of which newspaper proprietors have long been aware. These men, however, were exceptional and rare: the great majority, or at least their leaders down to platoon commanders and below, saw their situation in a different light: admittedly war was evil; nevertheless it was their duty to their country to fight, if necessary to the end, hoping rather pathetically, that this would be 'the war to end all wars'. Half-a-century later, in countless villages and towns in Great Britain and Northern Ireland, old men would make their painful way on 11 November to the local cenotaph, still sustained by the thought that they had not been found wanting in their country's hour of need; they would still retain their feeling of moral superiority over their contemporaries who had missed or evaded service in the front line, and often feel that in their own lives one thing at any rate had been worthwhile. So it would be in Australia on Anzac Day. Later generations may scoff at their ideals: the fact remains that they were ideals in which their ancestors profoundly believed. On the faith and devotion of these men, the vast inarticulate mass of the Army, the issue of the battles now ahead would depend.

The British generals in this war have been the target of more adverse criticism than those in any other. Whatever opinion of their capacity is held, this must be admitted: they realised that troops must not be allowed to sit and brood on the fact that 'they have a rendezvous with death' but that at all times, whether in or out of action, they must be kept profitably occupied so that in due course they will be able to eliminate their country's enemies efficiently and economically. The manner in which the 8th Division was handled in June and July is particularly illuminating. Since 21 March its casualties in the March retreat, at Villers Brettoneux in April and on the Chemin des Dames in May had exceeded 15,000, that is not far short of twice its infantry fighting strength and just 300 short of the Army record for the same period, held by the 50th Northumbrian Division, hard men from a harsh country who died game. Every battalion commander had fallen in action: some battalions had had three. To make up his losses Haig had been forced to break up seven divisions; nevertheless, in view of its fighting reputation, the

8th was not one of them. By the latter half of June, the survivors had been withdrawn to the coast south-west of Abbeville. This is how the divisional commander, Major-General Heneker, proceeded to rehabilitate it as reinforcements poured in from England and from the divisions which had been broken up:

'A programme of intensive training was carefully drawn up and put into operation with great thoroughness. Combined training in the morning and specialist training, lectures etc., in the afternoon formed the usual routine. The ranges were in constant occupation; intensive wiring and digging were frequently practised; regular attention was given to gas drill; particular stress was laid on training in manoeuvre and co-operation with the artillery. Night operations and route marches took place at intervals. No one was idle but at the same time the comfort and health of the troops was considered and the fact that many of them had just been through a prolonged period of extreme physical and mental strain was not forgotten.'

All this was done under the unrelenting, penetrating and ubiquitous eye of General Heneker; all units during the hours of daylight posted lookouts to ensure early warning of his approach. He expected to be saluted by everyone within eye range; his eagle eye could detect an unshaven chin, the need for a hair cut, a grease stain or an unpolished button at a considerable distance. His comments were unequivocally clear, vividly expressed and long remembered.

The Divisional History goes on to record:

'The weather during practically the whole period of the division's stay in this area was gloriously fine and full use was made of the opportunities for sea bathing. A divisional boxing tournament was held, and won by the 1st Worcestershires whose representative knocked out the Royal Artillery in the final round, and in addition to this divisional event, brigade and regimental sports were also organised. The 25th Infantry Brigade, in particular, held a most successful meeting on 10 July which the GOC and his Staff attended and the proceedings were enlivened by the presence of the divisional band. The programme would not have been complete without a

Divisional Horse Show which was duly held on 13 and 14 July and also proved a great success. (One topic dominated almost all others in conversation at this time: pressure by the French voiced by Foch himself to cut the British horses' rations from 22.2 lb. a day to 16.1 lb., the amount the French considered adequate. Indignation at all levels from driver to field-marshal raised the issue to the highest inter-Allied level. As a result the Americans had the deciding voice. Pershing came down on the side of the British.) Fine weather, hard work and amenities such as these kept the men in good health and helped to make them contented. . . . Indeed there must be many who, on looking back, will find that some of the pleasantest memories of their service with the division are bound up with the interlude, strenuous and hardworking though it may have been, which they spent during June and July in the summer sunshine and within sight of the blue water of the Channel on that strip of Picardy coast between St Valéry and Le Treport.'

These words were sincerely written just after the end of the war: the least that can be said of them is that they accord ill with the picture painted by the more celebrated writers of the period. For a later generation to enter into the minds of these First War soldiers and to comprehend their motivation is not easy. It is therefore necessary to record the fundamental articles of faith of their leaders, from lieutenant-colonel down to lance-corporal. In their eyes Courage was the highest of the virtues. Even if afraid, a leader must not show fear, above all in the presence of his inferiors in rank, age or status. Pain, cold, hunger, danger and discomfort must be endured without complaint: self-pity in any form must be treated with contempt. No comrade must ever be let down whatever the risk. Women and children must be protected. Animals must be treated with kindness. A man's duty to his King and Country in the last resort must come before all else. Finally their faith in Discipline exemplified in the national mythology of Blenheim, Ramillies, Oudenarde and Malplaquet, of Salamanca, Waterloo, Inkerman, the Charge of the Light Brigade, of the sieges of Delhi and Lucknow, and of Rorke's Drift had for them all the validity of religion. The Guards' memorial on the Horse Guards Parade and the Gunners' Memorial in St James's Park embody this spirit in stone.

Primarily the New Armies were an expansion on a vast scale of the regimental system of the Regular Army in which, theoretically at any rate, all officers and men were drawn from the same part of the country, speaking the same dialects, sharing the same suspicions and prejudices and united by a tribal loyalty. The bond between officer and man was thus very close, transcending any class distinctions. The new battalions had taken over the Regular Army's traditions and standards uncritically—the saluting, the insistence on close-cropped hair, the meticulous shaving, the emphasis on personal neatness and cleanliness, the polishing of boots and buttons and the rest. Perfect drill had been the secret of the Army's triumphs in the days of Brown Bess: it must therefore, they thought, be so in the age of the machine gun, in some mysterious way that no one could quite explain. When, however, they saw French soldiers slouching from place to place, dirty, unshaven and shabby, they knew they were fundamentally right. In fact, the mutinies in the French Army had been due as much to bad unit administration as to failure in battle. The British officer's sense of responsibility for his men was certainly greater than that of his French counterpart. The best of them who had survived the fighting of the past four years were now holding ranks which in their case would have been regarded as ridiculous both before and after the war. Lieutenant-Colonels of 25 were not unknown. The war at least had made the Army for the moment a career open to the talents with only one standard: courage and the capacity to command in battle. It is not in accordance with the facts for writers of repute to state that class considerations had any influence in the selection of officers in this period of the war. No other Army in Europe at this time was drawing its officers from more varied levels of society than did the British, or from so many careers in which individuality, resource and leadership were qualities which were essential to success. It is dishonest to misstate the facts of history to support the political dogmas of a later age.

At heart most of the brigade and divisional commanders were regimental officers. Whatever their deficiences in the sphere of tactics may have been, the best of them understood and insisted on the highest possible standards of unit administration. This had, in the end, been the secret of Marlborough's and Wellington's success and the fact had never been forgotten. Compared with the civil population in the United Kingdom, now feeling the pinch of food shortages, they were well fed. Supplies of clothing and boots were ample; pay was regularly forthcoming when out of the line and could be spent in well-stocked Expeditionary Force Canteens. Almost every farm would supply coffee, omelettes, fried potatoes, bread and butter. The number of estaminets in Picardy far exceeded the needs of the local population: they always seemed to be well supplied with beer of a sort and wine. The Quartermaster-General himself had now entered the brewing business, importing the malt and hops, thus saving shipping space and brewing beer locally to the strength required. Sympathy for the American troops condemned to war on a teetotal basis was widespread. That there was a lot of drunkenness in the British Army is quite untrue. Provided that brigade commanders would certify that the weather was inclement a rum ration could be issued. Thus, for official purposes, it rained every day in 1918. The rum, dark and syrupy, that came in stone jars marked SRD, popularly supposed to stand for 'Soon Runs Dry', had apparently been laid down at Deptford on the assumption that the South African War would go on for many more years than it actually did. Anyhow the supply never failed. Despite the widespread belief that sergeant-majors always had it in their tea, its issue had to be carried out in the presence of an officer: for many soldiers this constituted the highlight of the day. Music of some sort seems to be a necessity of life: the posterity of these men may well wonder what their ancestors did about it. In fact they generated their own. They sang on the line of march; every battalion had its concert party; every platoon its musician, usually on the Jew's Harp, and its comedian. It was these simple men, coarse and Rabelaisian if you will, who would now finally turn the tide of the war.

Haig's Army fell into two parts: the home-based divisions and those of the Dominions. Of the latter the Canadians and Australians constituted the major part. On the outbreak of war all had immediately proclaimed their support of the Mother Country: ever since, they had displayed outstanding eagerness to close with the enemy. With every justification they were the idols of the British public and press. The Canadians had been in France since early 1915: they had their own corps and their own sector about Vimy Ridge which they had captured in 1917 and on

which their monument now stands. About 50 per cent of their
four divisions were Canadian-born; among the rest the Scottish
element was very strong. They were better clothed, better fed
and better paid than the home-based troops and, on the whole,
bigger in stature. In their ranks were many men of great physical
strength, accustomed to a hard life in primitive conditions, and to
the use of their own initiative. All were volunteers. Their officers
on the whole had been selected on their ability to lead their
men in action and not for other reasons. By now they had considerable war experience behind them; fortunately they had not
been involved to any extent in the battles of March, April and
May. Their morale was high: they would soon show themselves
to be outclassed by no other troops in the Allied or German
Armies—with one exception.

All who fought in it gave the palm for the best infantry of the
war on either side to the Australians. There were five divisions of
them of which part of the 5th and the 1st alone had been caught
up in Ludendorff's offensives. Dressed in their rakish hats and
loose-cut uniforms, ever since the Dardenelles they had fascinated their English-born comrades including the Monarch
himself, King George V. Stories concerning them were legion.
As they would stand for neither criticism nor patronage, description of what they were like is best left to one of their own countrymen, Sir Frank Fox, who although over 40 had managed, after
being severely wounded on the Somme as a result of which he was
permanently lamed and deafened in one ear, to get back to
France after a year in hospital. Writing about this time he said:

'The Anzac striding or limping along with rakish hat and
challenging glance, for the first time brought Australasia
actually home to the Mother Country. These Australasians,
the men of the Bush, were as remarkable, as significant almost,
as the Dacians in the Army of another Imperial nation two
thousand years ago. Easily can they be picked out. They walk
the street with a slightly obvious swagger. When they are
awed a little, it is a point of honour not to show it. When they
are critical, a little of it peeps out. . . . He will often set up as a
protective barrier against real knowledge of him, a stubborn
taciturnity, or a garrulous flow of what Australasians call
"skite" and Londoners "swank".'

He went on to describe them as

'the young of the British, not of the English only, though English is the master element of the breed. The Anzac is a close mixture of English, Scottish, Irish and Welsh colonists with practically no *foreign taint*. There is however a wild strain in the mixture. One of the first tasks of Australasia was to take the Merino sheep of Spain and make a new sheep of it—a task brilliantly carried out. A concurrent task was to take black sheep from the British Isles and make good white stock out of them. The success in this was just as complete. The "rebels" of the Mother Country—Scottish crofters, Irish agrarians, English Chartists and poachers—mostly needed only elbow room to become useful men. Even for the Micawbers a land of lots of room was regenerative.

'Was it Charles Lamb's quip that the early population of the British Colonies should be good "because it was sent out by the best judges"? That was a truth spoken in jest. The first wild strain was of notable value to a new nation in the making. It came to Australasia not only from the original settlers but also from the rushes to the goldfields. . . . They have done, continue to do, their pioneer work well, but have always kept some time for the arts and humanities. . . . Australia produces a high rate of mental as well as physical energy. . . . The Anzac, faced by natural elements which are inexorably stern to folly, to weakness, to indecision but which are generously responsive to capable and dominating energy, had become more resourceful, more resolute, more cruel, more impatient than his British cousin. . . . Australian life leads to a certain hardness of outlook. Life is prized, of course, but its loss—either of one's own or of the other fellows—is not regarded with any superstitious horror. Certainly it is not regarded as the greatest evil. To go out with a mate and to come back without him and under the slightest suspicion of not having taken the full share of risk and hardship would be counted greater.'

It is not surprising therefore that the welcome of British units to the arrival of Australians in their neighbourhood was tempered with a note of caution. Their best horses were liable to vanish, apparently into thin air, in the night. Concurrently with the fighting a widely publicised salvage campaign directed by a brigadier-general was in full blast, inevitably on a competitive basis. The Australian divisions always won: it would be untrue to say, however, that the vast tonnages of rags, bones, swill, shell cases, tins and other bric-à-brac, for the collection of which they were officially given credit, had been meticulously picked up item by item on the battlefield. British units jealous of their own reputation in this widely publicised contest were driven to placing sentries over their own salvage dumps. Little parties of Australians apparently in search of unconsidered trifles were a feature of the rear areas; when bored they would look in behind the German lines as well. Stories concerning them were legion. In May their Army Commander wrote of them:

'They are certainly original fighters and up to all sorts of dodges, some of which would shock a strict disciplinarian. I hear that during the battle of Villers Brettoneux the village of Corbie was being shelled by 5.9s. Some of the German shells were falling short in the pools of the Somme river and exploding under water. Two Australians spent the day in a boat, rowing about and watching for a shell to explode and then picked up the stunned fish. They wore their gas masks to prevent recognition.'

In a private letter he said of them:

'Some of them are pretty tough customers. A party of them went off on their own the other day, got themselves photographed and sent the photo to the Provost Marshal at Havre with the following inscription: "With all respect we send you this PC as a souvenir, trusting that you will keep it as a mark of esteem from those who know you well. At the same time trusting that nous jamais vous regardez encore." Five of them were recognised as having done a term in Havre prison.'

According to Haig's Diary, in March the Australians had nine men per 1,000 in prison compared with 1.6 per 1,000 Canadians and 1 per 1,000 British.

The Australian nation had come of age on the shores of Gallipoli in 1915. When the Canadian Government had insisted on having a corps of their own the British government had agreed without demur in September of that year. Obviously it was to the advantage of all concerned that their troops, with their more lavish scale of provision than those of the United Kingdom, should be controlled at the corps level by a Canadian headquarters staff. South Africa was already conducting her own campaign in East Africa. Australian pressure therefore to form what was described as an 'Australian Army' came rather late on the arrival of their four divisions in France in 1916. This was met by a compromise—one Anzac Corps, which included the New Zealanders, under Birdwood and another under Godley. By November 1917 this had evolved into a single all-Australian Corps under Birdwood, of whom despite the fact that he was not one of their countrymen, both their Prime Minister Hughes and the troops approved. This esteem unfortunately was not shared by Haig who, with good reason, suspected Birdwood of ambition and looked with disfavour on his fondness for what he considered to be playing to the gallery. In the crisis of March and April Haig had chosen to employ the Australian divisions piecemeal, without any objection on their part, under British corps commanders. Then on 31 May the Fifth Army, which had been in suspended animation since the sacking of Gough in March, was revived. The opportunity thus arose to break the connection with Birdwood by giving him command of the Army and to promote an Australian in his place. Largely as a result of Haig's influence and Hughes' perspicacity the choice fell on Monash.

Up to this time little was known outside Australian circles of this remarkable man and then only with any true appreciation of his merits within his own division. In civil life he was an engineer by profession who had had much to do with the development of Australia's railways and bridges. In particular he was an expert in the use of reinforced concrete. In 1912 he had been elected President of the Victoria Institute of Engineers and a member of the Council of Melbourne University. Outside his civil profession his interests were wide especially in the fields of history and archaeology (like Moshe Dayan). Intellectually he outshone both his civil and military contemporaries. From early life, though in his heart he hated it, the Art of War had had a peculiar fascination for him and from 1887 he had held a commission in the Garrison Artillery of the Citizen Force. By 1913, at the age of 47, he had risen to the rank of colonel. In Gallipoli he had shown himself to be a sound infantry brigadier. His first encounter with Haig had come in December 1916. Thereafter the Commander-in-Chief had watched him carefully and been impressed by his handling of his division at Messines and in the Passchendaele operations both as a tactician and as an organiser. Each was quick to see in the other qualities which they both esteemed. Haig became a frequent caller at his headquarters: Monash recorded of him: 'He never departed without leaving a stimulating impression of his placid, hopeful and undaunted personality nor without generous recognition of the work the Corps was doing.'

Monash brought to the command of the corps an understanding of his men's physical, mental and emotional capacities as profound as that shown by Napoleon of the ragged and half-starved soldiers of the Army of Italy in 1796, as that shown by Rommel of the Afrika Corps, or by Montgomery of the Eighth Army. As an Australian he realised that he must appeal to their intelligence, their imagination, their adaptability, their high sense of comradeship, their capacity for independent judgment and their aggressive instincts. He would feed them on victory. He would teach them to believe, because of success, that they were invincible. He would make every man feel that what he was and what he did was vital. Above all he would convince every one of them that he would get a square deal.

He had little use for the discipline of the barrack square, for servile obedience of forms and customs or the imposition of a drab uniformity. What really mattered was discipline on the battlefield itself. Nevertheless he insisted on personal cleanliness, soldierly bearing, punctuality, spotless weapons and unquestioning obedience in action. He insisted that officers should place the needs of their men before their own and that staff officers should regard themselves as the servants of the troops.

Monash brought to the command of his corps something which his British colleagues lacked—experience of the planning and execution of large civil engineering projects. He thus realised that fundamentally the same principles which he obeyed in his civil capacity were equally applicable to the command of a corps. In both activities there was the same need for foresight, for flexibility, for economy, for cooperation and for fitting the right man to the job: the same need for appreciation of the time factor, for coordination and lastly for the delegation of authority.

Fortunately in Blamey, his Chief of Staff and the future Allied Commander-in-Chief in the South-West Pacific, he had inherited a man in the class of De Guingand and Bedell Smith. He was thus in a position to insist on meticulous planning and yet avoid becoming personally involved in excessive detail. By these means he was free to supervise the execution of his orders and at the same time free to plan in outline two operations ahead. Before every operation it was his habit to hold very carefully prepared conferences attended by the senior representatives of all the arms and services involved. These, with his powerful intelligence, speed in the uptake and willingness to listen to constructive comment, he completely dominated. Like Montgomery later he had the supreme quality of being able to express himself in terms of unmistakeable clarity and vigour. The result would soon be the development in his corps of mutual understanding, team spirit, tactical skill and offensive spirit which would outclass even the Germans in their prime at any stage of the war.

For the past three months Monash's corps had held the sector east of Amiens astride the Somme between Monument Wood, a mile south of Villers Brettoneux, and the Ancre south of Albert. South of the Somme, as far as the valley of the Luce, there stretched for about five miles an open and slightly undulating plateau virtually free of obstacles. There were few outlying farms and houses. The going for tanks was, in fact, almost perfect; there were few shell holes. Immediately north of the river the country was more involved but everywhere there were plenty of useful observation posts for the artillery. Contrary to their usual custom the Germans had done little to develop their forward defences since the front had stabilised at the end of April. Behind a chain of isolated forward posts almost unspoilt country stretched for about six miles to the labyrinth of the old Somme battlefields of 1916 running roughly north and south through Lihons. Opposing the Australians there were about nine divisions of the Second Army with four in reserve under von der Marwitz which had driven the British Fifth Army back from St Quentin to the eastern outskirts of Villers Brettoneux in March. Their fighting strength now averaged only about 3,000 in each division and their morale, partly on account of their losses and rather more as a result of three months in close proximity to the Australians, was in decline. Prisoners stated that Mangin's victory on 18 July had badly shaken the confidence not only of the Army but of the people at home. Monash's irrepressible, impudent and aggressive infantry patrols ranging everywhere by day and night made their lives a burden. Persistent Australian sniping kept their nerves on edge. In the air above them the 5th Brigade RAF of 17 squadrons reigned virtually unchallenged. When therefore on 21 July Rawlinson the Commander of the Fourth Army, at his head-quarters at Flexicourt, revealed to Monash and Currie that, subject to the approval of Foch, Haig proposed to launch them to the attack on the Villers Brettoneux plateau, von der Marwitz's head was already on the chopping block and the axe about to fall.

10

August the Eighth

Sentry: 'Halt! Who goes there?'
Voice from the dark: '* * * *!! * * *!!'
Sentry: 'Pass Australian.'

The most that can be claimed for Haig's Army Commanders, is a high level of mediocrity—with one exception: Rawlinson of the Fourth Army. There were in him elements of subtlety, imagination and wide vision beyond the scope of his equals in rank. Not for nothing had he earned in peacetime manoeuvres the nickname of 'Rawley the Fox'. Since the eighties when they had hunted dacoits in Burma together, he had maintained a very close relationship with his fellow Rifleman Wilson, the brilliant, voluble, and equivocal Irishman, now CIGS and intimate of Foch. His relations with Haig ever since the start of the war had therefore been characterised by reservations on both sides. Indeed, he had not hesitated on occasion to express strong disagreement with French and later with Haig.

He had all the graces expected in a higher commander in the heyday of the British Empire. Faultlessly dressed, he carried himself with an air of distinction. Despite the fact that he was an infantryman he could hold his own with most of the cavalry generals on a horse: he played polo well and enjoyed it. He was equally good at golf and tennis. Like many of his predecessors, especially in India, he was no mean artist in water-colour; his drawing, whether of figures or landscape, was good but his pleasure lay in colour boldly applied. Before and after the war he never missed a chance to set up his easel. Some of his pictures of the Seven Cities of Delhi and the Himalayas have considerable distinction; his caricatures combined wit and charity. His friends

Men of the 51st Battalion AIF, holding the dominating ground which they had just
ɔtured on the North Bank of the Somme, 13 August 1918

29 Australian Gunners in the Morcourt Gully, 14 August 1918

30 Infantry of the Fourth Army in action near Nesles, August 1918

31 HM King George V and Rawlinson leaving a gun position

32 Churchill and Lt.-Colonel—later Field Marshal—Montgomery at the Liberation of Lille, October 1918

included King George V and the East End Jew who rose to
become Lord Chief Justice and one of the greatest of the Viceroys
of India. He managed to combine a liking for the society of the
young and of witty and beautiful women with great understanding
and consideration for humble people normally considered of no
account. In public he spoke with a clarity and purpose which
no one could misunderstand. He loathed anything in the nature
of what he called 'ringing the bell' or self-advertisement: society
journals and all they stood for were anathema to him. Now at
55 he was at the height of his powers: apart from a brief period at
Versailles he had held high command of troops ever since 1914.
He had been quick to grasp the lessons of the fighting since the
spring. This was the man who more than any other would be
responsible for the planning and execution of the battle which
finally tipped the scales against the Germans. Its conduct and
lessons moreover not only set the pattern for the rest of the war
but also profoundly influenced both European and American
strategic and tactical thought for the next quarter of a century.
Indeed some of the great set-piece battles of World War Two are
merely sophisticated variations on the theme of Rawlinson's Battle
of Amiens. What actually happened in the battle, and what its real
lessons were, would soon after the war be obscured by the
protagonists of all-out armoured warfare and of their vilification
of the generals who did not share their point of view. The actual
form and content of the battle therefore repay consideration.

Time and again since the middle ages the River Somme has
been an important factor in the history of Europe: in the process
its eccentric course has done much to confuse the minds of the
young and others. In fact it runs due north as far as Péronne.
Here it takes an abrupt right-angled turn westwards towards
Amiens and the sea. When therefore historians and countless
schoolmasters have proclaimed for example that 'The English
Army then advanced across the Somme', the legitimate doubt
has arisen only too often as to whether they moved east or west
or north and south. It is within the amphitheatre provided by
this confusing angle that the Battle of Amiens would be fought.
The north–south course of the Somme to Péronne lay some 20
miles to the east of the line just east of Villers Brettoneux on
which the Germans had been finally halted at the end of March.
'The perfect tank country', made all the better by the dry weather

I

of June and July, of which Fuller, Liddell Hart and others were
later to write so much, stretched some seven miles from the
east–west course of the Somme near Villers Brettoneux as far as
the Luce, a marshy stream affording a measure of flank protection.
A mile or two to the east of the German front line lay the old
Inner Amiens Defence Line; six miles further to the east the old
Outer Amiens Defence Line provided a further clearly defined
objective. Both were seamed with rusty barbed wire obstacles.
About five miles further to the east, also running roughly north
and south, stretched the broad zone of the old Somme Battlefield of 1916, a veritable labyrinth of old trench systems partially
caved in, shell craters and belts of rusty barbed wire hidden by
long grass. Within this belt stood the Lihons Ridge, commanding
a fine view in all directions and especially over the railway
junction of Chaulnes, where met the four lines on which the
maintenance of the German Armies in the salient between the
Somme and the Oise ultimately depended. North of the Somme a
series of commanding spurs, including especially the one above
the village of Chipilly, stretched down to the river like the
fingers of a hand. Here ravines restricted the use of tanks and
provided a complex problem to the attacker. What seems obvious
to the observer on the south bank could be baffling to anyone
on the other side. Two great Routes Nationales from Amiens,
paved with granite blocks, straddled the battlefield, the one
running to Brie and the other to Roye, both lined by poplars and
straight as a die. These then were the major topographical
features which would dictate the form and course of the coming
battle.

    In essence, Haig and Rawlinson planned a great surprise
attack, using the Canadian and Australian Corps as the main
effort between the Somme and the road from Amiens to Roye.
This would be supported by the whole strength of the Tank
Corps, consisting of nine heavy battalions of Mark Vs and Mark
V Stars and two battalions of Whippets, over 2,000 guns and the
Cavalry Corps. The aim was to secure on the first day the Outer
Amiens Defence Line some six miles ahead and secondly, the
western edge of the old Somme battlefields west of Chaulnes
six miles further on. To secure surprise the Canadians now
about Arras would be brought in on the right flank at the
last possible moment. In the light of past experience working

with the French, Rawlinson for ease of control and simplicity
wanted it to be a purely British operation. When however Foch
gave his approval, he stipulated that the First French Army on
Rawlinson's right should be included in the assault and thus
ensure the sharing of any glory that was going, and incidentally
enable himself to intervene from strength should he find it
expedient to do so. He accordingly placed Debeney, the Commander of the First Army, nominally at any rate under Haig's
command. On the Soissons–Reims front operations were now
nearing their end, the Germans on the whole having withdrawn
according to plan and in the process exacted a heavy price from
the six American and four British divisions serving under
French command. Foch estimated that by 6 August he would be
in a position to close down operations here; determined to give
Ludendorff no respite he therefore fixed the date of the British
attack as 8 August.

The railway line from Amiens to Chaulnes provided a con-
venient dividing line between the Canadian Corps on the right
attacking on a frontage of three divisions with one in reserve
and the Australians on their left with two divisions forward and
the remaining three in depth behind them. To each corps Rawlinson allotted a brigade of four heavy tank battalions. When the
Amiens Inner Defence Line had been taken the Cavalry Corps of
three divisions with the two Whippet tank battalions under its
command was to break out, seize and hold the Outer Amiens
Defence Line till the Infantry and tanks arrived. Thereafter
exploitation to a depth of perhaps 20 miles was held out as a
pious hope in the general direction of Ham on the far side of the
Somme. Both corps would form up in depth on the principle that
those formations which had farthest to go formed up nearest to
the start line. One-third of the available artillery would provide
the creeping barrage covering the advance of the infantry and
the tanks and the other two-thirds, including all the heavies,
would concentrate on all known battery positions. North of the
Somme 3rd Corps with one heavy tank battalion under its
command was given the task of protecting the right flank advancing in the general direction of Etinhem. On the southern flank,
Debeney proposed to commit only one of his four corps, the
31st, and to cross the start line 45 minutes later than the British:
this would enable him to carry out a preliminary bombardment

of the Germans on his own front and to reap the full benefit of the surprise created by his Allies. Currie, the Canadian Commander, therefore arranged, very wisely as it turned out, for an Independent Force of machine gunners and cyclists under Brigadier Brutinel to look after this flank. Regrettably language difficulties on both sides nipped any prospects of close cooperation there ever may have been in the bud.

Salmond, the RAF Commander, proposed to use some of his aircraft in the hours of darkness before the attack to drown the noise of the tanks moving forward and, at first light, to deliver a concentrated attack with his bombers and fighters on the German airfields. Thereafter the day bombers would engage enemy reserves detraining at the railway stations of Péronne and Chaulnes; the fighters would stand by to engage whatever tempting targets cropped up. To ensure surprise, Salmond prescribed no abnormal air activity over the Fourth Army front before the battle. He did, however, plan a concentration at the very last moment on the front of the attack. In this he would be completely successful: on the day the main German air concentration was still on the Reims front. He thus achieved a superiority locally of seven aircraft to one. Furthermore, in the days immediately preceding 8 August, he staged a great increase in air activity over the fronts of the First and Fifth Armies in the north as his part of the general deception plan to lull the Germans into a false sense of security on the Amiens front by creating the impression that a British offensive was imminent south-west of Ypres. This indeed had been Foch's intention until Haig had persuaded him to drop it in the latter half of July. All the measures taken to ensure security revolved around this theme. A great increase in wireless activity was stimulated in the north. The major problem was to conceal the departure of the Canadian Corps from the First Army front to the neighbourhood of Amiens. To this end two Canadian battalions, two Canadian Casualty Clearing Stations and a Canadian wireless section were moved to the front opposite Kemmel Hill. A few tanks were given the task of raising a lot of dust and showing themselves around the sidings at St Pol. No Canadian troops were allowed to enter the zone of their battle position before Amiens until 7 August. In fact, they did not take over the front from which they launched their attack until two hours before zero hour.

Fortunately, the civil population had been evacuated from the city ever since April; within it straw was laid on the granite sets of the streets to drown the noise of the steel-tyred limbers and guns passing through. Elsewhere wheels were wrapped with ropes to deaden the sound. In the event, the 10 Army Field Brigades of 18 pounders and 4.5 howitzers, the divisional artilleries of the Canadians and the 25th Division, the 30 heavy brigades and the four siege batteries moved in unspotted by the German air force and registered silently, off the map, as the Germans had done in the big spring offensive. All forward movement and all dumping of ammunition were carried out by night: all preparations were openly described as preparation for taking over from the French thus deceiving enemy agents in the rear areas.

The mounting of the attack indeed did involve the taking over of some 7,000 yards of the French front by the Australians and their own replacement immediately north of the Somme by the 3rd Corps. The four divisions of this Corps had been severely mauled in the defensive battles of the spring and had now been made up with large numbers of boys of 18. Their losses, particularly in war experienced junior officers and NCOS, had been severe. Two days before handing over, the 5th Australian Division had felt that they could not leave the sector without a final expression of their opinion of the German troops south of Morlancourt. Attacking in the early morning of 29 July, using what they called 'peaceful penetration', two battalions advanced the line about 500 yards and captured 140 prisoners and 36 machine guns. Retaliation for the moment was slight. Two days later 3rd Corps on taking over found that the defences lacked the tidy character to which they were accustomed. The expected riposte came on 6 August when the 27th Wurtemburg Division, well rested, re-trained and re-equipped, attacked on a 4,000-yard front and drove the 3rd Corps back some 800 yards. Next morning the 18th Division partially restored the situation and took about 70 prisoners. Fortunately these operations did not result in any loss of secrecy but they did necessitate many last-minute alterations in start lines and barrage plans for the 18th Division on the morrow. Inevitably they were tired before the battle started; to add to their ill luck the Germans deluged them with gas shells whilst they were forming up, forcing them to put on their masks. South of the Somme, however, as the tanks, Canadians and Australians moved up to their final assault positions, all was quiet. The night was fine: there was no moon. About 3 a.m. ground mist began to form in the river valleys and to spread over the plateau. This is how Monash remembered the tension of the last ten minutes before zero at 4.20 a.m.:

'In black darkness, 100,000 infantry, deployed over 12 miles of front, are standing grimly, silently, expectantly, in readiness to advance, or are already crawling stealthily forward to get within 80 yards of the line on which the barrage will fall; all feel to make sure that their bayonets are tightly locked, or to set their steel helmets firmly on their heads; company and platoon commanders, their whistles ready to hand, are nervously glancing at their luminous watches, waiting for minute after minute to go by—and giving a last look over their commands—ensuring that their runners are by their sides, their observers alert, and that the officers detailed to control direction have their compasses set and ready. Carrying parties shoulder their burdens and adjust the straps; Pioneers grasp their picks and shovels; Engineers take up their stores of explosives and primers and fuses; machine and Lewis gunners whisper for the last time to the carriers of their magazines and belt boxes to be sure and follow up. The Stokes mortar carrier slings his heavy load, and his loading numbers fumble to see that their haversacks of cartridges are handy. Overhead drone the aeroplanes and from the rear, in swelling chorus, the buzzing and clamour of the Tanks every moment louder and louder. Scores of telegraph operators sit by their instruments with their message forms and registers ready to hand, bracing themselves for the rush of signal traffic which will set in a few minutes later; dozens of staff officers spread their maps in readiness to record with coloured pencils the stream of expected information. In hundreds of pits, the guns are already run up, loaded and laid on the opening lines of fire; the sergeant in charge is checking the range for the last time; the layer stands silently with the lanyard in his hand. The section officer, watch on wrist, counts the last seconds. "A minute to go", "Thirty Seconds", "Fire".

'And suddenly, with a mighty roar, more than 1,000 guns,

begin the symphony. A great illumination lights up the eastern horizon: and instantly the whole complex organisation, extending from back areas almost beyond earshot of the guns, begins to move forward; every man, every unit, every vehicle and every tank on the appointed tasks and to their designated goals, sweeping onward relentlessly and irresistibly. Viewed from a high vantage point and in the glimmer of the breaking day, a great artillery barrage surely surpasses in dynamic splendour any other manifestation of collective human effort.

'The artillery barrage dominates the battle and the landscape. The field is speedily covered with a cloak of dust and smoke and spume, making impossible at the time any detailed observation of the battle as a whole. The story can only be indifferently pieced together, long after, by an attempted compilation of the reports of a hundred different participants.'

In the thick mist, dense smoke and clouds of dust of the battle-field the Canadian and Australian infantry and the eight battalions of the Tank Corps groped their way forward making use of the noise of the barrage to keep direction. Typical of the hundred small battles fought in the chaos and gloom of the next few hours is the exploit of Private Croak of the 13th Battalion Canadian Infantry, Quebec Regiment, who becoming separated in the confusion from his section, suddenly came upon a German machine-gun post. This he bombed and jumping into it forced the crew to surrender. Despite a wound in his right arm, he now managed to rejoin his platoon which was held up by a strong-point stiff with men and machine guns. Croak dashed ahead followed by the rest of the platoon and bayoneted, or captured the whole of the garrison. A little later he was severely wounded and died in a few minutes. Corporal Good, another vc of the same battalion, when his company were halted at the very start by heavy fire from a post containing three machine guns, dashed forward alone, killed several of the garrison and forced the rest to surrender. Later on, still alone, he came upon a battery of 5.9 guns which were firing at the time. Collecting three men of his section, he charged the battery and captured the entire crews of three guns who had continued to fire point blank at them until the very last moment. On the Australian front, Lieutenant Gaby's company of the 28th Battalion, was halted almost at the outset by the wire of an enemy strongpoint. Gaby found a gap and entirely on his own tackled the garrison in the teeth of rifle and machine-gun fire. Running along the parapet, still alone, and at point-blank range, he emptied his revolver into the Germans, drove them from their guns and compelled all 50 of them to surrender with four machine guns. He then quickly reorganised his men and led them forward. Nothing could stop stout-hearted men like these: when the mist cleared about 10.30 a.m. the Australian flag was flying from the church tower of Harbonnières on their final objective. They had advanced six miles and in the process reaped a rich harvest in prisoners, food, canteen stores and the entire contents of a German pay office. For the tanks too it had been no easy passage: of the 5th Battalion on the extreme right only eight tanks reached the final objective: of the 4th Battalion 11 survived. The 14th Battalion had better luck, losing only five tanks. Only 11 tanks of the 1st Battalion were undamaged. On the Australian front the tanks had better fortune. Lieutenant Percy-Eade of the 2nd Battalion, seeing the infantry being enfiladed from the village of Marcelcave, attacked it single-handed with his tank and knocked out six machine guns. He then turned against a German battery and put the gunners to flight. In general on the Australian front the infantry and the tanks worked together: the tanks crushed the wire; those of the enemy who could not be disposed of by the infantry were erased by the tanks. As a result the tanks too were on their final objectives by 10.30 a.m., after an advance of six miles.

Now that the mist had gone the whole plateau south of the Somme, seen from the air, was dotted with parties of infantry, field artillery, cavalry and tanks moving forward. Staff officers were galloping about, many riding horses for the first time; prisoners in formed bodies were marching back with hardly more escort than the Canadian wounded they were carrying, while overhead the planes of the RAF were flying noisily to work. Indeed at this stage there was more noise of movement than of firing, as the heavy batteries, almost wheel to wheel, with their muzzles cocked up to the highest elevation were no longer in action for the infantry had gone so far that it was no longer possible for them to shoot. Here and there little parties of Germans were putting up white flags or waiting under cover to surrender. No German guns were firing. In the eastern sky some eight Allied aircraft were shooting up enemy troops on the roads and tracks leading forward from the Somme south of Péronne. A gap 11 miles wide was rapidly developing. Now, if ever, was the time for exploitation by the Cavalry Corps, to thrust forward a further six miles to the line of the old Somme battlefield between Roye and Chaulnes. They were in fact well forward. The 3rd Cavalry Division had passed through the Canadians about 11 a.m. but had soon run into opposition from scattered machine guns. Despite this check they had reached their final objective, the Outer Amiens Defence Line, soon after noon. Here they halted and awaited orders from the Headquarters of the Cavalry Corps. None came. The 1st Cavalry Division on the Canadian front had moved through the leading infantry soon after 9 a.m. but were soon held up by machine guns until relieved by the infantry. They also when they reached the Outer Amiens Defence Line halted and awaited orders. Most unfortunately the two Whippet battalions had been placed under command of these two cavalry divisions. A more unhappy marriage, characterised by recrimination on both sides, could hardly have been devised. When there was no enemy opposition, the horsemen outstripped the tanks which were capable of little more than four miles an hour across country: when enemy machine guns opened up, the Whippets got forward and the cavalry were paralysed. It was a sorry story mitigated by the exploits of the 16 cars of the 17th Armoured Car Battalion which, driving straight down the Route Nationale towards Brie, reached the Morcourt Valley ahead of the infantry. Here they shot up a panic-stricken crowd of Germans milling around like a disturbed ant heap. Leaving the survivors to be dealt with by the Australians, the cars drove on towards the east, fired on large dumps near La Flaque and, most dramatic target of all, a railway train loaded with troops which they soon reduced to a complete wreck. Two miles further on they ran into a vast traffic jam and having saturated it with fire split into two parties. One party turned southwards and at Framerville caught a whole Corps staff seated at lunch. The other party went northwards towards Proyart where it encountered long columns of horse transport which it shot to bits. The cars then roamed across the front for some hours shooting up stray columns of Germans to their hearts' content until they ran out of petrol and ammunition. The story of 'Musical Box', a Whippet of the 6th Battalion,

Tank Corps, is equally dramatic. First near Warfusée Abancourt
it attacked a German battery from the rear and put it out of
action. It then moved towards Harbonnières where it caught a
large party of Germans packing up their kits and wrote off about
60 of them. It then engaged line after line of troops in retreat and
finally closed with a transport column. All alone and subject to
enemy machine-gun fire, with petrol from pierced cans on its
roof pouring down its sides, it continued to fire at retreating
Germans till about 3 p.m. when a direct hit from a field gun set it
on fire. Its commander, Lieutenant Allen, managed to drag out
his two men and to extinguish the flames. His driver however was
killed: the full story of this exploit was not known till after his
release from a Prisoner of War Camp at the end of the war.

What would have happened had the Cavalry Corps now been
ruthlessly launched in the direction of Chaulnes and Roye will
never be known: probably the slaughter would have been on the
scale of Balaclava for their day had gone. The old battlefield
around Lihons and Chaulnes was virtually impossible for horsemen or for that matter, tanks. What is certain so far as the
cavalry were concerned is that the will to go forward, whatever
the cost, was there. This cannot be said of Debeney's Army.
At 11.30 a.m. Haig sent a staff officer to his headquarters request-
ing him to send forward all his mounted troops to operate on the
right of the British Cavalry and to extend the breach in the
enemy's front southwards by moving in rear of the Germans
holding Montdidier. Debeney replied that his cavalry were too
far away to be able to intervene before noon next day: anyhow
the roads were blocked by infantry. Haig therefore in the afternoon called on him in person and pressed him to send forward
his cavalry to join the British. Debeney was much distressed at
the failure of some of his troops. With the best will in the world
it cannot be said that the First Army's operations on this day
were characterised by the traditional French *élan* or even *bonhomie*. The Canadians were abreast of Mézières at 10.30 a.m.:
the French did not take the town before 3 p.m. and they did
not link up with the Canadians on the final objective till the light
was fading.

North of the Somme the operations of the 3rd Corps lacked
distinction. Unlike their countrymen south of the river, the
Wurtemburgers were expecting retaliation for their own attack on

this front forty-eight hours previously. They had ample artillery support. The element of surprise was therefore lacking. For the 3rd Corps it proved to be a day of confused fighting. Only one tank battalion was available to support them. The infantry were heavily shelled with gas whilst forming up; last-minute alterations in the artillery fire plans were imperfectly understood; the tanks failed to link up with the infantry they had been ordered to support; most of those concerned seem to have been tired and exasperated before the battle started. In the end, however, the three attacking divisions did indeed capture their first objective. Thereafter what was politely described at the time as the 'fog of war' and, impolitely, in words considered unprintable in those days, descended for the rest of the day on the northern bank of the Somme. All attempts to capture the Chipilly spur which gave excellent observation over the Australians immediately south of the river broke down. This was exasperating: indeed the Australians had another word for it; but it was in no way decisive. There is no justification for the British Official Historian's fatuous comment that the attack 'with well trained troops and more experienced company commanders should have been a complete success': nor for Liddell Hart's unworthy accusation of 'lack of ardour'. Most of the experienced company commanders had been written off in the fighting of March and April; criticism of the courage of others comes ill from men who were not present and whose own experience of the hazards of the forefront of the battle can by no stretch of the imagination be described as great. The commanders of the divisions involved may have been deficient in the qualities which gain the accolade of academic historians and civilian military experts but lack of guts, driving power, force of character and vigour of expression were not among them.

The results of the day can be well left to the Germans themselves to sum up. According to the Official Monograph *Die Katastrophe des 8 August 1918*:

'As the sun set on 8 August on the battlefield the greatest defeat which the German Army had suffered since the beginning of the war was an accomplished fact. The position divisions between the Avre and the Somme which had been struck by the enemy attack were nearly completely annihilated. The troops in the front line north of the Somme also suffered seriously, as also the reserve divisions thrown into the battle in the course of the day. The total loss of the formations employed in the Second Army is estimated at 650 to 700 officers and 26,000 to 27,000 other ranks. More than 400 guns, beside a huge number of machine guns, trench mortars and other war material had been lost. More than two-thirds of the total loss had surrendered as prisoners [the actual number was 15,000].'

In sharp contrast British casualties, apart from 25 per cent of the tanks, had been light.

Despite their losses, however, by nightfall the Germans had managed to patch up some sort of line and to reinforce it with three fresh divisions by dawn on the 9th; three more would arrive during the day and a further three on the 10th. When therefore the Canadians, Australians and the 3rd Corps resumed the offensive, somewhat late in the day, apart from the brilliant capture of the village of Le Quesnel soon after daybreak by the Canadians, they met ever increasing resistance. Only 145 tanks were now left of the 415 which had attacked on the previous day: the German 77 mm guns, sited well forward and in depth, had exacted a heavy toll. It was another hot day with a cloudless sky. Communications were now becoming increasingly difficult and lack of experience of mobile operations on the part of the staffs was beginning to betray itself. Nevertheless the Canadians and Australians made a further three miles in the day, taking 12,000 more prisoners and 130 guns. North of the Somme the 58th and 12th Divisions, reinforced at their own request by the United States 131st Regiment, finally carried the Chipilly spur. According to the Fourth Army Official Record:

'Although the Americans had to double for the last mile in order to reach their assembly positions, they advanced in fine style. Led by their commander, Colonel J. B. Sambon, the Americans swept everything before them and the German resistance collapsed. So precipitate was the retreat of the enemy that a German Battalion Commander fled from his dugout abandoning his orders, map and telephone switchboard. The Americans were so impetuous that they outstripped the British on their left and it was due to them that the objective was so quickly and rapidly gained on the front of the 58th Division.'

On this day the 3rd Corps captured over 3,000 prisoners and 70 guns. They could thus hand over the Chipilly spur to the Australians with a clear conscience; this solution satisfied both parties: the 3rd Corps got rid of an uncongenial liability: Monash, with an eye to operations in the future, ensured that he, and he alone, would decide what was to be done, not on one but on both banks of the Somme. Already in his mind the form of battles still to come was taking shape. On the French front, pressure on Debeney by Foch 'to push forward the 31st Corps, drums beating, on Roye, without losing a moment and preventing any delay and hesitation' produced only a sluggish response. Haig, visiting him again at 4 p.m., found him frankly uncooperative. Foch's wishes with regard to a musical accompaniment had apparently fallen on deaf ears. Fortunately for Debeney the Germans soon solved his problem for him. That night Ludendorff agreed to the withdrawal of von Hutier's 18th Army facing the French who thus were able to get forward on the morrow.

Mist on the morning of the 10th ushered in another sultry day. There were now ever increasing signs that the offensive was running out of momentum. Infantry casualties were increasing: only 67 tanks were now fit for action. The Canadians and Australians had in fact closed with the overgrown trench systems of the old Somme battlefield now held by nine fresh divisions. German resistance, though unavailing against the Australian attack on Lihons Ridge, had become bitter in the extreme. The tangle of trenches of the old Somme battlefield offered every advantage to the defenders and none to the attack. Ten tired British divisions now faced 12 German divisions fed into the battle since the 8th. Nevertheless Foch arrived in mid-morning at Haig's headquarters train at Wiry, still cock-a-hoop with offensive zeal. The Germans, he said, with Gallic emphasis, were utterly demoralised. The Fourth Army must press on their heels a further eight miles to the Somme. At the same time, Haig must go over to the attack with his other Armies, capture Aubers Ridge, thrust on Bapaume and take Monchy Le Preux. That afternoon at the headquarters of the Canadian Corps in some dugouts at Demuin, Haig passed on Foch's orders to Rawlinson. What exactly passed between the Commander-in-Chief and the Commander of the Fourth Army has not been recorded. It is however known that Rawlinson went to the verge of insubordination when told by Haig that it was the wish of Maréchal Foch that he should at once press on towards the Somme regardless of the cost in British life, replied: 'Are you commanding the British Army or is Maréchal Foch?' Haig departed to visit the Canadian divisions. Rawlinson was right; the offensive had shot its bolt.

Early next morning Haig continued his tour of the front, calling on all five Australian divisions: that morning they had beaten off all German counter-attacks and finally consolidated the Lihons Ridge. They were tired but undaunted. At Monash's headquarters he met Byng by appointment and told him to get ready to attack in the direction of Bapaume. Going on to the 3rd Corps headquarters he found its commander, Butler, his late Deputy Chief of Staff, suffering from insomnia and sent him off on leave for a fortnight ordering Godley, now back from the operations about Reims, temporarily to take his place. Finally, on his way back to his train, he called again at Fourth Army Headquarters in Villers Brettoneux.

That afternoon Rawlinson addressed a conference of corps commanders and their staffs. It was evident, he said, that the enemy had been strongly reinforced and that he was now holding a broad belt of country virtually tank-proof and impenetrable to infantry without overwhelming artillery support not feasible for the present. The tank crews were exhausted and their machines needed overhaul before they could fight again. Twenty-four German divisions had been engaged and defeated by three cavalry and 13 infantry divisions and part of an American division. In the air, the redoubtable Richthofen Circus had appeared and the formidable Hauptmann Goering and the advantage the RAF had enjoyed on the first day had gone. For the moment it was not possible to bring forward all the heavy artillery and the vast tonnage of ammunition required for another set piece battle. Our casualties at about 22,000 had been light as compared with the prisoners taken and the number of Germans killed: they were however increasing. He therefore announced that, with Haig's approval, he had decided to suspend the operations for the time being. At long last a commander had emerged who realised that an operation should be closed down when the element of surprise has gone and when, in terms of human life expended, it has ceased to pay a dividend.

Rawlinson, indeed, had brought to a successful conclusion the limited operation he had originally planned. Exploitation to the line of the Somme had been a concept grafted on to it almost as an afterthought by Foch and Haig, regardless of the barrier imposed by the old Somme battlefield. He had thus levered open the way for the advance of the Third French Army, now gathering momentum in the face of the German voluntary withdrawal. His Army and the 31st French Corps had advanced 12 miles in four days, taken 30,000 prisoners, 500 guns and vast stocks of ammunition and stores at a cost of less than one-third of the casualties on the first day of the Battle of the Somme in 1916. If the First French Army had attacked simultaneously and with enthusiasm equal to that of the Australians, the Canadians and the Tank Corps the bag would have been greater still.

If the 3rd and 6th Battalions of Whippet tanks had been employed independently of the cavalry and followed up by infantry in lorries, as Fuller had suggested at a conference before the battle, there is little doubt that they could have seized the vital high ground of the Lihons Ridge by noon on the first day and, thus blocking the German rail communications, would have precipitated a retreat—provided, that is, that the First French Army showed greater eagerness than they actually displayed. This arrangement would have deprived the commander of the cavalry corps of his traditional role as the master of the pursuit— a step only possible with the approval of Haig, and he was a cavalryman. The 3rd Corps, given by far the hardest task and only one battalion of tanks, had been out of luck: the attack on their front had come as no surprise to the Wurtembergers who in every respect were of superior quality to those of the rest on the Fourth Army front. The comparative failure of this Corps, however, on the first day was a nuisance but it did not greatly affect the course of the battle as a whole. Over the whole front after the first day the command machinery, inevitably as a result of primitive communications and staff lack of experience of mobile war, began to creak. Nevertheless the initiative had never been lost.

Fuller, who saw something of the battle, and Liddell Hart, who did not, proclaimed that it was the tanks who virtually alone 'crushed the fighting spirit of the enemy and paralysed his will to endure'. Their acolytes would continue to echo these sentiments for the next half-century despite the fact that the Germans had achieved equally spectacular advances in March, April, May and June without the aid of a single tank. Edmonds, the British Official Historian, would claim that 'the infantry with the machine guns was the instrument of success but its vital assistant was the artillery'. There was indeed an element of truth in this view. The artillery, especially in the development of counter-battery technique in cooperation with the RAF, had since 1917 made an immense step forward in accuracy and fire effect. The fire of no less than two-thirds of the available artillery, including all the mediums and heavies, literally blasted most of the German batteries out of the ring at the outset; the lines of the bursting shells of the creeping barrage guided and shielded the infantry and the tanks as they advanced. Without this support it is unlikely that many of the tanks would have survived for long. Victory in fact had been the reward of all arms skilfully acting in combination with one single aim. Fifty years later it is clear that the last word can be left with Rawlinson himself writing in his diary on the second day of the battle. After commenting on the fact that surprise had been complete, he wrote: 'While everyone did splendidly, I think the spirit of the Colonial Infantry was probably the decisive factor. The result of this victory should have a far-reaching effect on the Boche morale.'

This was in fact the truth. Its significance lay more in the sphere of morale than in terms of prisoners and guns captured and ground gained. Within the Fourth Army's cages many Germans could not conceal their delight at being captured and greeted new arrivals with loud cheers. On interrogation the majority, both officers and men, stated their conviction that Germany could no longer win the war. On the other side of the lines reports of panic and of troops surrendering without a fight suddenly brought home to Ludendorff that the German infantry were no longer of the quality of the men who had fought so stoutly in 1916 and 1917 and swept all before them in the spring. His manpower resources were running low. With defeat before Amiens coming on top of the loss of the Marne Salient Ludendorff, overworked, irritable and frustrated, suddenly

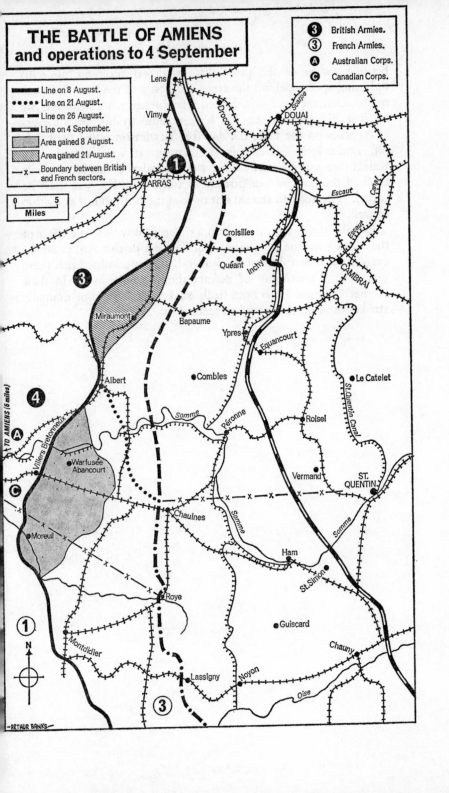

THE BATTLE OF AMIENS
and operations to 4 September

3 British Armies.
③ French Armies.
A Australian Corps.
C Canadian Corps.

- ▦▦▦▦ Line on 8 August.
- •••• Line on 21 August.
- ‑‑‑‑ Line on 26 August.
- ▤▤▤▤ Line on 4 September.
- ▨ Area gained 8 August.
- ▧ Area gained 21 August.
- —x— Boundary between British and French sectors.

0   5
Miles

Lens

Vimy

Drocourt

DOUAI

Scarpe

Escaut

①

ARRAS

Croisilles

Escaut

Escaut Canal

Quéant

Inchy

CAMBRAI

3

Miraumont

Bapaume

Ypres

Equancourt

St. Quentin Canal

Le Catelet

4

Albert

Combles

Somme

Péronne

Roisel

TO AMIENS (6 miles)

Villers Bretonneux

A

Warfusée Abancourt

C

Vermand

ST. QUENTIN

—x—x—x—x—x—

Chaulnes

Somme

Moreuil

Somme

Ham

Roye

St. Simon

①

N

Montdidier

Guiscard

Chauny

3

Lassigny

Noyon

Oise

~ARTHUR BANKS~

became aware of the possibility of defeat looming up with lightning speed. Behind the arrogant façade of the First Quartermaster-General there now lurked a frightened man. Momentarily he lost his grip. When the Kaiser came to his headquarters at Avesnes on the 11th, the day that Rawlinson called the battle off, Ludendorff offered his resignation. It was refused. The Kaiser then said: 'I see we must strike a balance. We have nearly reached the limit of our powers of resistance. The war must be ended.' The rot had started not only at the bottom but at the top as well.

Equally significant, though in a different way, was the effect of the victory on the officers and men of the British Army. Never even in the worst days of the spring had they admitted that there was even a possibility of defeat: their faith however in their Higher Command had been badly shaken. Now, in one dramatic stroke, the Fourth Army had restored it.

The Silences of
Field-Marshal Haig

Here lie six Boches.
They met a Digger.

*Inscription on a rough wooden cross seen on
the battlefield of St Quentin in late 1918*

An atmosphere of Wagnerian gloom pervaded the Crown Council
when it met under the presidency of the Kaiser himself on
13 August at Spa in Belgium. Of the 201 divisions in France
over half were reported as fit only for a defensive role. Kaiser
Karl of Austria, when pressed to provide troops for the Western
Front, not only refused to do so but said that in his opinion his
own army would not face another winter. Bulgaria and Turkey
were known to be on the way out. The war at sea had been
irretrievably lost. Within the Reich itself there was discontent
and even hunger in the towns. In the past, however, the German
people had faced and survived far greater threats and would
again in the distant future. In 1757 and again in 1759 Britain's
ally Frederick the Great, the Kaiser's ancestor, outnumbered
and surrounded on all sides by the converging armies of the
French, Russians, Austrians and Swedes, had fought them one by
one, and in the end, partly by military and political skill and
partly by sheer good luck, had saved Prussia from extinction. An
infinitely worse situation would confront his successor Adolf
Hitler in September 1944, caught between the jaws of the Western
Allies and the Russians and under the hammer of vastly superior
air forces, who would succeed in prolonging the war for another
six months and would give the Allies an unpleasant shock in the
Ardennes. Now in mid-August 1918, the outlook was by no
means hopeless. The Fatherland was intact, the Russians were
out of the war and the industrial area of north-east France and

practically all Belgium were firmly held. Admittedly the initiative had been lost and must be regained. If this was to be done the bulk of the Army would have to be pulled out of the line, re-habilitated and re-trained so that in due course, before winter finally congealed the front, it could stage a come-back either in another surprise offensive or in a defensive battle which would enable it, at worst, to remain on French soil. The means were there.

In March 1917 the Germans, by falling back to the shelter of the Hindenburg Line, had not only deranged the Allies' strategic plans for the year but had also shortened their front by 20 miles and thus saved 13 divisions. At the same time they had con-fronted the Allies with the problem of attacking one of the most formidable defensive systems ever constructed and had finally used it to cover the mounting of their great Spring Offensive only four months previously. The most important section of it, known as the Siegfried Line, lay some 36 miles to the east of the British front line and at the time of the end of the Battle of Amiens stretched for about 90 miles from near Arras via St Quentin to the Aisne east of Soissons. The chief architect of this masterpiece of field fortification, Colonel von Lossberg, had embodied in its design all the experience gained in the great battles of 1916. As a result he had sited the main defences not on forward but on reverse slopes with the artillery observation posts well back. The attackers could thus be caught in the fire of the guns as they came over the crest. The system was at least 12,000 yards deep, was divided into three zones—an outpost zone, a main zone and a reserve zone—and was sited with meticulous care. Over 50,000 Russian prisoners of war and all the French and Belgian craftsmen and labourers who could be rounded up took part in its construction. Veritable forests of barbed wire, so sited as to drive the attacker into the arcs of fire of concealed machine guns, straddled the entrenchments in great depth. The garrison of the outpost zone, designed to take the weight of the enemy's initial artillery bombardment, was small; the main zone, however, was held in greater strength. Machine guns in concrete emplacements sited to fire in enfilade studded each zone. Underground passages and shell-proof dugouts, liberally provided with bunks, gave ample cover against bombardment and the weather. A comprehensive drainage scheme made the going in the actual trenches relatively easy. Deep ditches made each zone virtually tank-proof. Underground cables linked the various headquarters and battery positions. Within the system men could live in comparative security and comfort for months on end in sharp contrast to the conditions it imposed on the attackers. In front of the position every fold in the ground had been registered, all shelter from the weather had been destroyed, every well had been blown up and every tree cut down. Streams had been dammed and bogs created.

A further 15–20 miles to the east of this system was another defensive position running from the Verdun area to the head waters of the Lys and Scarpe; roughly a further 25 miles to the east nature provided in the line of the Meuse from Sedan to Namur and thence to Antwerp a defensive barrier of great strength celebrated ever since the days of Marlborough and Louis XIV. Finally, on the German frontier lay the prewar frontier defences running from the Argonne and the wooded Ardennes to the Dutch border. If therefore a respite could be secured for the troops by a clean-cut withdrawal to the Hindenburg Line, as von Lossberg and other senior German commanders advised, morale could be restored and the opportunity created to inflict such losses on the British and the French as would shatter the will of their peoples and governments to continue the war. At the very worst the prospect of another winter of war with their armies called upon to endure the discomfort of badly sited, waterlogged and shelterless trenches might well induce their leaders to accept a compromise peace whatever the Americans said or did.

The Allied command system, to give it a title it did not deserve, in no way resembled the elaborate structure evolved by the British and Americans in the Second War. Montgomery might argue with Eisenhower and, indeed, did; in the end, however, whether his wishes were met or not, he loyally, without exception, accepted the decisions of the Supreme Command. Eisenhower's Headquarters resembled a vast cantonment mobile only with the assistance of an inordinate fleet of transport; Foch's could have been transported in half-a-dozen cars plus a lorry or two. Haig and Pershing, and sometimes Pétain too, disputed almost every issue with Foch and obeyed his orders with reservations and when it suited them to do so. As the Allies had no common war aims there was always the chance that they would fall out amongst themselves. Even to the most politically dumb German general or statesman it should have been apparent that the Americans, including as they did many officers and men of German descent, would not be inclined to pull either British or French chestnuts out of the fire or to strip the Germans of their dignity, but in all good faith would try to secure an end to the war which would satisfy the dictates of President Woodrow Wilson's sensitive conscience, the reputation of the American Army and the material interests and aspirations of the people of the United States. Admittedly this would not be easy. To the German generals, however, the art of politics consisted of reconciling the irreconcilable; that was what politicians were for. If therefore, to use the Kaiser's own words at this juncture, 'the termination of the war must be brought about by diplomacy', there was sense in the advice of von Lossberg, now up-graded to Chief of Staff of the Army Group most closely concerned, that the Army should fall back immediately to the Hindenburg position and not allow itself to be destroyed, bit by bit, by Allied offensives delivered in relatively rapid succession.

Ludendorff, like Hitler, in not very dissimilar conditions in Russia in the Second War, and for similar reasons, would not agree: no argument could shake his pig-headed determination to carry on with the fight with the armies where they now stood. Voluntary retirements, he said, although they economised divisions, also allowed the enemy to do the same and to build up reserves; besides, they were bad for morale. The most he would consider was a withdrawal, should the necessity arise, to the line of the Somme south of Péronne and along the Canal du Nord to the north of it. Von Lossberg protested that it would take a long time to reconnoitre and dig a defensive position here: he was overruled. Strategically, as the event proved, there was nothing to be said for Ludendorff's decision: tactically, however, so far as the immediate situation on the British Fourth Army front was concerned, he was on firmer ground. South of Péronne the devastated grass-grown jumble of shell holes, rusty wire and collapsed trenches of the old Somme battlefield provided the Germans with a succession of defensive positions easy to hold with machine guns sited in depth, virtually tank-proof and inevitably costly and tedious to attack as Rawlinson and Haig had long since realised. A direct order from Foch, therefore, to resume the offensive on this front on 16 August, inevitably brought Haig in person to Foch's headquarters at Sercus to protest.

Although he was in his 67th year, Foch had lost none of his energy and determination. In conversation he employed gestures to emphasise his words: two blows in the air with his fists, followed by two kicks, used to show the fate he reserved for his enemies. He had a way of dismissing difficulties with his hands. In explaining his own views he would say: 'Ah si, Ah si', in a firm and persuasive manner, or if he disagreed 'Ah non, Ah non', in a very decided way. These Latin histrionics cut little ice with the inscrutable, tongue-tied British Commander-in-Chief. Haig made it unequivocally clear that to resume the attack on Rawlinson's front at this moment would involve expenditure of British life on a scale which he considered to be unjustifiable. He, and not Foch, was responsible to King George V and his Government for the tactical handling of his own army. In any case, he was not prepared to accept a degree of subordination any greater than Foch exercised over Pershing, or for that matter Pétain, who only obeyed when it suited him. Haig however, was willing to extend the general offensive northwards on 21 August between Albert and Arras, where the ground was suitable for tanks, using at first his Third Army and later his First. The aim of these operations would be to turn the line of the Somme south of Péronne by striking the northern flank of the Crown Prince's Army Group and hustling them back to the Hindenburg Line destroying as many as possible in the process. Haig went on to point out that the Germans were deployed to meet attack from the south; attack in the north on the lines he proposed might therefore once again, as on 8 August, reap the rewards of surprise. By now Foch had learnt that to attempt to argue with a Lowland Scot once he has made up his mind is about as rewarding as offering food to the lions in Trafalgar Square. He therefore bowed to the inevitable and let Haig have his way. Some have seen in his almost simultaneous withdrawal of Debeney's Army from Haig's command as an indication of his displeasure. This is doubtful: the French Official History, drafted under the critical eye of Pétain after the war, merely records that the need for their retention under British command had passed. In the Battle of

Amiens the French First Army and Debeney had done little to endear themselves to their British Allies. They would not be missed. If Haig however had been a little-minded, hyper-sensitive man, he could have legitimately expressed his resentment at the unfortunate wording of a letter from Foch received on 20 August on the very eve of the Third Army's offensive. That morning, Mangin's Tenth Army west of Soissons had advanced 3,000 yards: in passing on the glad tidings to Haig, Foch wrote:

> 'I therefore count on the attack of your Third Army, *already postponed to the 21st, being launched that day with violence,* carrying forward with it the neighbouring divisions of the First Army and the whole of the Fourth Army. After your brilliant successes of the 8th, 9th and 10th *any timidity* on their part would hardly be justified in view of the enemy's situation and the moral ascendency you have gained over him.'

The suggestion that British soldiers would be guilty of timidity was at best tactless and at worst an insult: coming from a Frenchman it was doubly offensive. Haig chose to carry on with the war without comment.

In World War Two Eisenhower's operations were, with a brief exception, characterised by an underlying theme evident to all: this cannot be said of the next six weeks ending on 26 September with the completion of Stage One of Foch's broad strategic plan as laid down in late July, that is, to recapture the ground facing the Hindenburg Line which had been lost in the German spring offensives. Some have claimed to see in these battles the triumph of a policy of indirect leverage, deftly executed and perfectly timed, which kept the Germans off balance. According to Monash, who militarily and mentally made all the other generals look, to use Montgomery's description of a fellow Army Commander whom he did not admire, like good plain cooks, the truth is that on the British front all the commanders were opportunists. One idea dominated them all: to hit the Germans on their immediate front with all they had got, as often as they could and, when not actually attacking, to make their life as unbearable as possible by means of fighting patrols, by raids, by snipers and by machine gun and artillery fire round the clock. British munition production, directed by Winston Churchill, was now at its peak: between 8 August and 11 November no less than 621,289 tons of ammunition would be fired into the German lines on the British front alone. Furthermore, a new Haig seemed to have emerged: he lived near the front, moving his headquarters train, like Montgomery with his small Tactical Headquarters in a later war, to those points where success was most conspicuous or failure most glaring, like a high-power 'whipper-in' in a fox hunt. At last, backed by an efficient staff he had his finger on the pulse of the operations; and the commanders under him, with one or two exceptions, realised that they must succeed or accept transfer to that limbo from which those found wanting seldom in any war ever return.

The many battles which now followed never at the time captured the imagination of the war correspondents or the public: their very names in fact had to be invented by official historians after the war. For the French they are the Battles of Picardy, Montdidier, Second Marne and Noyon; for the British the battles of Albert, Arras, the Scarpe, Péronne–Bapaume, Drocourt–Quéant, Outersteene Ridge, Havrincourt and Epéhy; for the Americans St Mihiel. The majority were on the British front and were mounted and executed in the spirit of, and in accordance with, the general design of the Battle of Amiens. All in all they constitute the most impressive chain of victories in the history of the British Army since the Peninsular War. Among them the capture of Mount St Quentin and Péronne by the Australian Corps, according to Rawlinson, stands out as the 'the finest single feat of the whole war'. The breaking of the Drocourt–Quéant Line by the Canadians on 2 September was undoubtedly a triumph, equalled only by the forcing of the Canal du Nord on 4 September by the Fourth Army.

There was certainly no lack of that violence which Foch had ordered Haig to inject in the Battle of Albert which opened on 21 August or any indication of that timidity which he had requested him to avoid. Blasted in by over 800 field guns and some 500 heavier pieces, and supported by rather less than 200 tanks, three corps of the Third Army carried all before them and despite heavy tank losses from close range artillery fire, by nightfall had taken practically all their objectives except on their extreme right amongst the swamps of the Ancre. At first light next day Fourth Army, supported by the Fourth Tank Brigade, entered the fray, wiped out the salient lying between the Ancre and the Somme and forced their way into the ruins of Albert, to find that, at long last, the hanging Virgin had fallen from the church tower. Ever since the days of the Somme battle of 1916, the superstition had been widely held that when the Virgin fell the end of the war would be at hand. The news flashed from one end of the British Army to the other.

The whole British front as far north as Arras was now aflame. The attack of the Third Army had lured the German reserves in their direction: Rawlinson therefore was able to launch the Australian Corps once more into battle in the valley of Chuignes with the certainty of success. The valley itself constituted the last stretch of habitable country before the devastated area began. The Germans had therefore concentrated in it many of their reserves and administrative troops: upon them now descended, like the wrath of God, the 1st Australian Division supported by the 32nd British Division. There followed a day of blazing heat and close-quarter fighting in the tangled valleys. On approaching Herleville all the officers of the leading battalion were shot down; in the resulting confusion there was grave risk that all would be annihilated. One of the officers of the supporting battalion, Lieutenant Joynt, sized up the situation at a glance, rushed forward over the open in the teeth of devastating machine-gun fire and rallied the survivors in a piece of dead ground. Then linking them up with his own men he led them all forward in a wild charge with the bayonet which by its very audacity got the whole front once more on the move. Later, when the advance was checked again by fire from a wood, he worked his way round the rear of it with a small party of volunteers and in hand-to-hand fighting so demoralised the enemy as to turn a stubborn defence into abject surrender. Lieutenant McCarthy's valour on this day was equally astonishing. In the course of the fighting he crawled into a disused trench and under a block over which an enemy machine gun was being fired. He therefore tunnelled a hole under it, pushed his head and arm through and shot dead the two men firing the gun. Then, using German stick grenades, he proceeded to bomb his way up the enemy trenches, killed one German officer, wounded another and captured three machine guns. A non-commissioned officer now joined him; all told they captured five machine guns and 50 prisoners. Altogether Lieutenant McCarthy killed 20 of the enemy on this day. By nightfall, the

Australians were the undisputed masters of the whole valley of Chuignes: in the process they had taken over 3,000 prisoners and 21 guns and written off the greater part of three German divisions.

It was a good day too for the Third Army north of the Somme. Here seven divisions attacking on an 11-mile front, advanced roughly two-and-a-half miles, captured a number of villages and drove the Germans out of their last defensive position, the strongly fortified embankment and cutting of the railway between Arras and Albert. Here, too, it was a day of disaster for the Germans, 5,000 of whom ended up in the cages of the Third Army. On the 24th the weather broke; nevertheless the Third and Fourth Armies remorselessly continued their attack both north and south of the Somme. The Germans flung in 11 divisions but to no avail. By the evening of the 25th the Fourth Army was approaching Péronne; north of the Somme the Third Army threatened Bapaume. The time had now come for another devastating blow.

Ten days previously Haig had ordered Horne, the Commander of the First Army, to plan an attack south-east from the direction of Arras designed to pierce the formidable defences of the Drocourt–Quéant Line which anchored the northern flank of the Crown Prince's Army Group. He was then to swing south and threaten the rear of the Germans facing the Third Army. The time for the delivery of this attack had now come. On the morning of 26 August the Canadian Corps, consisting of the 2nd and 3rd Canadian Divisions and the 51st Highland Division, burst out and by nightfall had advanced four miles near Monchy Le Preux. Thus threatened from the north by the First Army, driven in by the Fourth and Third Armies from the west and under pressure from the French in the south, Ludendorff faced the fact that if he did not withdraw at once his Armies would be destroyed where they stood. That night he ordered his battered troops to fall back some ten miles to the line of the Somme south of Péronne and thence to Noyon. Two days later at Ypres, the mere threat of attack by the Second and Fifth British Armies stimulated Ludendorff to sanction the abandonment of all the gains they had made here in the spring. The whole British front was on the move: morale was high. On the Third Army front, a London boy of the 18th Division, hearing that the troops in front were short of ammunition, fell in 50 prisoners of the Second Guards Division who had just surrendered, made each of them pick up a box of ammunition and carry it up to the front line in front of him. Bapaume, which had resisted capture in the First Battle of the Somme in 1916, fell to the New Zealand Division on the 29th: by the evening of the next day the Australians had closed with the angle of the Somme opposite Péronne and, thanks to Monash's foresight in insisting that both banks of the westward course of the river should be within his domain, established their 3rd Division on the north bank at Cléry: due south of this village they had two crossings of sorts at Omiécourt and Buscourt. Before them however there stretched a prospect which would have shaken the nerve of any Army in any war. Opposite the town itself lay a marsh 1,000 yards wide: through this the river sluggishly made its meandering way. West of the marsh flowed a canal. All the bridges had been destroyed and all boats removed. It was obvious that the front here was impregnable to frontal assault. A mile to the north of the town stood a low hill absolutely destitute of cover known as Mount St Quentin. On this hill an elaborate network of trenches festooned with thick belts of barbed wire completely dominated both arms of the Somme. They were garrisoned by elements of no less than five divisions some of whom were high-grade troops. When Monash told Rawlinson that he proposed to carry this immensely strong defensive work by storm he was incredulous.

In the morning mist of 31 August, the 5th Brigade of the 2nd Australian Division, only 70 officers and 1,250 men strong, advanced to the assault of this formidable fortress. No tanks were available to support them. Now began a day of battle in which the infantry with little outside support fought their way forward on their own. Fighting every inch of the way, they had by nightfall, despite 15 counter-attacks during the day, secured a foothold on the mountain. That night Monash passed the 5th Australian Division over the river and into the attack. There now followed two days of close in-fighting, ending with the capture not only of the mountain but of the town as well. No less than eight Victoria Crosses were won by the Australians in these amazing battles. Amongst them was Private Curry who advanced alone against a German machine gun holding up his battalion, shot dead the entire crew and captured the gun. There was also Private Macatier who single-handed killed 15 Germans and captured 20 and Sergeant Lowerson who captured 12 machine guns and 30 prisoners and who, when badly wounded in the right thigh, refused to be evacuated. Rawlinson and indeed the whole British Army were astounded by the surpassing courage and enterprise of the Australians. Unquestionably the capture of the fortress of Péronne without the aid of tanks stands out as the greatest infantry exploit of the war. Meanwhile the 3rd Australian Division immediately to the north had literally destroyed the Germans holding the Bouchavesnes spur.

In the north astride the Arras–Marquion road the Canadian Corps had now reached the elaborate trench system, concrete defences and wire entanglements of the Drocourt–Quéant switch, an outwork of the main Hindenburg Line and the northern bastion of the existing German front. So great had been the strain on the Tank Corps and so heavy the wastage that only 50 tanks could be produced for their support. Nevertheless attacking at dawn on 2 September the Canadians, despite bitter resistance which cost them dear, burst right through the German defences and by noon reached the open country beyond. With Péronne gone, the Third Army pressing eastwards from Bapaume and now the loss of the Drocourt–Quéant switch, Ludendorff admitted defeat. At 2 p.m. he ordered withdrawal for about 20 miles to the shelter of the Hindenburg Line, thus abandoning all the ground gained since the spring. At dawn next day, patrols probing their way forward in the half-light along the whole British front, returned to report that the enemy forward defences had been abandoned. The news galvanised into life all the headquarters right back to the base. By 9 a.m. the leading troops of the First, Third and Fourth Armies were on the move.

In refusing to cut his losses a fortnight earlier and husband his resources in a systematic and orderly withdrawal to the Hindenburg Line, Ludendorff had lost some 115,600 men, 470 guns and vast quantities of stores on the British front alone. Haig, using a mere 34 divisions, had defeated 66 German divisions, admittedly some of poor quality and low in strength, prised them off the line of the Somme and smashed the Drocourt–Quéant Line. In the process his losses at 89,000 killed and wounded, mostly infantry, had been comparatively light. The morale of his troops was high. In sharp contrast, it was a badly shaken German army, short of sleep and numb with exposure, which was now falling back before them. Nevertheless the hard core of the Army, notably the machine gunners, as Hitler would claim not without an element of truth in later years, were still prepared to fight and if necessary to die for their country. Foch's insistence that the Germans were now 'retreating in disorder' and that Haig must 'continue the pursuit' regardless of risk, flank protection, administrative considerations and, indeed, common sense bore no relation to the actual situation.

Haig had already decided that the German withdrawal would be conducted in accordance with the technique with which he was familiar. The normal indication of a step back on the part of the enemy would be a sudden increase in the weight of artillery fire as their gunners used up their dumped ammunition. Actual withdrawals would be covered by high-velocity guns firing at long range. Single-gun detachments in woods and copses and well-concealed machine guns with a covered getaway would hang on till the last moment, inflicting heavy losses on the impetuous and unwary. In their withdrawal they would deliberately destroy all habitable shelter and water supplies and leave behind them booby traps sited with considerable ingenuity and malice. All cross roads would be cratered and for some queer reason all fruit trees cut down. This was how they had carried out their withdrawal in March 1917: this was how they would do it again. The decisive battle had still to be fought on the main Hindenburg Line. Inevitably the cost would be high: if it was not to be prohibitive, planning and preparation would have to be carried out in great detail. Roads and bridges would have to be repaired; vast tonnages of ammunition and stores would have to be brought forward. Troops must be rested, made up to strength and retrained. Intelligence with regard to the actual German defences must be brought up-to-date and widely disseminated. Fortunately, on 8 August the Fourth Army had captured a defence scheme complete in every detail for the Hindenburg Line between the Oise and Bellicourt. It showed all the trenches and wire, gave the position of every battery, its calibre, barrage lines and observation posts; the position of all sound-ranging and flash-spotting sections; the location of all infantry and artillery headquarters, dug-outs and machine-gun emplacements. It also revealed the divisional sectors, the ammunition and supply dumps, the signal communications and electric power installations. It was in fact a triumph of German staff work of which the British now prepared to take the fullest advantage.

Haig accordingly forbade operations on a large scale until further orders, pulled back the maximum possible number of his troops into reserve and contented himself for the time being with ensuring that contact with the Germans was not lost as they fell back. Meanwhile the administrative staffs concentrated on the build-up for the grand attack.

Just before the Battle of Amiens there had arrived at Haig's headquarters a remarkable document from Henry Wilson, the CIGS, dealing with long term policy. It was over 10,000 words long and it bore all the marks of the mercurial mind of its author. 1 July 1919, wrote Lloyd George's chief military adviser, must be the date when the Allies' preparations for the decisive struggle must be complete. He visualised about then a grand Allied attack in a 50-mile front by 70 divisions and eight cavalry divisions supported by 10,000 tanks of which 3,000 would be British. Fuller had been sent back to England to work out the details of this fantastic scheme. On 21 August, Winston Churchill, the Minister of Munitions, had arrived at Haig's headquarters to discuss, in the light of Wilson's illuminating forecast, the production programme for the coming winter. That night, Haig wrote in his dairy: 'He is most anxious to help us in every way . . . his schemes are all timed for completion next June. I told him we ought to do our utmost to get a decision this autumn.' From now until mid-November the will of this stubborn Scot would be the decisive factor in the war.

Haig now, at the very moment when the rest of the Allied Higher Command, such as it was, were thinking in terms of another year of fighting on the Western Front, made a suggestion to Foch which would profoundly influence Pershing's plans for the first grand all-American attack of the war at St Mihiel and the subsequent line of advance of his armies.

12

St Mihiel

Timeo Danaos et dona ferentes
(I fear the Greeks most when they come bearing gifts)
Virgil

Tongue-tied though he may have seemed to many, Haig could express himself on paper with grace, force and clarity. On 25 August there had arrived from Foch yet another exhortation to press on with what he described as the pursuit. In reply, after compliments, Haig gently hinted that others might well be urged to do a little more: indeed, at a time when all his five Armies were advancing, he was strongly of opinion that American divisions might, for the general Allied good, take a more active share in the battle without further delay. He himself was thrusting in the direction of Cambrai whence he could threaten the complex of railway junctions around Aulnoye which controlled the German main lines of communication to Liège, Aachen and Cologne. If Pershing and Pétain could be encouraged simultaneously to attack from the south towards Mézières, so as eventually to converge with his own advance, the results might be far-reaching. Foch, although he had not actually revealed his intentions for the development of operations after the ground lost since the spring had been re-conquered, had obviously not overlooked this possibility: Haig, in all probability, knew this when he wrote. Both he and Foch were now fully aware of the discontent and disillusion in Germany and the precarious political position of the Kaiser's government. A huge Allied pincer movement ending in more heavy losses and further retreats before the autumn rains slowed down the pace of operations might well strengthen the arms of those in Germany who were clamouring for peace. Foch

33 The Americans attack—St Mihiel, 12 September 1918

34 Men of 21st Battalion AIF moving forward to the attack on Mont St Quenti
1 September 1918

35 American Gunners support the Infantry with rapid fire, St Mihiel, 10 September 19

therefore accepted Haig's proposals with alacrity: all that now remained to be done was to secure Pershing's agreement. At last the Allies would have an overall strategic plan for bringing the war to an end. Armed therefore with new proposals on these lines, Foch and Weygand on 30 August arrived at Pershing's residence in the ancient little town of Ligny-en-Barrois 25 miles south-west of St Mihiel.

For the past year Pershing had missed no opportunity of making it clear to his Allies that his aim was the creation of an independent American Army with its own theatre on the Lorraine front, supplied from the west coast ports of Bordeaux and St Nazaire by a good rail system, now, thanks to his own persistence, largely manned by American operators. All his depots, hospitals, communications and indeed his whole logistic system had been built up on this assumption. An American offensive in the direction of Metz would eventually cut the vital German lateral railway running from Lorraine to Mézières and threaten the Briey iron basin on which the German munitions industry at this time largely depended. At the Bombon Conference of 24 July when Foch had given the Allied Armies their respective tasks, the reduction of the St Mihiel Salient had been prescribed as the major American effort for the immediate future. The First American Army accordingly had been activated on 10 August and, when Foch arrived on the 30th, had just finished taking over the sector from the French. Their plans for a 25-mile advance from St Mihiel to the line Marieulles–Mars La Tour-Étain, ten miles beyond the base of the salient, with a view to the eventual invasion of Lorraine, were already far advanced.

The meeting started badly and it went from bad to worse. In brief, Foch explained his plan to make the main Franco-American effort an all-out attack, tentatively in about a fortnight's time, north-west towards Mézières to meet Haig's thrust in the direction of Cambrai. It would therefore be necessary, he said, to reduce the scope of the St Mihiel operation to the elimination of the actual salient only. Pershing's proposed attack on the western face in addition to that on the southern face would therefore be a waste of effort. Any further advance beyond the base of the salient would be in the wrong direction. For the Allied main operation towards Mézières Foch suggested the placing of some four to six American divisions under command of the French

L

Second Army between the Meuse and the Argonne. Between the
French Second and Fourth Armies a new American Army would
be formed with its axis astride the River Aire. Foch would be
delighted to make available the services of Generals Degoutte
and Maclor to supervise the staff work of this new Army. In
other words, Pershing would be relegated to look after the
moribund sector of St Mihiel, all his plans for an independent
American Army would be wrecked and all credit for such success
as might be achieved would go to the French. His reactions were
those which might have been expected from the leading American
actor of the period, John Barrymore, if, when cast as Hamlet, he
had been asked instead to play the part of one of the grave-
diggers. At long last Foch had overreached himself. In the
course of heated exchanges Pershing made it clear that he could
stand no more. The American troops, their Government and their
people at home expected their Army to operate as a whole and
would not countenance its dispersion in this way. Eventually,
Foch said, with the sarcasm for which his countrymen are
renowned and which other races find particularly offensive: 'Do
you wish to take part in the battle?' Pershing replied: 'Most
assuredly. . . . Marshal Foch you have no authority as Allied
Commander-in-Chief to call me to yield up my command of the
American Army and have it scattered among the Allied forces
where it will not be an American Army at all.' Foch remained
adamant. Finally, both rose from the table. Then Pershing said:
'Marshal Foch, you may insist all you please, but I decline
absolutely to agree to your plan.' Foch picked up his maps and
papers and, very pale and apparently exhausted, handed him a
memorandum: then, with the remark that after careful study of it
he would change his mind, abruptly left. The memory of all that
Lafayette had done to help the Americans to throw off the British
yoke, so vivid a year ago, had now grown very dim.

Pétain was no friend of the British either in this or in the
Second War. Whether he was aware of the fact that Foch's
proposal originally came from Haig is unknown. Pershing certainly
was not. It is impossible, however, not to admire the military
statesmanship with which he handled this Franco-American
deadlock. When on the following day Pershing called on him in
his headquarters train at Nettancourt to discuss the St Mihiel
operation, first on the agenda was Pershing's proposal that there

must be an attack on the western face of the salient as well as on the south. Pétain most cordially agreed: that was the very conclusion he himself had reached. In any case whether to attack on the west flank as well as the south was a matter for the Army Commander concerned and no business of the Generalissimo. In fact, as only American troops would get killed in the process, Pétain did not mind how they did it so long as they attacked but he did not say so. With regard to Pershing's proposals for a subsequent advance towards Metz he observed that he himself had similar ideas but that, in his opinion, an offensive in the direction of Belgium should be executed first to ensure a secure flank. Speaking as one soldier to another, he fully realised the need for an independent American Army and the folly of splitting it up into two parts with some divisions under French command. Both agreed that the sooner the Americans took over the whole front from the Meuse to the Argonne the better. Pétain, who knew this most unpleasant sector only too well and the likely cost of an offensive there, found no difficulty whatever in agreeing with Pershing.

As a result, when Foch summoned them both to meet him at Bombon on 2 September all went well. Firstly, it was agreed that the St Mihiel attack should not for the time being proceed beyond the base of the salient; secondly, that the American Army should take over the whole 90-mile front from the Meuse to the Argonne and from there launch an offensive on 25 September in the direction of Mézières in cooperation with the Fourth Army on its western flank. Thus, largely owing to Pétain's diplomacy, Franco-American unity was once more restored. All the Allied Commanders had good reason to be satisfied: Haig because he got the Franco-American attack towards Mézières to converge with his own towards Cambrai which he himself had suggested. Furthermore, it would be launched twenty-four hours in advance of his own and thus might be expected to attract German reserves away from his own front. Pétain got the Americans to undertake an inevitably costly and difficult offensive in ever-deteriorating weather: he would thus save the lives of many Frenchmen and be able in addition to pull others into reserve to rest. Foch had at last got an overall strategic plan which might well imperil a German withdrawal through the Liège Gap and thus precipitate an early demand for an armistice. Pershing at long last got the chance to exercise his own hand in a large-scale battle free from interference and to exploit the offensive enthusiasm of his soldiers. Success at St Mihiel would give the people at home the victory they had so long awaited, strengthen the hand of the Government, stimulate subscription to the Liberty Loan and war production and enhance the prestige of the United States throughout the world. He and his Army had in fact undertaken at short notice a gigantic task: he had agreed to launch with practically the same army, within the next 24 days, two great attacks on battlefields 60 miles apart, connected only by three roads—a task which in the circumstances of the First War was calculated to strain to the limit the capacity of the most experienced Army staff German, French or British.

The number of staff officers in the American Army who had qualified at Fort Leavenworth was small but their quality was high. Like the British opposite numbers from Camberley they had a common tactical attitude: all spoke the same military language and believed in the same military doctrine. Coming from a small peacetime army had its advantages: they knew each other well. Without the knowledge, skill and devotion of these men an Army over a million strong and destined soon to reach the two million mark could never have been committed to the large-scale operations now imminent. Brigadier-General Conner, Pershing's Chief of Operations, was a very able man who spoke French well. Brigadier-General Drum, aged 39, the Chief of Staff of the First Army, had boundless energy and good judgment. He got on well with Pershing's Chief of Staff, MacAndrew. Under him as Chief of Operations, was the brilliant Colonel Marshall, now aged 37 and destined to rise in the Second War to the very top of the Army and world-wide fame. His outstanding capacity was already apparent: it would soon be demonstrated in striking form.

The St Mihiel Salient was a bulge of some 200 square miles protruding between the Meuse and the Moselle, 18 miles across the base and 13 miles deep. Its western face was dominated by the wooded heights of the Meuse: the remainder consisted of the Woeuvre plain which included a number of lakes and woods. At the apex stood the little town of St Mihiel; across the base stretched the Michel Line, part of the Hindenburg system. Since 1915 this part of the front had been quiescent and both sides had used it as a rest area for battle-worn divisions. With their usual skill and industry the Germans had converted it into a vast fortress with elaborate defences and amenities such as electric light and a piped water supply. In the first week of September it was garrisoned by some nine divisions for the most part below strength under General von Fuchs. Like all salients it was vulnerable to converging attacks, from both flanks. This concept in fact governed Pershing's plan for its reduction.

No commander ever realised more clearly that whenever possible troops in their first battle should be given an easy task and be supported by overwhelming force. If initiated comparatively gently in this way they are likely to go from strength to strength. He therefore demanded from his staff meticulous and detailed preparation and arranged for the maximum possible fire support and air cover. Altogether over 500,000 Americans, over 110,000 Frenchmen, nearly 3,000 guns, 200,000 tons of supplies and 50,000 tons of ammunition had to be assembled.

Pershing proposed to make his major attack against the southern face with the 1st Corps under Liggett on the right and the 4th Corps on the left under Dickman: here altogether seven divisions were involved. The 5th Corps were simultaneously to attack the western face and the 2nd French Colonial Corps to make a holding attack at St Mihiel itself against the nose. A mixed American, French, British and Italian Air Force, including the British Independent Bombing Squadrons, some 2,000 aircraft strong, under Mitchell, provided air support on a grand scale both over the immediate battlefield and in the enemy's rear. It is of some interest to note that, in sharp contrast to the Second War when the United States were able to supply their Allies with equipment on a lavish scale, that none of the aircraft and none of the guns were of American manufacture. Roughly half the artillery was manned by Americans and the rest by the French. Delay in the arrival of French heavy artillery from Mangin's front at Reims resulted in the attack, originally planned by Pershing for the 7th, being postponed to 12 September. This was unfortunate as Ludendorff on the 8th had ordered the gradual evacuation of the salient and when the American attack eventually went in on the southern face at 5 p.m. in drizzling rain after a four-hour preliminary bombardment by the 3,000 guns, the withdrawal of the heaviest guns had already started. All went well: the counter-battery bombardment had been particularly successful. Trained teams of pioneers and engineers with Bangalore torpedoes, a British invention, wire cutters and axes drove gaps through the dense barriers of barbed wire. Leading troops carried rolls of chicken wire which they flung over the entanglements to form a bridge of sorts across it. Thus easily was a problem which had absorbed immense and disproportionate effort on the part of the other Allies solved with apparent ease. By the afternoon most of the objectives on the southern front had been gained. The 2nd French Colonial Corps, attacking an hour after the 1st and 4th Corps, had little difficulty in occupying St Mihiel itself. The 5th Corps attack on the western face which was not delivered until 8 a.m., reaped some of the advantages of the success of the other three Corps, but in its advance in difficult country in the direction of Vigneulles met tougher resistance. Nevertheless, after pressure from Pershing, a strong force of the 56th Brigade reached its objective during the night and linked up with the 4th Corps at dawn on the 13th. By the afternoon the whole of the salient had been erased and 15,000 prisoners and 450 guns were in American hands. American casualties at 7,000 only testified to the care and skill lavished on this first all-American large-scale operation.

It was a triumph not only for Pershing but for Pétain too. On the afternoon of the 13th, Pershing's birthday, both generals went together to the Hotel de Ville in St Mihiel to be greeted by the Assistant Mayor and the populace waving French flags. Why the Mayor was absent is not known. Pétain, addressing the citizens, explained that the French coloured troops who had driven the hated enemy from the town on the previous day were in fact part of an American Army which had smashed both flanks of the salient. Thus did Pétain, as Clausewitz prescribed, accomplish his military and political end with the utmost economy in French life and, at the same time, maintain the prestige of the French Army. That the Germans were caught on the point of withdrawal does not detract from the fact that this first American battle of the war on a grand all-American scale was a remarkable achievement, executed as it was, with the notable exception of the veterans of the 1st, 2nd, 4th, 26th and 42nd Divisions, by a newly-raised Army Staff and large numbers of troops with no previous battle experience.

Some German authorities, at this time and later, asserted that if the advance had now been continued towards Metz, as Pershing had originally planned, spectacular results might have been achieved. This certainly was the opinion of MacArthur, who as a brigadier-general had established his headquarters in the jumping-off trench and led his troops throughout from the front. On the 14th he personally made a daring reconnaissance towards Metz. Such was the shock which had been administered to the Germans that the partially completed fortifications of the Michel Line might well have been carried had the 1st and 4th Corps been allowed to continue the pursuit. The morale of the German troops was low. The roads to Longuyon on the lateral railway and to Lorraine were open. The guns of the fortress of Metz had been removed for use on other parts of the front. This too, was the opinion of Dickman. Liggett, however, of the 1st Corps did not share it. He thought at the time and subsequently that 'the possibility of taking Metz and the rest of it, had the battle been fought on the original plan, existed, in my opinion, only on the supposition that our Army was a well co-ordinated machine, which it was not as yet'. Pershing himself would never cease to regret that he had committed his army to the Meuse–Argonne operation as the main American effort. The recollection, however, of what a pursuit towards Metz and Longuyon might have achieved would profoundly influence the imagination and the plans of American commanders, notably Bradley and Patton, in this very same part of France a quarter-of-a-century later.

As it was, Pershing and the American people had good reason for satisfaction: much had been accomplished and much learnt. Their all-American Army had stepped off on the right foot. The mission Foch had given them of removing the threat to the Paris–Nancy railway had been accomplished with skill and expedition. The right rear of the offensive towards Mézières now in preparation had been made secure. The Allies were also now in a position at a later date to launch an offensive towards Metz, into Lorraine and perhaps later down the Moselle to the Rhine itself at Coblence. The widespread and quite unjustified suspicion in the British ranks that the Americans were dragging their feet had at last been removed. Furthermore, the victory had demonstrated Pershing's own capacity to command an Army in battle and that he had under him commanders and staffs fully capable of conducting operations on their own without Allied assistance and, in particular, unsolicited advice. It had also been demonstrated that the offensive spirit already displayed at Château Thierry and Reims extended to the whole army. Pershing would now call upon virtually the same troops within a fortnight to launch another great offensive 60 miles to the west, in unfamiliar country, commanded on the east by the heights of the Meuse and on the west by the hilly, tangled Argonne Forest in which the Germans had built a defensive system as elaborate and ingenious as any on the Western Front, roughly 12 miles deep, bristling with barbed wire, mutually supporting concrete strong points and machine-gun nests in great depth.

Pershing had confronted his staff with a stupendous task. The concentration on the new front involved the move of some 600,000 Americans and 93,000 animals from St Mihiel to the Meuse–Argonne front and the move out of 220,000 French troops by rail, bus and on foot under cover of night. For the 4,000 guns to be employed in the new attack 40,000 tons of ammunition would have to be dumped by the 25th of the month: thereafter expenditure of 350,000 rounds per day would have to be met. As many as 19 railheads and 100 depots would have to be opened to meet the needs of the Army and elaborate arrangements made for the reception and onward transmission of the large number of casualties expected. All this had to be done in 14 days over roads designed only for the peacetime requirements of a rural area. All preparations had to be camouflaged; vast tonnages of engineer material had to be accumulated; new water supplies on a large scale had to be opened up. Marching men, horse-drawn transport, tracked vehicles and motor lorries, each with their individual rate of movement, presented a traffic control problem of extreme intricacy. Only a staff officer of genius could have produced the solution to this logistic nightmare at short notice; only staffs of outstanding flexibility of mind and energy could have ensured that it was carried out. Probably only Pershing would have ordered them to do it. For the moment then they can be left to their labours while a glance is taken at the British front.

Here the slow and methodical German withdrawal towards the main Hindenburg Line continued. At night, the glare of burning villages behind the German Lines reddened the sky; the days were punctuated by the dull thud of explosions as the Germans blew up the ammunition they lacked the transport to remove. Determination to reduce to a desert those parts of France they were compelled to relinquish characterised their every move. They even chopped down the apple trees. For the British the need now was to close with, and penetrate, the outer zone of the Hindenburg system and to get observation over its main features so that the grand attack towards Cambrai, which Haig was now planning for the end of the month by his Third and Fourth Armies, could be mounted. Accordingly on 12 September while the St Mihiel battle was in progress, the New Zealand, the 37th and 12th Divisions had attacked at Havrincourt and captured part of the Hindenburg defences. Four days later near Épehy, the Third and Fourth Armies attacked on a seven-mile front north of St Quentin, secured a good jumping-off line for the attack on the main Hindenburg position and took over 9,000 prisoners. Thus, by the evening of 19 September, Haig was able to report to Foch that he would be ready on 26 September for the grand assault. The morale of his young soldiers rose from day to day: he and his commanders were now certain of success. Since 8 August the British Armies had pushed the Germans back on a 40-mile front across damnable country, intersected with trenches, pitted with shell holes and bedevilled by the forests of barbed wire of old and new battlefields, at a cost of 180,000 casualties, almost exactly the same number as those sustained by the British and Canadian Armies from Normandy to the Baltic in the Second World War. This, in terms of First War butchers' bills, was a comparatively low figure: for the Somme Battle of 1916 it had cost 420,000 casualties to advance eight miles in four-and-a-half months. The recovery of the British Army since the reverses of the spring must be voted remarkable by any standard: in the past six weeks they had taken over 50,000 prisoners and killed large numbers of Germans with ever-increasing efficiency as they adapted themselves to the demands of increasingly fluid operations.

Foch, in fact, had since July made his main effort on the British front because the British were ready and willing while the French were unenthusiastic and the Americans were still in the throes of building up their Army almost from scratch. In July his hopes for the rest of 1918 had gone little further than the liberation of the mines around Lens to ensure France's coal supply for the winter. Theoretically, the British effort had been applied in the wrong place. Most of the German forces were immediately west of Reims: their communications ran east and west. An all-out offensive here therefore offered better prospects. The British instead of threatening the German communications had been engaged in pushing them back frontally along them. As a result Foch had condemned them to a series of battles of attrition. His persistent nagging of Haig to press on regardless of loss and the tactical situation had been, to put it mildly, not in the best of taste. No commander can be happy with his immediate superior continually breathing down his neck—a fact which commanders in the future and indeed prime ministers could have remembered with advantage. Incidentally, in the actual operations, it would have been an exaggeration to describe the cooperation displayed by Debeney and his Army on the British immediate right as efficient, effusive and generous.

Whether at any time since 8 August much more could have been achieved is very doubtful. Haig had hoped that the Third Army would not only break in but break out as well and that he would be able to pass the Cavalry Corps through so as to swing south and thus envelop the Germans facing the Fourth Army. It was now clear, once and for all, that no horseman could survive for long on the Western Front. The mere sight of a single rider near the front line brought down a hail of bullets: an infantryman could fall flat on the ground; a cavalryman stood up like a pea on a drum. For a battalion commander to gallop round his companies when deployed was courting suicide. That the two battalions of Whippet tanks were not more effectively used in the exploitation role is unfortunate. They could not by any later standard be described as efficient. Their range was only 40 miles, they were difficult to drive and their commander with only one gunner to help had not only to fire his four machine guns from a fixed turret but manoeuvre as well. The Mark V and Mark VI tanks with which the rest of the Tank Corps were armed could cross a ten-foot trench and climb a four-foot slope: this was the limit of their capacity. In fact they had been designed for advances of about 4,000 yards and no more. At this time probably Fuller alone had grasped what the ultimate capabilities of the tank would be. In any case their high wastage rate and mechanical shortcomings had prevented them from playing a conspicuous part in the semi-mobile operations which had followed the victory of the Battle of Amiens.

At first, with the notable exception of the Australians, the infantry had found it difficult to shake off the tactical inertia born of trench warfare: they did, however, improve from day to day as they gained experience. The problem of satisfactory communication between the infantry and the artillery was never solved in this war and indeed would remain unsolved until the advent of radio. Efficient inter-communication too between the troops on the ground and the pilots in the air was a dream of the future. What is remarkable at this late stage of the war is that with 50 per cent of the infantry under 19 years of age they fought as well as they did against the battle groups of machine guns, single artillery pieces and specially selected small infantry detachments which the enemy employed to cover his withdrawal. These were handled with great skill; all available cover and shelter was deliberately booby-trapped and fouled; every likely approach or forming-up place was carefully registered. Vast craters were created at every cross roads. That this type of opposition was successfully overcome says much for the initiative and courage of the junior officers and non-commissioned officers and the daring and drive of the battalion commanders, the majority of whom were now under 30 years of age. Far greater care than had been the case in 1917 had been taken to ensure that troops were properly rested and fed between battles, that hot tea and rum were got forward to the leading infantry at least once every twenty-four hours and that operations, once they had ceased to pay a dividend, were promptly closed down.

In these last days when the British carried the main burden of Allied operations Haig seemed to have grown in stature. Throughout, he kept his headquarters train close to the headquarters of the Army making the major effort at the time. Monash saw much of him; Rawlinson, who also saw much of him at this time, describes him in his diary as being 'in great form' and convinced that he and his army would finish the war before the end of the year. This is the image of Haig which should go down to history and not that which others with no personal knowledge and negligible battle experience have gone out of their way to defile. He was certainly better advised by his Intelligence Branch and better served by his Staff at all levels than in 1916 and 1917. His relations with Pershing had been frank and straightforward and indeed characterised on both sides by mutual respect and good manners. Understandably, he did not like the withdrawal of American divisions from behind his front and would have welcomed their aid in the front line so that his own infantry could be given a brief respite from contact with the enemy before proceeding once more to the assault. Pershing's insistence, however, on an independent American Army had his every sympathy. In the matter of overall strategy he was loyal to Foch: he did however resist persistent French attempts to get control of British resources and to squander British lives in reckless advances the French themselves showed little disposition to undertake. He now faced with equanimity, despite a warning from Lloyd George by way of Henry Wilson, the CIGS, that he must not, at his peril, incur heavy casualties, the prospect of launching his Army into an attack on the very heart of the Hindenburg Position; three defence systems in depth, 3,000–5,000 yards apart, covered by tank-proof obstacles, bristling to a great depth with forests of barbed wire and concrete, criss-crossed by the arcs of fire of countless machine guns firing in enfilade, and with their main lines of resistance sited behind the reverse slopes of many undulations. To the south in the Argonne with equal confidence and equanimity Pershing and his Army stood ready on 26 September, twenty-four hours before the British, to attack German defences quite as formidable and at least as stoutly manned. It was three years to the day since the Battle of Loos when a similar army mainly of wartime levies had faced the ordeal of a bitterly contested battle for the first time.

13

Meuse–Argonne or the Valour of Ignorance

Everyone is to attack as soon as they can, as strong as they can,
for as long as they can.

Foch

The grand assault by 12 Allied Armies, comprising over six
million men, that was now about to break all along the line
surpassed in scope, weight and numbers any offensive on the
Western Front in World War Two. Cost what it might in terms
of human life, Foch and Haig were determined on a supreme
effort to get a decision before the late autumn rains once more
engulfed the battlefield in one huge slough of mud. Only thus
could the aged, the mothers and the babies, the widows and the
orphans of France be spared the cold horror of another winter
in houses unheated for lack of coal and the mass of the British
people saved from semi-starvation, similar to that of the German
population, who subsisted on a diet mainly of potatoes so that
their soldiers could be adequately fed. The Americans were spared
such strains as these on their morale.

Judged by the experience gained in the Passchendaele battles of
the previous year, the thrust ordered by Foch of the British
Second Army and the Belgians under the command of King
Albert was of little promise: it could only succeed if the main
effort by the First, Third and Fourth British Armies towards
Cambrai and Maubeuge managed to smash the Hindenburg Line
at its strongest point and thus turned the southern flank of the
German Armies near the coast. To reach the key railway junctions about Aulnoye, the British, after breaking the Hindenburg
Line, would still have over 40 miles to go over country which was
one vast defended area, straddled by rivers and dykes and studded

with bottomless fields and patches of industrial slum. At first glance therefore it seemed that the First American and Fourth French Armies, with only 30 miles separating them from the vital German supply line at Sedan and Mézières, had the easiest assignment. In electing to commit his Army between the Meuse and the Argonne Forest, Pershing had taken over a sector which conventional military opinion at the time regarded as impenetrable. Pétain made no secret of the fact that he considered stalemate for the winter about Montfaucon a likely possibility. Foch's original offer of the front between the Argonne and Reims tactically would have been an easier proposition: so too would have been the advance over the open and level plains of the Woeuvre and the Moselle which Pershing had originally proposed. In the event his acceptance of Foch's decision in the interests of Allied solidarity would cost 26,227 American killed and 95,788 wounded over a period of 47 days, that is over 6,000 more dead than in the Battle of Normandy in 1944 and more wounded.

Apart from the Vosges it would have been difficult in First War terms to have found anywhere on the Western Front giving greater advantages to the defender. The 24-mile front selected for the American attack lay between the Meuse and the western edge of the Argonne Forest. Roughly parallel to the Meuse on the eastern edge of the Argonne Forest flowed the River Aire. Between these two rivers the Heights of Montfaucon, Cunel, Romagne and Barricourt, rising to 1,000 feet, provided natural strongpoints with all-round observation. The heights of the Meuse immediately east of the river completely dominated the valley on the west bank and the bluffs above the Aire river on the eastern edge of the Argonne Forest overlooked the valley below. The forest itself, 1,000 feet above sea level, was thickly wooded and, like all French and German woods, bottomless in wet weather. Only three metalled roads of doubtful quality led into the area which abounded in deep ravines and, quite apart from the forest, in wooded uplands and dense thickets which provided abundant cover from view. In four years, virtually undisturbed by the French, the Germans with all their normal industry and engineering skill had exploited the defensive possibilities to the full. Countless machine-gun posts in concrete, sited to fire in enfilade, dominated the position to a depth of ten miles: the magnificent facilities for observed artillery fire both in enfilade and to the front had been fully developed. Thick entanglements of barbed wire had been so sited as to lure the attacker into the arcs of the machine guns. Not until he had penetrated the first and second line of defence and advanced ten miles would he come up against the hard core of the position. This was the Kriemhilde Stellung, part of the Hindenburg Line running from Brieulles on the Meuse to Grandpré at the northern end of the Argonne Forest, the strength of which was unknown to the Americans at the time. Five miles further on the way to Sedan lay yet another defensive position—the Freya Stellung along the Barricourt Ridge. It was the time of the equinox when the normal autumn rains were liable rapidly to reduce all roads and tracks to quagmires. The position was known to be held by five divisions which Pershing's staff rightly estimated could be reinforced by a further 15 within three days. An attack on this labyrinth was the nightmare problem which Pershing in the early days of September called upon Drum and his staff to solve while the preparations for the St Mihiel attack were nearing their final stage. The newly formed Army Headquarters was thus confronted by all the bedevilments involved in planning and executing two major operations at the same time. At first glance the theme of the plan which they evolved bears a remarkable resemblance to Montgomery's for the Alamein battle in 1942—the punching of two corridors through the defences on either side of the Montfaucon feature, followed by a rapid advance. In fact there was no alternative to thrust lines up these two valleys. Pershing therefore proposed to bank on achieving surprise and to impart such momentum to the attack as would carry it in a giant stride of ten miles right up to the Kriemhilde position. The advance would then be continued throughout the succeeding night.

The very audacity of Pershing's plan, for his was the responsibility despite the fact that Drum and his staff had worked out the details, expresses the spirit of the man himself, his immense faith in the destiny of his country and in the courage of his soldiers. His aircraft would completely dominate the sky over the battlefield. The five German divisions in the line would be swamped by a human sea of a quarter-of-a-million assault troops outnumbering them by eight to one, advancing with reserves in great depth ready to leap-frog forward as the opportunity arose. They would be supported by the fire of 2,700 guns. It was a concept before its time and unfortunately without the means.

Surprise was the very essence of the plan. For this reason the French continued to hold the outpost position until the night of 25 September. All American reconnaissances were carried out by officers wearing the horizon-blue overcoats and elegant steel helmets of the French Army. Artillery registration was kept to a minimum and wireless activity maintained at the average level of July and August. Troops moved forward by night only and spent the days in overcrowded billets or dripping woods. Regrettably, these precautions failed to keep the Germans in the dark. French deserters gave warning of the offensive which the Germans concluded would come in the Argonne on 25 September. It was not, however, till 2 a.m. on the 26th, the actual day of the attack, that the capture of a prisoner from the 4th Division near the Meuse revealed the presence of Americans.

The risks were enormous: probably only Pershing would have dared to take them. The operation had to be mounted in a hurry at a time when the majority of the seasoned divisions were locked up at St Mihiel. A large number of troops without battlefield experience would therefore be going into action for the first time. Some had only four months' service and in some cases no more than six weeks. The story is told of drafts who were so green that on arrival they willingly paid old soldiers five francs to show them how to load their rifles. A high percentage of the staffs had only been together for a few weeks. Qualified staff officers were very thin on the ground. Most of the commanders were untried. Inevitably therefore the command machinery would creak and the primitive communications would be overstrained. Traffic congestion on a large scale would certainly arise. Even First Army Headquarters itself was only newly formed; Pershing personally was carrying on his shoulders the burden of the dual role of Army Commander and Commander-in-Chief of the AEF with all its logistic and political ramifications. Nevertheless, he never for a moment doubted that the high morale of his troops, the superiority of which over that of his Allies which he so frequently stresses in his own book, would triumph over all difficulties. In the end, and at a cost which the United States could well afford, he would be right.

In precise terms he had the 3rd Corps on the right next to the Meuse, the 5th Corps in the centre facing the dominating Mont-

British Mark V tanks with 'cribs' to enable them to cross the Hindenburg line near Bellicourt, 29 September 1918

British Infantry crossing the bridge over the St Quentin Canal captured by the 46th Division, 2nd October 1918

38 Foch visits Haig's advanced GHQ train, late Autumn 1918

39 American Artillery in action at Varennes in the Meuse–Argonne Battle, first we of October 1918

faucon feature and the 1st Corps on the left, with a further four divisions in reserve and a French Cavalry Division. On his immediate left the French Fourth Army, of six corps of 22 divisions and a cavalry division, carried on the front of the attack to the River Suippe. Phase One of the Allied plan envisaged a combined Franco-American advance of 12 miles to link up at Grandpré: in Phase Two it was proposed to press forward to the line Le Chesne–Stenay, a further ten miles ahead, and thus outflank the whole German position behind the Aisne and open the way to Mézières. Throughout, the Franco-American offensive would be attacking at the seam where the boundaries of the Crown Prince's Army Group and that of Gallwitz met—theoretically one of the classic recipes for victory.

That the concentration, grouping and forming up of the nine double-strength assault divisions was achieved in time with the means available and the difficulties to be overcome constitutes one of Marshall's many claims to take rank beside Berthier, Napoleon's Chief of Staff, and the elder von Moltke as one of the great staff officers of history. The French had to pull out and simultaneously the Americans move in over the same roads, by night in bad weather. Pétain gave immense help in the matter of guns, tanks and transport; Marshall's French assistant, Captain Gorfu too earned a mention in American History. Incredibly, at 2.30 a.m. on 26 September, all was ready when the 2,700 guns supporting the attack opened up: for three hours they pounded every known enemy battery, machine gun emplacement, position and communication trench within range. Awed and expectant the infantry in their jumping-off trenches listened to the steady thud of the bombardment and gazed at the flashes of the bursting shells against the night sky.

It was a fine night; dawn came with heavy mist thickened by the smoke of the preliminary bombardment. Then at 5.30 a.m., as one man, the serried lines of infantry plunged forward along a 20-mile front behind the barrage into the murk ahead. At first, so stunned were the enemy, only a few machine guns opened up: the main difficulty was the rough going amidst the shell holes and barbed wire overgrown with brambles. The 'fog of war', to use the contemporary British expression, now came down on the battlefield like a blanket: what little news filtered back at first by

M

messenger or walking wounded seemed good. On the right of the 3rd Corps, Major William H. Simpson, the G3 of the 33rd Division, the future Commander of the Ninth Army was able to report that his division had crossed the Forges creek and, thanks to good artillery and machine-gun support, had gained its objective by 9 a.m.

Elsewhere, the advance seemed to be going well with little loss except in the centre on the 5th Corps front where under the dominating feature of Montfaucon the situation was for a long time obscure. Here the hard going caused the infantry of the 79th Division to lose the barrage. About 9 a.m. therefore the leading companies of the 313th Regiment found themselves pinned to the ground by strongly entrenched machine guns at a clearing called the Golfe de Malancourt. Simultaneously, the 314th Regiment became hotly engaged in the ruins of Malancourt village. In their rear, Germans, who had been passed over in the advance and not mopped up, now sprang to life: casualties mounted. Inevitably there was some confusion and it was not until the late afternoon that Colonel Claude B. Sweezy was able to mount an attack against Montfaucon supported by French tanks. After forty-five minutes, in a tornado of fire in the valley below the commanding hill, the French officer in charge of the tanks insisted on pulling out. In consequence when night closed in at 6.45 p.m., although K Company had reached the outskirts of the town, the key position on the whole front remained untaken and violently belligerent.

During the day the 37th Division on the immediate left of the 79th Division had got well forward: in mid-afternoon their 145th Regiment could see the ruins of Montfaucon a mile away. Although the place was outside their boundary they had promptly attacked but had been driven back. A second attempt proved equally abortive. It was on the right of the 79th Division, however, that the 4th Division, with whom so far all had gone well, were later judged in some circles to have missed a great opportunity to envelop Montfaucon from the north. It does seem that they could have taken the village of Nantillois a mile in rear of Montfaucon with little difficulty had they been prepared to go outside their boundaries. By nightfall however, the Germans had strongly reinforced this village. If satisfactory communications between the two Corps commanders involved had been feasible, perhaps Montfaucon might have been taken on the 26th: in fact it was not. If those concerned in the Fourth Division had used their initiative and moved out of their own sector to envelop it they might have been successful. When they tried to do so next morning at 5.30 a.m. it would be too late. Thus when night closed in with the confusion inevitable at the end of the first day's fighting, the Montfaucon bastion projected like a giant thumb between the two flanking corps.

These two corps had done well. By the end of the day the three divisions of the 3rd Corps nearest to the Meuse had overcome stiff resistance from enemy machine guns, penetrated the German second position and beaten off all counter-attacks. The First Corps under Liggett on the left had also pushed rapidly forward. In support of the 35th Division attacking on the right of the Corps down the valley of the Aire, were the Provisional Squadron and the Light Tank Brigade, commanded by Lieutenant-Colonel George S. Patton. He had 189 French Renault tanks, 141 of which were manned by Americans. These tiny little two-man tanks were lightly armoured and mounted either a 37 mm gun or a machine gun. Their speed was five miles per hour on favourable ground. Owing to the haste with which the operation had to be mounted, time did not permit Patton to arrange for the infantry he was supporting and his own crews to get to know each other, let alone have a trial run. As a result they seem to have fought entirely independent battles. Patton, characteristically, was quite prepared to take on the whole German Army on his own: anyhow he had captured the little town of Varennes by 9 a.m. Four further hours elapsed before the infantry he was supposed to be supporting appeared upon the scene. Meanwhile Patton had rounded up a number of other bewildered infantrymen who happened to be in the neighbourhood and led them forward behind his tank, urging them on with the vividly worded exhortations for which he would later become famous. In the process a burst of shrapnel hit him in the midriff. Before losing consciousness he had time to give out his orders for the further conduct of the battle: he then collapsed and was evacuated. After he had gone his brigade fought on till practically all its tanks had been put out of action by enemy fire. Thus ended the most noteworthy American tank action of the First War. Twenty-six years later, Patton, now an Army Commander, would return to

Varennes as he stormed through this country of forests and vineyards, hell-bent once more towards the heart of Germany. Not far away from him on this day was another American destined to play an even greater part in his country's history—Captain Harry S. Truman of Battery D, 129th Field Regiment. The casualties in his division were severe: nothing, however, in his subsequent career indicated that his experience on this day in any way affected his spirits then or later.

West of Varennes the French during the day had got forward about two miles on the average against comparatively light German opposition. Now, however, the Germans were thoroughly alerted; their morale, if it ever had been as low as the intelligence experts had claimed, was certainly restored. Daylight when it came revealed broken-down communications, movement over the open inevitably bringing down a hurricane of enemy fire, large numbers of men separated from their units and uncertain of their whereabouts, bewilderment arising from the loss of key commanders at all levels, organisational chaos, large numbers of men incapable of rational thought as a result of shock combined with exposure, lack of sleep and hot food and drink, all the horror resulting from the suffering of the wounded and the mutilated bodies of the dead. Now that the element of surprise had gone the battle there inevitably developed all the characteristics of the British and French battles of 1916 and 1917 with some of those of Loos and Suvla Bay as well. About noon, after an abortive attack at dawn, the 79th Division finally took Montfaucon: a further twenty-four hours would elapse before they caught up with the divisions on their flanks by capturing Nantillois.

Much censorious capital would later be made by writers of the failure of the 79th Division before Montfaucon on the 26th and the apparent lack of initiative shown by the flanking divisions and Corps. A large part of this criticism can be dismissed as academic and uncharitable. Pershing had only taken the risk of employing inexperienced divisions because he was led to believe that German morale was lower than it turned out to be: only by laying down boundaries in detail could he hope to control the movement of the large numbers of troops involved. Communications being what they were, any movement outside the corridors prescribed would inevitably have resulted in chaos: artillery would have fired on their own troops; there might well have been battles between one American unit and another. On the overcrowded battlefield the telegraph wires run out by the signallers were soon cut by traffic: the only certain means of inter-communication was by orderlies who, in the confusion of the battle, often lost their way or were misdirected. Commanders had no means of transporting themselves in the forward area: they moved about on foot or not at all.

After three days' intensive action the sheer physical exhaustion and disorganisation of some of the troops in the raw divisions compelled Pershing to pull them out and replace them by veteran divisions from St Mihiel. The resulting increase in two-way traffic across the old No-Man's-Land finally broke the back of the only three roads. On the 27th heavy rain fell; it continued on the following day. Earlier in the war the French had blown enormous craters in the roads themselves to stop any German advance. A belt of deep shell holes fringed the whole original front line. Years of neglect and frequent bombardment had left scarcely more than a trace of the original road surface. As the Germans withdrew they exploded contact mines in it. In the incessant rain, trucks and guns became bogged; huge gangs of men struggled to haul them out with ropes. Inevitably there was congestion. As a result, too, of using inexperienced troops a considerable number of men had become separated from their units: these and the large numbers of wounded clogged the crowded roads. An outbreak of influenza further added to the traffic problem.

Uninvited, on Sunday 29 September Clemenceau chose to visit the First Army. After expressing his congratulations on the capture of Montfaucon, he announced his intention of going to see the ruins there and then. Pershing strongly advised him not to do so for the very good reason that the place was under incessant shell fire: if anything had happened to him, Pershing's would have been the responsibility. In later years Eisenhower would have similar trouble with Churchill at the time of D-Day and at the Crossing of the Rhine—a classic contest between a Commander-in-Chief and a Prime Minister ending in a draw. Eisenhower got his way over D-Day: Churchill beat Eisenhower in crossing the Rhine. Pershing, faced with the alternative of applying physical force to a head of state in his own country and letting the old man run the risk of getting killed, gave way. That morning the road to Montfaucon was even more tightly jammed than usual by the trains of the 1st Division going in and the 35th Division coming out. Clemenceau never reached Montfaucon. Nevertheless, in spite of the ever-recurring traffic jams of marching men, horses, trucks and tractors going in and similar columns including ambulances moving out, somehow or other the dense columns moved in and out in fits and starts. The problem was no new one: it had arisen in every Allied offensive; it would arise again in the Second War. Clemenceau's presence on the battle-field may well have inspired the French: in this instance his appearance was ill-timed, unfair to Pershing and apparently productive of criticism of the American forces which in no way helped the Alliance.

Despite the congestion on the lines of communication there was no let-up in the battle. The Germans with their normal resilience were quick to reinforce the threatened sector. One division arrived on the afternoon of the 26th; by the 30th no less than six additional fresh divisions had been fed into the line; a further five were available in immediate reserve. They contested every foot of the ground with the desperate courage and the skill born of years of experience. Their discipline remained unshaken. If their morale was in decline then large numbers of them concealed the fact very effectively from the American infantry. Nonetheless by 30 September, despite the wet and the ever-increasing fatigue of the troops, the First Army except in the Argonne Forest were about ten miles ahead of their original start line: on their western flank the French Fourth Army had advanced a similar distance. Between the eastern edge of the Argonne Forest and the Meuse they now faced about Brieulles, Romagne and Exermont the formidable defences of the Kriemhilde Stellung, the third and main line of defence which the Germans were determined to hold whatever the cost, to protect their vital railway communications and the flank of the Crown Prince's Army Group opposing the French Fourth Army. Altogether the American offensive had drawn towards it 27 German reserve divisions. Pershing therefore decided to suspend the offensive for a few days, to reorganise his forces and to put in hand the many preparations necessary for the elaborate set piece battle now obviously imminent.

Meanwhile in the north, between La Fère and Lens, another great battle now raging on a front of 50 miles had taken a dramatic turn which would not only unpin the main German defences but precipitate a political landslide within Germany itself.

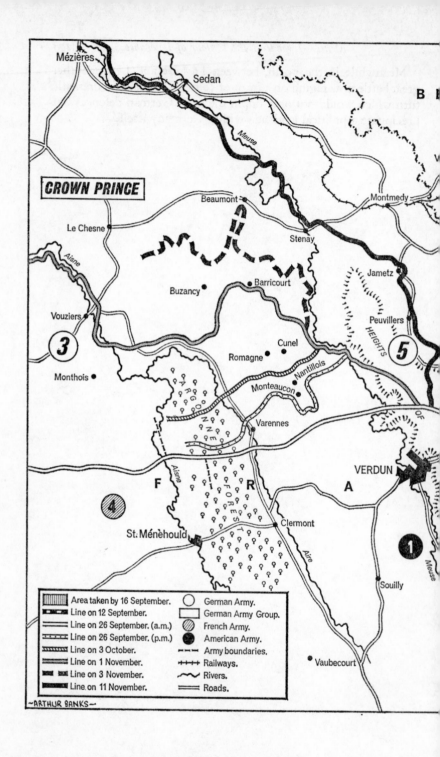

CROWN PRINCE

Mézières

Sedan

B

Meuse

Beaumont

Montmedy

Le Chesne

Stenay

Aisne

Jametz

Barricourt

Buzancy

HEIGHTS

Vouziers

Peuvillers

3

Cunel

5

Romagne

Monthois

Nantillois

Monteaucon

Varennes

VERDUN

F

Aisne

R

A

4

Clermont

St. Ménèhould

Aire

1

Meuse

Souilly

Vaubecourt

▦ Area taken by 16 September.	○ German Army.
▰▰ Line on 12 September.	☐ German Army Group.
══ Line on 26 September. (a.m.)	▨ French Army.
▱▱ Line on 26 September. (p.m.)	● American Army.
⟋⟍ Line on 3 October.	- - - Army boundaries.
▰▰ Line on 1 November.	+++ Railways.
▰▰ Line on 3 November.	⌇ Rivers.
▰▰ Line on 11 November.	══ Roads.

~ARTHUR BANKS~

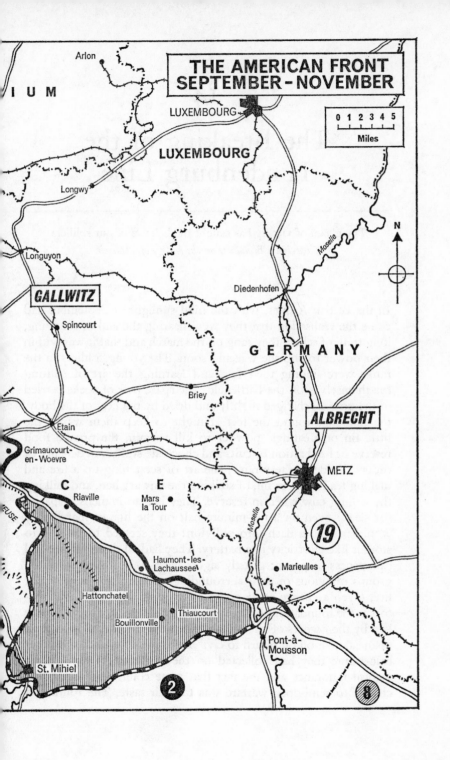

THE AMERICAN FRONT
SEPTEMBER – NOVEMBER

Arlon

LUXEMBOURG

LUXEMBOURG

Longwy

Longuyon

GALLWITZ

Spincourt

Diedenhofen

GERMANY

Briey

Etain

ALBRECHT

Grimaucourt-
en-Woevre

C   E

Riaville   Mars
               la Tour

METZ

19

Haumont-les-
Lachausseel

Marieulles

Hattonchatel

Thiaucourt

Bouillonville

Pont-à-
Mousson

St. Mihiel

2   8

Moselle

0 1 2 3 4 5
Miles

N

14

The Breaking of the Hindenburg Line

The gleam of victory has caught the helmets of our soldiers.
Churchill's Broadcast on the victory of Alamein

In the British Armies, with the mild sunlight of September had come the realisation that they were nearing the end of the 'long, long trail' of which they sang on the march and that it was within their power to end the war and soon. The young soldiers in the ranks were finding their feet and learning the art of shifting for themselves on the battlefield: the spare pair of socks carried in the pocket, changed nightly and dried by the heat of the body, the sandbags round the feet at night to keep them warm, the little tin of Keatings' powder to kill vermin, the private food reserve of hard ration biscuits and chocolate stuffed, in defiance of orders, inside the respirator, the art of scratching up a fire and making tea in a mess tin, of stalking the unwary hen, and milking the willing cow when in reserve. They had an immense capacity for sleep: even on a ten-minute halt on the line of march they would pass in a flash into oblivion: they seemed to be able to store it like electricity in a battery. They had all the resilience and callousness of youth: ghastly sights were soon forgotten. Little groups oblivious of their surroundings would, even under shell fire, given a chance settle down to interminable games of 'Pontoon'; the foundations of many a small business after the war were laid by the owners of Crown and Anchor sets; others owed their financial take-off on return to civil life to the false teeth and other bric-a-brac they had collected on the battlefield. Despite their tactical ignorance and the fact that none could read a map the change to semi-open warfare was to their taste. The routine of trench warfare had been boring almost beyond belief: a tour in the front line had seemed an eternity. Now there was a continual change of scene, there was scope for the exercise of curiosity and initiative; there was the hope too of picking up something portable of value such as a watch or a fountain pen or even cash.

To some extent the class distinctions of British society, which made it so different from the Australian and American attitude in this respect, had been replaced, at this stage of the war, by those of rank. This made for ease of living together: everyone knew exactly where he stood. Uncritically, the wartime Armies had taken over the Regular Army's tradition of the sharp distinction between the officer and the other rank. This, in war in those days, had its good side: familiarity did breed contempt. The emphasis was on privilege based on the obligation of the officer to take the greatest risks and place the welfare of his men and his regiment before his own. The junior officers of the Army were now a cross-section of British society; nevertheless they had been quick to absorb this tradition. Indeed the humbler their social origin, the more conscious they were, in many cases, not only of their privileges but of their obligations. The British Regimental System, giving names and not just numbers to units, conferred a collective personality on battalions and regiments. It gave them an identity which men could grasp: an unemotional man cannot feel inspiration from a number or a string of initials. When sick or wounded, men strove to get back to their own units. Their horizon indeed seldom stretched far beyond these little worlds. Many were illiterate: literature for them was represented by extracts from the *News of the World* read out with appropriate comment by some scholar in the ranks. Even among the officers it was surprising how many, nurtured at public and grammar schools, mainly on a diet of the Classics, had succeeded in evading whatever they had to teach, apart from the overriding need for courage and Spartan standards of living. Only a tiny minority had ever bothered to think about the moral issues of the war, whatever they may have been. Regrettably the war had taken the Church of England by surprise: bewildered parsons, suddenly shot out of the peaceful life of country vicarages, jumble sales and the Mothers' Union, found difficulty in adjusting their approach to the coarse but hearty life of the front line and were liable only too often to be esteemed more for the cigarettes they distributed

than for their sentiments. It was all very different from the
Second War when the Tiger tank and the Nebelwerfer stimulated
a regrettably temporary interest in religion.

The new dispensation at GHQ had been quick to produce an
immense improvement on the administrative side. The people at
home went hungry; at the front there was ample food especially
tinned beef from the Argentine and unlimited tea. When possible
there was fresh bread from the field bakeries and large quantities
of jam and cheese. The Army was no longer verminous. Seventy
years before a Crimean general had said: 'Where there's hair
there's dirt and where there's dirt there's disease.' His aphorism,
still relevant in 1971, had been taken to heart. Every company
had its barber ever ready in a pause in operations to remove
superfluous hair. The nit nuisance had thus disappeared (only
to return in the Second War with the Women's Services, many of
whom had invested capital in permanent waves); so to a great
extent had the louse—fortunately, as in the dug-outs of the
Hindenburg Line the troops were now beginning to encounter
a particularly vigorous Teutonic strain with iron crosses on
their backs. Improvised bath houses and laundries quickly
followed the advancing troops: men discarded all their clothing
as they entered, scrubbed themselves in the tubs with red carbolic
soap and on emerging put on a completely fresh outfit from top
to toe. Admittedly the bodies of the previous owner's lice,
dessicated and dead, fringed the seams of the new garments;
they had, however, ceased to bite and the new owners no longer
needed to sit in the sun naked to the waist, picking out what
they called 'little strangers', like monkeys in the Zoo.

Sarcastically men would quote the old Army aphorism of the
disgruntled: 'The only thing worth having in the Army is leave.'
It was now coming round every six months and each man in a
good unit knew exactly where his name stood on the list. He thus
had something to which to look forward. Most of the worst
scandals in the rest camps and on the lines of communication had
been eradicated—though, as the War poets were quick to point
out, in all wars the nearer the base the less attractive the company.
Such disciplinary trouble as there was occurred mainly in the
rear areas among men separated from their units or men in base
employment whose personalities were so repellent that their
own battalions had been only too glad to find an excuse to get

rid of them to empty latrine buckets at the base. Within the English Regiments there was virtually no difficulty in maintaining discipline. Field punishment meant forfeiture of pay and consequent hardship to dependants: officers therefore loathed having to impose it. When it was necessary the offenders concerned often had a criminal record in time of peace: in their case public opinion in the ranks was behind the officers as indeed it had been ever since the days of Marlborough. Such was the rough and robust school in which most of the commanders of the Second War served their apprenticeship. It had its compensations. To be a captain and commanding a company of 130 men at 19 was good for a young officer's self-esteem; it was good to be fully stretched. Responsibility, quick promotion, decorations, extra pay all came their way. Only one casualty in ten, they reasoned, was fatal. It was worth the risk. Why worry? The odds were on survival. They would learn their trade by trial and error in the British tradition. Now there was the chance to return with interest to the Germans some of the very medicine they had themselves administered to them in the spring.

Thus with soldiers whose battle experience and will to win increased from day to day, under proved commanders and efficient staffs who had digested the lessons of the fighting since the spring, Haig now proceeded to mount what would prove to be the decisive battle of the war—the smashing of the Hindenburg Line, a gigantic operation surpassing in size anything before 1945 in World War Two. At last all had faith in victory and, what was quite as useful, for the first and only time in the war, 30,000 tons of mustard gas shells, the weapon to which the Germans owed much of their success in the spring. They had, too, '106' fuses for the shells fired by the medium and heavy artillery which were so sensitive that they caused wire entanglements to disintegrate: they were most efficient man-killers as well. The Germans were now about to find themselves subjected to their own Bruchmüller technique with added British refinements—a gas bombardment starting at 10 p.m. on the 26th, to be followed by forty-eight hours sustained shelling of batteries, dug-out entrances, headquarters and wire. For this purpose a million-and-a-quarter rounds of ammunition would be expended. To teach the British new tricks of the trade and then themselves be overwhelmed by them seems to be a fate to which the Germans are historically prone—as Rommel, at the moment fully occupied on the Italian front, would discover in the Western Desert in the Second War.

Haig's grand design in brief was to strike with the First, Third and Fourth Armies, comprising 41 divisions in all, on a 35-mile front between St Quentin and Lens, with the First French Army protecting his right flank north of La Fère. He proposed to open the battle with the Third and First Armies on a 13-mile front north of Péronne on 27 September and two days later to deliver his decisive blow with the Fourth Army at the very heart of the Hindenburg Line immediately north of St Quentin. To them he gave ten of the 14 tank battalions, most of his 1,500 heavy guns and the support of over 1,000 aircraft.

Of all the captures on 8 August in the Battle of Amiens, the most valuable was the copy complete with elaborate maps of the defence scheme of the sector of the Hindenburg Line between Le Tronquoy and Vendhuille which the Fourth Army was about to attack. It showed all trenches and wire, the position of every battery and observation post, the locations of all headquarters, every dug-out and concrete emplacement, the rear dumps, the signal communications, billets and camps. It was a masterpiece of German staff work which saved the intelligence and counter-battery staffs immense time and labour. As a guide as to where to drop the gas shells it was to prove invaluable. Nevertheless, the task confronting the Fourth Army was awesome to a degree. Two widely differing types of obstacle had to be surmounted. The southern half of the German defences stood on the eastern side of the St Quentin canal, with thick wire on the western side and concrete machine-gun posts within the banks of the canal cutting, inaccessible to the British artillery and sited to fire in enfilade. Part of the canal had been dammed at Bellicourt to ensure sufficient depth of water. In the northern half of the front the canal ran through a tunnel. The defences here were exceptionally strong: there was a lot of concrete and three belts of wire. The tunnel itself, connected by numerous passages with ground level, gave almost perfect cover for reserves. The villages of Bellicourt, Bellenglise and Bony were strongly fortified. Altogether the system was about two miles deep. Behind it from Lesdins to Le Catelet, there was another strong support system and, four miles behind that, the Beaurevoir Line designed on the same principles as the forward zones.

For the initial assault Rawlinson and Braithwaite, the Commander of the 9th Corps, gave the terrifying task of swimming the canal in the teeth of enemy fire at Bellenglise to the 46th (North Midland) Division. They were Territorials from one of the less glamorous parts of England; they did not belong to that part of the British Army which has always delighted in picturesque costumes, weird musical instruments, eccentric mascots or obscure languages and rites intelligible only to the initiated; no one had ever suggested that they should specialise in ceremonial. Their commander, Major-General Boyd had risen from the ranks after winning the Distinguished Conduct Medal—traditionally awarded by the War Department with great reluctance as it carried a microscopic pension. This 100 per cent English division was about to bring off a spectacular exploit, equalled only by the Australian capture of Péronne. To cross the water obstacle they were given 3,000 lifebelts collected from the Channel steamers, a few light portable boats and a number of ladders. 'These,' solemnly records the Official History, 'on the day prior to the attack, they tested with success on the banks of the Somme.' In allotting the northern half of the front where the canal ran underground to the Australian-American Corps, it seemed at the time that they were being given the easier task. Here the 30th American Division on the right and the 27th American Division on the left, the whole on an 8,000-yard front, were to take the defences around Bellicourt and Bony to a depth of not more than 4,000 yards, a straightforward advance behind a barrage with no obstacles other than wire. It was then proposed that the 5th and 3rd Australian Divisions following close on their heels, with the Second Australian Division in reserve behind them, should leap-frog through. Meanwhile their flank to the north would be protected by an attack on the high ground about Vendhuille by the 3rd Corps.

Neither the 2nd American Corps nor its two divisions, numbering 50,000 men, had any artillery of their own. Their signals were also incomplete. These therefore had to be found from British and Australian resources. The Corps Commander, Major-General Read, his staff and troops had no previous experience of organising and executing an operation of the magnitude now contemplated. Rawlinson therefore decided that the Corps should be affiliated to the Australian Corps and fight under the direction of Monash and his staff; in all other matters they would remain under Read—surely one of the most anomalous arrangements for a battle ever made. In fact it worked, firstly because Monash and his Chief of Staff, Blamey, unquestionably outshone all their British counterparts in ability and battle expertise, secondly because Read and his staff showed sound sense, courtesy and clear judgment and, thirdly, because of the Australian Mission under Major-General Maclagan consisting of 217 specially selected and very experienced officers and non-commissioned officers superimposed on the American organisation at all levels down to battalions. Thus it became possible to talk with the whole American Corps in Australian military language, the members of the Mission acting as interpreters of the technical terms and usages customary in the Australian Corps, both in orders and on maps, with which the Americans were completely unfamiliar. Only by these means was it possible to ensure cooperation between two forces whose war experience, outlook, attitude towards their problems, training and temperament were so entirely different. Of these American troops Monash later wrote:

'It is not necessary to indulge in either a panegyric or a condemnation of these American divisions. Neither would be deserved or appropriate. They showed a fine spirit, a keen desire to learn, magnificent individual bravery, and splendid comradeship. But they were lacking in war experience, in training and in knowledge of technique. They had not yet learnt the virtues of unquestioning obedience, of punctuality, of quick initiative, of anticipating the next action. They were, many of them, unfamiliar with the weapons and instruments of fighting, with the numerous kinds of explosive materials, or with the routine of preparing and promulgating clear orders. They seriously underrated the necessity for a well organised system of supply, particularly of food and water, to the battle troops. They hardly as yet appreciated the tactical expedients for reducing losses in battle. . . . Yet all these shortcomings were the results only of inexperience. . . . It greatly added to the burden cast upon the American divisions that they were called upon to fight almost as soon as they had taken up duty in the line.'

It was on 25 September that the 2nd American Corps assumed

responsibility for the front between Bellicourt and Bony. The 30th American Division on the right was already on its start line for the grand attack now fixed for 5.30 a.m. on 29 September. Unfortunately, however, the front line of the 27th Division was about 1,000 yards short of their's. Here the enemy still held a strong defence system around the ruins of Quénnemont Farm and Gillemont Farm. Rawlinson therefore decided that this defect must be made good on 27 September. Haig was averse to the Americans being given the additional burden of this preliminary step and said they should be kept fresh for the main attack. Rawlinson, however, made difficulties, submitted lengthy reasons in writing and Haig, unfortunately as it turned out, gave way. Accordingly the 27th American Division, assisted by tanks, attacked at 5.30 a.m. on 27 September under cover of a powerful artillery barrage. Their luck was out. A fresh German division, the 54th, had just taken over, prepared to fight to a finish. A bitter struggle developed: the Germans promptly launched a strong counter-attack whenever the Americans gained ground. The situation became most involved and it was not until the afternoon that it became clear that small parties of Americans had reached their objectives and were gallantly maintaining their hold: the rest had been pushed back to their start line. What actually happened that day will never be known. The preliminary bombardment for the main attack had started at 10.30 p.m. the previous night and would continue till 'zero' at 5.30 a.m. on the 29th. Here then, with isolated parties of Americans still holding out despite the fact that they were surrounded and some of their wounded still uncollected, was a damnable situation. To pull back the opening line of the barrage on the 29th to the Americans' start line on the 27th would be to bring it down on our own troops. Monash hastened to Rawlinson to suggest a postponement of the main attack to give the 27th Division another chance to retrieve the situation.

Because the operations of three Armies were committed to attack on the 29th, Rawlinson decided that it was now too late to alter the intricate artillery programme. The 27th Division were therefore ordered to form up for the attack as near the Army start line as possible one hour before 'zero' and, assisted by additional tanks, fight their way forward for a 1,000 yards to reach the opening line of the creeping barrage at 5.30 a.m.

N

Monash hoped that this would enable the division to catch up with the southern half of the battle line: in the event he was doomed to disappointment. None of the commanders concerned, with the exception of Read and perhaps Monash, can escape criticism; Butler, the commander of the 3rd Corps who, before handing over part of his line to the Americans, should have ensured that they got a clean start in their first big battle; Rawlinson who did not insist that Butler did so before handing over and thus imposed upon the Americans a task for which they lacked the training and Haig, who realised that Rawlinson was asking too much of the Americans and did not overrule him. Regrettably in war it is sometimes necessary for Commanders to appear high-handed and even personally offensive in their personal relations: this was one of them. This lesson was to be well digested by some British commanders in the Second War. Fortunately, in this instance, the Third Australian Division were at hand to retrieve the situation but, as Wellington observed of Waterloo, it would be 'a damned near thing'.

Meanwhile starting at first light on 27 September, without any preliminary bombardment, the First and Third Armies had assaulted in the general direction of Cambrai. On the front of the Canadian Corps all went well: the Third Army on a front of two corps faced a maze of trenches in great depth. Nevertheless by the end of the day the Canal du Nord had been crossed on the whole front, 10,000 prisoners been taken and 200 guns. Next morning the advance continued and by nightfall a breach 12 miles wide and six miles deep had been made in the German defences. That morning the King of the Belgians about Ypres had launched his nine divisions, the French Sixth Army and the British Second Army to the attack in the general direction of Ghent. By the end of the day the British had carried the Passchendaele Ridge; on their left the Belgians had cleared the Germans from the stumps of Houthulst Forest.

In the last hours of the night of 29 September the last of the 46th Division, the 30th and 27th American Divisions filed into their assault positions, some in shell holes, some in trenches, in No-Man's-Land: under foot the ground was slippery on the surface but firm underneath. The rhythmic throb of the aircraft overhead drowned the noise of the move forward of the tanks to their start line. Now and then an aeroplane dropped a bomb somewhere behind the German lines. With the approach of dawn the din of the bombardment rose to a crescendo. At 5.55 a.m., just as a faint silver streak appeared in the eastern sky, down came the creeping barrage with an appalling crash 200 yards in front of the infantry. Shadowy shapes surged forward towards the flashes of the line of shells bursting in the thick morning mist. Simultaneously the tanks rumbled forward into the smoke. The shrapnel balls rattled down like hail in front of the advancing infantry: overhead the swish of machine-gun bullets could be heard intermittently in the din. The acrid smell of high explosive was in every man's nostrils.

With all its three battalions in line the 137th Brigade of the 46th Division, followed closely by the other two brigades, each on a one battalion front, under cover of the fog and smoke swamped the German trenches west of the canal, killing the garrisons as they thrust forward. The 1/6th South Staffordshire on the right found little water in the canal as they scrambled across to storm Bellenglise with such speed that they trapped the Germans coming out of the tunnels in which they had been sheltering, killed some and forced the rest to surrender. The other two forward battalions, however, the 1/5th South Staffordshire and the 1/6 North Staffordshire on their right, found a considerable depth of water in the canal. Their officers therefore immediately plunged into the water trailing ropes, followed closely by their men using lifebelts, rafts and a few portable boats. A bridge was found intact and captured before the German Pioneers could ignite the demolition charges. Pushing on a further 700 yards the forward brigade captured four guns. At 11.29 a.m. the other two brigades of the division leap-frogged through and regardless of the situation on their flanks forged ahead. The morning mist had now gone. Intense machine-gun fire now greeted them: a German battery quickly knocked out all their tanks. Nevertheless, almost clinging to the barrage they reached the high ground near Le Haucourt. Here there was a check. Lieutenant-Colonel William Vann, commanding the 1/6th Sherwood Foresters, in civil life a clergyman of the Church of England, realising that everything depended on keeping close to the barrage, rushed to the front and led the whole line forward. Meanwhile another party killed all the gunners of the batteries which had destroyed the tanks. A gallant German officer on horseback struggled to rally the men of the 79th Reserve Division; both he and his horse were promptly shot dead; his men bolted. By 3 p.m. the 46th Division were on their objective for the day. Hot on their heels, the 32nd Division, ignoring their flanks, passed through and in the teeth of opposition reached the Le Haucourt Ridge, the Army objective for the day. By any standards the achievement of the 46th Division was magnificent. Of the 5,100 prisoners and 90 guns captured on this day they had taken 4,200 and 70 guns. The dash, determination and initiative of their junior officers and non-commissioned officers on this day reached a standard not surpassed even by the Australians.

The 30th American Division on their left had more chequered fortune. They struck exceptionally intricate German defences from the start and by the time they reached the tunnel had lost the barrage. Nevertheless, with reckless gallantry, they carried the ruins of the village of Bellicourt and the southern end of the tunnel. Beyond this it is difficult to say how far they actually got in the dense smoke and thick mist. Some parties certainly reached Nauroy, two miles within the German position: many later attached themselves to the 5th Australian Division and fought the rest of the day with them. Like the British on the Somme in 1916, they had not yet realised the need for 'mopping up'.

When they had passed, Germans oozed up from the ground behind them to shoot them in the back. The 27th American Division on their left had bad luck from the start. Of the four German divisions on their front, one was completely fresh. Twelve of the 39 tanks supporting them were knocked out almost at once, seven broke down and only one succeeded in crossing the line of the tunnel. When the 3rd Australian Division came to their aid, Quénnemont Farm and Gillemont Farm were still in German hands: they were thus confronted by the task which the 27th Division had been unable to complete, with the added complication that there were now even more isolated pockets of Americans intermingled with the Germans. Meanwhile the 5th Australian Division swept through Bellicourt towards Nauroy. By mid-afternoon Monash had the 5th Division firmly established east of the canal and the 3rd Division at death grips with the enemy about Quénnemont Farm. It was on this day that Major Wark of the 32nd Australian Battalion gave as fine a demonstration of leadership as any in the whole war in a battle around Bellicourt and Nauroy in which over 200 Americans fought side by side with the Australians. Night closed in with heavy rain which soaked friend and foe alike to the skin on a confused battlefield, with Monash reluctant to use his artillery in case he shelled American wounded lying out ahead and many Americans temporarily serving in, and unwilling to leave, Australian battalions. That night, Rawlinson took the only decision possible in the circumstances: to pull out the Americans for reorganisation. Of them he wrote: 'Only the most fearless and self-sacrificing troops would have faced the fire to which they were subjected from the moment the attack started, and it is to their undying credit that they did what they did and broke the backbone of the tunnel defences.'

Despite these setbacks it had been a good day: the Fourth Army had forced a wedge into the German defences at their strongest point to a depth of 6,000 yards on a front of about 10,000 yards; another blow by the Australian and the 9th Corps and the whole defensive system around the tunnel would collapse. They, the First and Third British Armies, the First American Army on the Argonne front and the King of the Belgians' Army Group in the north had by their efforts set off a chain of events beyond the battlefield which would lead to the end of the war. That very morning at 10 a.m. while the death struggle in Bellicourt and Bellenglise was at its height, Hindenburg and Ludendorff in the Hotel Brittanique at Spa, near Liège, confronted the Kaiser's Foreign Minister, von Hintze, with a demand for an armistice 'to save the Army from catastrophe'. The situation said Ludendorff, 'admits of no delay, not an hour is to be lost'. The three agreed that this could best be brought about by approaching President Woodrow Wilson for a cessation of hostilities with his Fourteen Points as a basis for negotiations: they were so imprecise and idealistic that it should not be difficult to twist them to Germany's advantage. To give these proposals a veneer of respectability they suggested that Prince Max of Baden, well known for his idealistic liberal socialist sympathies, should be offered the Chancellorship; thus the existing social order in Germany would be preserved and the Army enabled to make its exit from the war with its position in German society and its military reputation intact. The Kaiser agreed. Accordingly,

Hindenburg and Ludendorff drove back that night to OHL at Avesnes to face in an atmosphere of Wagnerian gloom the ghastly reports from the front between Cambrai and St Quentin and the Argonne.

Next morning, 30 September, the 3rd Australian Division grimly got down to cleaning up their front. Gillemont Farm fell; by nightfall they had advanced 1,000 yards in the labyrinth of trenches and wire. The 5th Australian Division too made progress: on their right the 32nd Division advanced another mile. German resistance in the Hindenburg system on the Fourth Army Front was nearing its end. That night the Headquarters of von Boehn's Group of Armies facing the British reported to OHL that they had no reserves left and that their troops were exhausted. Hindenburg and Ludendorff decided that the only course open to them was to yield ground bit by bit and defend every yard in the hope that British losses and German political manoeuvres would save them from defeat. At 1 p.m. on 1 October, Ludendorff telephoned Major von der Bussche, his liaison officer with the Reichstag, telling him to inform Prince Max in the presence of the Vice-Chancellor and the Foreign Minister that:

'If before 7–8 p.m. this evening assurance is given that Prince Max of Baden will form a government, I agree to postponement of the demand for an armistice until tomorrow morning. Should, on the other hand, the formation of the Government be in any way doubtful, I maintain that the issue of the declaration to the foreign governments is required this very night.'

Ludendorff had not only lost his head but forgotten his manners as well.

Accordingly, next morning at 9 a.m. Major von der Bussche gave the Reichstag party leaders an account of the situation and told them 'the war is lost'. For Prince Max of Baden the Chancellorship was indeed a barren inheritance. In Macedonia, the Allied Armies under Franchet d'Espéry had just broken the Balkan front and the Bulgarians had asked for a suspension of hostilities. A week previously Allenby had finally defeated the Turks at Megiddo and was about to enter Damascus. The Navy had failed to keep its promise to prevent the arrival of American troops in Europe. At home there was widespread discontent amongst the workers and real hunger within the country as a result of the Allied naval blockade. Major von der Bussche went on to say that every twenty-four hours delay only made the situation more desperate.

Meanwhile the 9th Corps, the Australian Corps and the Third Corps continued their merciless pressure through the last remnants of the Hindenburg Line and now approached the Beaurevoir Line (or Hindenburg Reserve System) further east. Next morning, the 3rd, Rawlinson launched the 9th Corps, the Australian Corps and the 13th Corps into a final grand attack supported by every gun, tank and aeroplane he could bring to bear: three further days of desperate fighting lay ahead. Slowly but remorselessly the British widened the breach they had created on 29 September. The Germans fought on with the courage of despair, launching no less than 13 counter-attacks. The villages of Séquehart, Montbrehain, Le Catelet and parts of Beaurevoir were taken, only to be lost and then regained. Altogether the Germans launched no less than 20 different divisions into the cauldron. On 5 October the Australians finally threw the Germans out of Montbrehain, six miles east of Bellicourt, and handed it over to the American 2nd Corps, now rested and reorganised. This was their last and by no means least glorious battle. Eleven Australian battalions, whose average fighting strength was 260 rifles, had been engaged in the fighting; their casualties were less than 1,000. One of their German officer prisoners paid them a compliment which they appreciated far more than from anyone else: 'You Australians are all bluff; you attack with practically no men and are on top of us before we know where we are.' Since 8 August they had been almost continuously in action. They had fought their way forward for 37 miles, liberated 116 villages and towns, captured 610 officers and over 22,000 soldiers from 30 different divisions and 332 guns. By the evening of 5 October the whole of the main Hindenburg position had been lost and a wide gap driven through the Beaurevoir Line. The Fourth Army was at last out in open country bearing few traces of war: there were no prepared lines of defence ahead. The Germans had sustained a great defeat. Now that the Hindenburg defences had gone they had no option but to withdraw all their forces facing the British Third, First and Fifth Armies. About Reims their Armies were already falling back; in Flanders withdrawal had already started.

Only continued resistance to the British Fourth, Third, First and Fifth Armies could save them from irreparable disaster.

On this day, President Woodrow Wilson received a telegram via the Swiss Government: it read:

> 'The German Government requests the President of the United States to take in hand the restoration of peace, acquaint all belligerent states of this request, and invite them to send plenipotentiaries for the purpose of opening negotiations. It accepts the programme set forth by the President of the United States in his message to Congress on January 8th and in his later addresses, especially the speech of September 27th, as a basis for peace negotiations. With a view to avoiding further bloodshed, the German Government requests the immediate conclusion of an Armistice on land and water and in the air.
>
> Max, Prince von Baden
Imperial Chancellor.'

Thus the ultimate control of the destinies of the peoples of Europe passed out of the hands of the generals into those of the politicians. Meanwhile, in mud and rain as the days grew shorter and the nights longer and colder the soldiers fought on.

THE BRITISH ADVANCE TO VICTORY
8 AUGUST – 11 NOVEMBER

0   5   10
Miles

N

NORTH SEA

BELGIAN ARMY

OSTEND
BRUGES
GHENT
ANTWERP
Nieuport
DUNKIRK
Dixmude
Schelde
Lys
Audenarde
Grammont
Ath
Ypres
TOURCOING
ROUBAIX
Tournai
Hazebrouck
Armentières
LILLE
Merville
Lys
Mons
Binche
Béthune
Orchies
Scarpe
Condé
Sambre
Lens
Douai
Sensée
Bavai
Maubeuge
Arras
Schelde
Valenciennes
Selle
Sivry
Cambrai
Wassigny
Avesnes
Bapaume
Landrecies
Albert
Bray
Somme
Péronne
Oise
Guise
St.Quentin
AMIENS

BRITISH ARMIES

② ⑤ ① ③ ④

FRENCH FIRST ARMY

▲▲▲ GERMAN DEFENCE LINES
① Drocourt-Quéant.
② Hindenburg.
③ Beaurevoir.

= = British sector boundaries.
x x British army boundaries.
•••• Starting line 5 August.
▪▪▪ Starting line 8 August.
Starting line 31 August.
▪•▪• Starting line 27-29 Sept.
▲▲▲ Starting line 14 October.
Starting line 17-20 October.
Starting line 4-8 November.
Armistice line 11 November.
⊥⊥⊥ Canals.

—ARTHUR BANKS—

The Politicians Take Charge

Saying, Peace, Peace; when there is no Peace.
Jeremiah 6, 14

A fortnight previously Allenby, after his victory at Megiddo in Palestine, had brought off an annihilating pursuit of the Turkish Armies as decisive as Napoleon's after Jena. It is relevant therefore to ask why Haig and Rawlinson failed to exploit the breaking of the Hindenburg Line and why the Germans were now able to stage a controlled withdrawal of nine miles to the line of the Selle and later to evade destruction as they fell back.

These huge muscle-bound armies on the Western Front, made possible by the development of railways, were in many respects almost as immobile as those of Marlborough and Louis XIV. Each of the 200 and more Allied divisions demanded at least a standard train a day to carry its supplies: a high proportion of this was forage for the animals. Furthermore, a division normally consumed a train load of artillery ammunition every day. Each set-piece battle demanded hundreds of additional train loads of shells. As the Germans fell back they completely wrecked the railways, blowing up the culverts and bridges and smashing the turntables and workshops. They thus confronted the Allied transportation engineers with a vast reconstruction problem across a devastated area already some 30 miles wide. Rawlinson was advised by his experts that it would be the end of October before a general advance could be considered, and that if the Germans continued to destroy the rail system, there was little likelihood of reaching the German frontier before February. So effective too had the destruction of the roads been that it was only with the greatest difficulty and delay that the heavy artillery could be brought forward and the limited resources in motor transport used to meet the deficiencies of the railways. In Flanders, east of Ypres, the roads had completely collapsed in a sea of mud and virtually immobilised the northern armies after their capture of the Passchendaele Ridge.

Although the Germans had been thrown out of the Hindenburg Line, they continued, admittedly with diminishing enthusiasm, to fight on with courage and skill. The British still had 30 miles to go to reach the vital lateral railway. Strong German rear-guards, consisting primarily of machine gunners supported by long-range artillery, forced them to fight for the crossing of every stream and defile. In the past month the British had lost over 140,000 men: many units therefore needed time to absorb replacements into their ranks and to enable fresh junior leaders to find their feet. Furthermore, the Germans having destroyed all the houses on their way back, it was difficult to provide troops in reserve with cover from the weather. The strain, therefore, on the administrative services to find the means to keep the troops fighting fit was great.

British hopes that the other prong of the Allied offensive in the Argonne and on the Meuse would draw large numbers of German reserves away from them had not been realised. The French, having induced the British and Americans to attack each side of the neck of the great German salient, had shown themselves quite happy to offer their congratulations and to await developments which would enable them in due course to go forward with the minimum loss. The Americans temporarily were stalled in front of the Kriemhilde Position in what, without question apart from Ypres, was the most difficult sector of the whole front. The dominating features of Romagne and Cunel commanded all the approaches: the heights of the Meuse completely overlooked the west bank. The roads had virtually disintegrated and it was only with the greatest difficulty that supplies could be got forward. The weather now broke. As a result, the troops were not only exposed to almost continuous shell and machine-gun fire but soaked to the skin as well and often without hot food and drink for days. Pershing described the period, 1–11 October, as involving the heaviest strain he and his Army had to endure in the whole campaign. Nevertheless, when requested by Foch to renew the offensive on 4 October, he loyally obeyed. There now followed some of the most confused, bitter and costly close-quarter fighting of the war in the dense woods and deep ravines of the Argonne Forest and around the sinister Heights of Cunel and Romagne. Not until 10 October were the last traces of resistance in the forest eliminated. For a whole week, east of the Meuse, the French 17th Corps and the 33rd Division under Pershing's command struggled with Germans ready to die where they stood in positions which gave them every advantage. Here the 33rd Division, despite 2,000 gas casualties, fought a see-saw battle for nearly a month until completely exhausted.

Thus by the second week of October, with the Americans held up at the Kriemhilde Stellung and the British, stationary for the moment on the Selle, Ludendorff's spirits revived. He now proposed gradually to shorten his front, cut down the length of his lines of communication and thus reduce the Allies' advance to a snail's pace by systematically devastating what was, after all, not German territory. By these means he hoped to get the Allies, faced by the prospect of another winter of war, to agree to a negotiated peace on terms not unsatisfactory to Germany. In this optimistic frame of mind he set off to attend the Council of War held between OHL and the War Cabinet on 17 October to consider the reply to be sent to President Wilson's second note. This told them bluntly that if they wanted an armistice they would have to deal with the Allied military authorities and that, in any case, he was not prepared to deal with individuals who had sanctioned atrocities such as the sinking of the Irish Mail Boat on 10 October, with the loss of a large number of women and children. Unrestricted submarine warfare must stop at once. Before deciding on their reply the Council obviously needed a clear assessment of the military situation. Here they found the man who all his life had seemed to be a plain, dedicated soldier strangely equivocal. 'War,' he patronisingly informed them with the pompous omniscience of the expert, 'is not like an arithmetical sum. In war there are many probabilities and improbabilities—in war you need "Soldiers' Luck"; perhaps Germany will still enjoy "Soldiers' Luck" once more.' Sensing lack of conviction on the part of the rest of the Council, Ludendorff threatened to resign if other generals were asked to express their opinion and denied accusations that the Army was guilty of looting and wanton destruction. Finally he concluded by saying that the situation had taken a turn for the better and that, provided he received reinforcements and Allied pressure declined, the front could hold out till the spring. The Conference dispersed without reaching a decision and Ludendorff set off on his return journey. On arrival at OHL at Spa he was greeted with the news that during the day the British Fourth Army immediately south of Le Cateau with the 9th Corps on the right, the 2nd American Corps in the centre and the 13th Corps on the left, had forced the passage of the Selle, broken deeply into the Herman Stellung and established itself on the broad ridge which separates the valleys of the Selle and the Sambre and had captured Le Cateau. So much for 'Soldiers' Luck'.

Next morning Prince Max received a letter direct from Crown Prince Rupprecht commanding the Northern Army Group reporting with emphasis a rapid decline in his soldiers' morale and stressing the need for speed in securing an armistice 'before the enemy breaks through into Germany'. Princes do not usually tell each other lies. Prince Max therefore, despite further pressure from Ludendorff not to abandon submarine warfare, decided to agree to President Wilson's terms and sent a note to that effect. Ludendorff would linger on at OHL for a few more days but his power and prestige were at an end. Meanwhile the British advance continued: by the 19th the Fourth Army was six miles beyond the Selle, on a front of seven miles, had captured 5,000 prisoners and 70 guns and was pressing forward.

On the Argonne front there was no let up in the bitter ding-dong battle: the Kriemhilde Line was the veritable corner-stone of the Antwerp–Meuse Position: in no circumstances could the Germans afford to let it go. On 14 October, in conformity with the French Fourth Army, Pershing staged what was to be his final operation as an Army Commander against the Kriemhilde Stellung near Romagne. Here the key to the position was a ridge, shaped like a crescent, called the Côte Dame Marie which had so far resisted all efforts by the 32nd Division, now diluted by partially trained reinforcements, to take it. When once more a desperate assault by all three regiments seemed to be getting nowhere, Captain Edward B. Strom and a patrol of seven men managed to work their way up a steep slope to a position only

150 yards away from the guns holding up the division. He and his men then proceeded to bombard them with rifle grenades with deadly effect; finally they rushed forward and captured no less than ten machine guns from the survivors of the crews. His battalion then quickly seized the ridge. The 5th and 42nd Divisions on this and the following day were less fortunate but finally, on the 16th, MacArthur's brigade carried the Côte de Chatillon in style. With the capture of these two ridges the objectives prescribed for 26 September had at last been gained.

Pershing now had over two million men in France. He therefore decided that the time had come for him to hand over command of the First Army to his obvious successor, Liggett, and to activate a Second American Army under Bullard at St Mihiel, thus raising his own status to that of an Army Group Commander and Commander-in-Chief. For three weeks the First Army had been fighting without respite in unspeakable conditions and had paid dearly with over 100,000 casualties for its advance of ten miles. Liggett, despite pressure originating from Foch to continue the all-out attack, decided that there must now be a pause to enable his Army to rest, re-organise, re-group and plan for the next offensive. Within the next fortnight this remarkable man, by methods not dissimilar to those of Montgomery before the battle of Alam Halfa, transformed what was a brave but somewhat baffled army into an efficient war-winning machine. At his headquarters Lieutenant-Colonel George C. Marshall became Chief of Operations. War-worn divisions were pulled out of the line; the gaps in the ranks were filled; men who had lost their units were returned to them and in some cases punished. Arrangements for rounding up stragglers in future were tightened up. Drastic steps were taken to improve cooperation between the infantry and the artillery: flying officers were given a spell of duty with the infantry in the front line to enable them to grasp the needs in the matter of air support of the men on the ground. The lessons of the recent fighting were widely publicised. In no uncertain terms Liggett spared no effort to ensure that junior officers realised their personal responsibility for the enforcement of discipline and for seeing that their men were properly fed. Meanwhile planning for the final drive to Mézières went on.

North of Le Cateau under relentless pressure from the five British, Belgian and French Sixth Armies the whole line was now wavering back like a vast receding tide leaving behind it the wreckage of a storm. On the 19th, Foch on a note of triumph, issued his last directive: the King of the Belgians' Army Group which included the British Second Army, were to force the lines of the Scheldt and the Dendre and thrust towards Brussels; the British Armies would continue to push back the Germans on their front against the Ardennes barrier and cut their main lateral railway about Aulnoye and Maubeuge. They were also to do all they could to help the King of the Belgians' Army Group to get over the Scheldt and the Dendre; the French First and Tenth Armies were to operate in the general direction of Givet on the Meuse south of Namur whilst the French Fifth and Fourth Armies and the American First Army continued their offensive towards Mézières and Sedan.

On 28 October, Foch called a conference of Commanders-in-Chief at Senlis to settle the terms of the armistice to be offered to the Germans. The Fourteen Points were no business of theirs. In fact, when they were mentioned, a newspaper had to be produced to find out what they were; Pétain and Haig had no instructions from their governments on the subject. Opening the proceedings Foch said that in his opinion the overriding consideration was they should make it impossible for the Germans to resume hostilities. Haig then spoke; he said that the Germans were still capable of withdrawing to a shorter front and of putting up an effective resistance for several months; British and French manpower resources were diminishing; he therefore recommended that the Allies should be satisfied with the complete evacuation of France and Belgium and the occupation of Alsace and Lorraine and the fortresses of Metz and Strasbourg. If he had to fight them again, he said, he would prefer to do so on the Old Frontier rather than on the Rhine. On the whole he was in favour of moderation. Pétain pressed for much harsher terms: the Germans must immediately withdraw their armies to the east bank of the Rhine on a strict schedule which would compel them to abandon the greater part of their equipment. Substantial Allied bridgeheads must be established across the Rhine at Mainz, Coblence and Cologne.

Of the four commanders present Pershing showed himself to be the most ruthless and uncompromising, stating in unequivocal terms his opinion that the Germans must be called upon to lay down their arms where they stood. He added that the military situation was far more favourable to the Allies than Haig seemed to think and that the American Army, now two million strong, was only just getting into its stride. When it did the Germans would be inevitably doomed. In any case, all U-boats and U-boat bases must be surrendered and free passage across the seas ensured: all French and Belgian rolling stock must be returned. After further discussion Foch closed the conference, all concerned having agreed to submit their proposals to him in writing. So strongly did Pershing feel with regard to the terms which should be exacted from the Germans that he now stepped right out of his own province as a Commander-in-Chief into the sphere of politics and, without permission from President Woodrow Wilson, told the Allied Supreme War Council formally in writing that the Allies had an advantage of nearly 40 per cent in men and guns, and that the Germans were already beaten. He went on to assert that an armistice would revivify their spirits and 'would deprive the Allies of the full measure of victory by failing to press their present advantage to its complete military end'. He doubted the sincerity of the German leaders and was convinced that they would exploit any cessation of hostilities short of capitulation to their own ends. He concluded: 'Finally, I believe that complete victory can only be obtained by continuing the war until we force unconditional surrender from Germany.' Reprehensible though this direct approach to the Allied Supreme War Council may have been from the point of view of protocol, it can be claimed more than half-a-century later that, if Pershing's advice had been taken, the German Armies would never have been allowed to march home unmolested in formed bodies with drums playing and carrying their side arms. Hitler and his followers would never have been able to seize power on the plea that the Army had been stabbed in the back by traitors. This admittedly is speculation but it can be firmly said that events in the next fifty years would have taken a different course and that course could not possibly have been worse than what actually happened.

Despite continual pressure from Foch to attack regardless of circumstances, Pershing, when he had handed over the First Army to Liggett, had the wisdom and generosity to let him fight the Meuse–Argonne Battle in his own way. Liggett, like

Montgomery before Alamein, was determined to resume the full scale offensive when he was ready and not before. To describe the last fortnight of October, however, on the Meuse–Argonne front while he was preparing for the final advance and pursuit as a lull, would be an understatement. Not for one moment were the Germans allowed any rest. About Grand Pré two ridges, the Bois de Bourgogne and the Bois des Loges, dominated the plateau and would have to be taken before the French Fourth Army could advance. To get them cost the 78th Division 4,000 casualties; nevertheless after four days' intensive fighting they were taken. On the rest of the front the Germans, though amazed at the Americans' lack of concern for heavy losses, showed few signs of any inclination to abandon the struggle and fought on with all their normal efficiency, turning the fields, hills and woods near Cunel into veritable death-traps. Nevertheless, these last days of October were a terrible time for them too, their casualties rising to 25,000 in less than a fortnight. They could not hope to continue the struggle on these terms much longer.

Behind the screen of this battle of attrition, Liggett went ahead with his preparations for the final attack now fixed in agreement with Gouraud for 1 November. Once again the 5th Corps under Summerall with the 1st Corps on its left and the 3rd Corps on its right would make the main effort with seven veteran divisions to seize the Barricourt Heights five miles ahead and thus unpin not only the American front but that of the whole French Fourth Army as well. The build-up of supplies and ammunition and the engineer preparations were impressive. All troops were thoroughly briefed: all available air support was concentrated on the 5th Corps front. Summerall got an additional 608 guns to blast his way through. For days before the attack 14-inch naval guns under Rear-Admiral Plunkett hurled 1,400 huge shells into the German rear areas. Then on 28 October the artillery shelled the German battery and reserve positions with over 40 tons of gas shells. When therefore in the cold and foggy dawn of 1 November the assault battalions of Marines and infantry of the 5th Corps advanced to the attack they found the resistance less than anticipated. By nightfall they had fought their way forward with such speed that they completely swamped four German divisions, two of which were of high quality, and

o

seized the heights of Barricourt. The other two corps took all their objectives. Next day the advance continued with ever-increasing momentum enabling the French Fourth Army too, to get on the move. The Germans were now in full retreat towards the Meuse. On 6 November the 1st and 42nd Divisions carried the heights overlooking Sedan. Their guns now commanded the vital lateral railway. Seven miles up stream the Fifth Division now had a substantial bridgehead across the river at Brieulles. Liggett paused for the moment to prepare for a further advance on Montmédy and into the heart of the Rhineland.

On the British front all their five armies were now pressing forward over broken-down roads in vile weather. In the north the Germans managed to hold on to the line of the Scheldt until 8 November: they then fell back allowing the Northern Army Group an unimpeded crossing. On the 1st the British First and Third Armies had forced the line of the Rhonelle and captured Valenciennes. Three days later, the Fourth and Third Armies in heavy mist fought their final full dress battle on the Sambre. Here the 1st, 32nd and 25th Divisions were at the top of their form establishing three out of four bridgeheads over the 70-foot obstacle within less than three hours. The crossing at Catillon was made memorable by the personal courage and example of a subaltern of the Irish Guards aged 23, named Marshall in command as a Lieutenant-Colonel of the 16th Lancashire Fusiliers. When enemy artillery fire broke down the bridge, he stood on the bank directing the repairs and as soon as they were done led his men across and was killed at their head. He had been wounded ten times before. Three other vcs were won at the crossing of the Sambre on this day. Once across, the 9th and 13th Corps found the going easier although the German rearguards continued to fight on with all their normal malice and obstinacy. Nevertheless prisoners, including officers, were now being taken in a drunken condition: all expressed themselves as glad to get out of the war. On the whole demolitions and the collapse of the roads now slowed down the advance more than the Germans. Half-starved civilians now began to emerge from their cellars in a state of great excitement. Some offered brandy: one old lady hung a garland of chrysanthemums round an embarrassed colonel's neck. It was common knowledge that OHL on 6 November had ordered a general withdrawal to the line Antwerp–Namur–

River Meuse–Sedan. To all it seemed evident that the cease-fire order would come any time now.

In fact, on the very day when the British had forced the line of the Sambre, revolution had broken out in Germany. Disillusion, a sense of betrayal by their leaders, and hunger took charge. The Navy, when ordered to put to sea and go to the bottom in one final glorious battle with the British, not unwisely mutinied. Bulgaria, Turkey and Austria had already negotiated armistices with the Allies. Ludendorff, having published without the Kaiser's permission an order of the day declaring an armistice unacceptable, had offered his resignation and departed. Other generals, when consulted, advised that the military situation was hopeless. Gröner, Ludendorff's successor, was a transportation expert, a mere juggler with timetables and statistics, not a strategist. To Prince Max and Hindenburg, convinced that there was a real threat of revolution, an armistice seemed the only course open. Accordingly, a German delegation headed by Herr Erzberger left Berlin on 6 November and crossed the front line on the night of 7th–8th. They were sent on at once by special train to Foch's Advanced Headquarters at Senlis. Here at 11 a.m. they were handed the terms of the armistice and given seventy-two hours to make up their minds. At 2 p.m. on 9 November, Germany was proclaimed a republic: Prince Max handed over the Chancellorship to Herr Ebert: the Kaiser, on Hindenburg's advice, left Spa for Holland early on the 10th. In the small hours of the 11th the German delegation received orders from Berlin to accept the Allies' conditions for an armistice.

Throughout the 10th every road in north-east France and western Flanders had been packed with dense columns of men and horses all marching eastwards in the rain. From Bruges to St Mihiel the German Armies were in retreat. When night closed in about 5 p.m. the Belgians had reached the line of the Ghent Canal; on their right the French Sixth Army and the British Second Army were over the Scheldt and pushing on to the Dendre. The British Fifth Army and the Cavalry Corps were 12 miles east of Tournai; the British First Army was once more back in Mons where it had fought its first battle of the war in 1914; the Third Army was eight miles east of Maubeuge and over the frontier into Belgium hot on the heels of the retreating enemy. Further south the advance guard of the British Fourth Army, consisting of one cavalry brigade and one infantry brigade, had pressed hard all day against enemy rear-guards. On their right the French First, Third and Fifth Armies prolonged the advancing Allied line as far as Mézières. The American First Army were now across the Upper Meuse as far as Mouzon and thence on the west bank of the river to Sedan; the heights of the Meuse too were in American hands. The threat to Verdun since 1914 was at an end. In the Woeuvre, Bullard had set the Second Army in motion towards the Briey iron basin. At Pershing's headquarters planning was far advanced for a grand Franco-American Offensive to be delivered on the 14th in the direction of Metz and Sarrebourg. The American Army in France had now passed the two million mark: they had tasted victory and their morale was high. In fact only six German divisions, three of them Land Landwehr, stood in the way. What the result would be was a foregone conclusion. To Pershing this was not the moment to forget the tradition of Yorktown and Appomattox: when the American Army went to war it saw the grim business through to a decisive and unequivocal end. In the event it would be another twenty-seven years before Bradley, Hodges and Patton would go that way.

At 5.5. a.m. on 11 November, in Foch's headquarters train in the Compiègne Forest, near Rethondes, Herr Erzberger and the rest of the German delegation put their signatures to the Armistice agreement. Neither Haig nor Pershing was there. The news reached the headquarters of the five British Armies just as day was breaking:

'Hostilities will cease at 11.00 hours today, November 11th. Troops will stand fast on the line reached at that hour which will be reported by wire to Advance GHQ. Defensive precautions will be maintained. There will be no intercourse of any description with the enemy until the receipt of instructions from GHQ. Further instructions follow.'

It soon became known throughout the Allied Armies that although the Germans were to surrender the greater part of their war equipment and the whole of their fleet, they would nonetheless be allowed to march home in formed bodies and carrying their personal arms. When Mangin heard this he burst into tears:

'No! No! No! We must go right into the heart of Germany. The Armistice should be signed there. The Germans will not admit that they are beaten. You do not finish wars like this . . . and who will see that the conditions are enforced? The Allies? A coalition has never survived the danger which has created it. It is a fatal error and France will pay for it!'

On a far lower level the adjutant of the battalion whose impressions of the front line on New Year's Day 1918 are recorded on the first page of this book, spent the night of 10–11 November on the floor of a miner's cottage in a squalid suburb of Mons. They had arrived after dark at the end of a long day spent marching in the rain. Hardly a man remained who had been present on 1 January. The adjutant himself had been away for eleven weeks after being wounded on the Somme in April. Two signallers with the field telephone to Brigade Headquarters were close by. Every inch of floor space held a man snoring to high heaven. At 7.30 a.m. they were due to pass through the outposts half-a-mile or so down the road. About 6 a.m. one of the signallers woke him up and handed him a message from Brigade Headquarters which he read by the light of his electric torch. It read: 'No move till further orders. Acknowledge.' So that was it! For several days there had been rumours that the war was coming to an end. Automatically he reached for his message pad and wrote on it, 'Stand fast till further orders', called for a runner and handing it to him told him to take it to the four companies and the transport officer. There was no point in waking the commanding officer: he might as well sleep on till Reveillé at half-past six. Men soon began to stir all around him. There was a clatter of steel-shod boots and mess tins and the rattle of arms and equipment. An iron-tyred limber rumbled over the cobblestones of the road outside. Men lumbered in with great black dixies of dark brown tea; a quartermaster-sergeant handed out biscuits, tins of jam one between three and corned beef one between two. The adjutant's batman brought him a canvas bucket of water from the pump outside: he washed and shaved. About 9 a.m. another message arrived. This read: 'Hostilities will cease at 11.00 on November 11th aaa Troops will stand fast on line reached at that hour which will be reported aaa Defensive precautions will be maintained aaa There will be no intercourse of any description with the enemy.' Once again the adjutant took his message pad and wrote: 'To all Companies. Hostilities will cease at 1100 today. Acknowledge hereon.' It was timed 0904. He then handed it to a runner. Half-an-hour later it was back with all the company commanders' signatures on it. The officer commanding D Company had added to his 'Acknowledged with thanks'. This morning the brigadier who was in the habit of calling every day soon after dawn was late. The worse things were as a general rule, the more cheerful he always seemed to be. When he did turn up he was unsmiling. 'They've been allowed to get away with it,' he said, 'we haven't finished the job.' The adjutant too had an uncomfortable feeling that it would all have to be done all over again. The Boche were like rhubarb; cover up a plant with concrete and it would in the end break through. His commanding officers' main worry seemed to be the thought that he would soon lose his acting rank of lieutenant-colonel and revert to captain. As for the troops, there was no cheering or demonstration of emotion. When 11 a.m. approached, most of them, grateful for the chance to shelter from the rain and get off their feet for a bit, were fast asleep. They had earned a rest: since 8 August they and their like in the five British Armies had taken 188,700 prisoners and 2,840 guns.

On the Fourth Army front, at two minutes to eleven, a machine gun, about 200 yards from the leading British troops, fired off a complete belt without a pause. A single machine-gunner was then seen to stand up beside his weapon, take off his helmet, bow, and turning about walk slowly to the rear.

That night the officer of a British battalion responsible for keeping up the War Diary made the entry for the day:

'November 11th—Armistice with Germany commenced.
Weather: fairly heavy rain.'

Bibliography

Ash, B. *The Lost Dictator* Cassell 1968
Balland, Cdt. Article in *Revue D'Infanterie* (October 1935)
    Charles Lavauzelle et Cie, Paris 1935
Barclay, C. *Armistice* J. M. Dent and Sons 1968
Barnett, C. *Britain and Her Army* Allen Lane 1970
    The Sword Bearers Eyre & Spottiswoode 1963
Boraston, J. H *The Eighth Division in War 1914/18* Medici
    Society 1926
Brogan, Sir D. *The Development of Modern France* Hamish
    Hamilton 1967
Bugnet, C. *Mangin* Plon, Paris 1934
Carrington, C. *Soldier from the Wars Returning* Hutchinson
    1965
Churchill, Sir W. *The World Crisis* Thornton & Butterworth
    1923
Coffman, E. M. *The War to End all Wars* Oxford University
    Press, New York 1968
Connell, J. *Wavell—Scholar and Soldier* Collins 1964
Cooper, D. *Haig* Faber & Faber 1935
Cutlack, F. M. (Editor) *War Letters of Genral Monash* Angus
    & Robertson 1935
Edmonds, J. E. *Military Operations in France and Belgium, 1918*
    (Five volumes) Macmillan & Co. 1935 et seq.
Esposito, V. J. *The West Point Atlas of American Wars* Praeger
    1957

Falls, C. *The First World War* Longmans 1960

Feuchtwanger, E. J. *Prussia: Myth and Reality* Oswald Wolff 1970

Fox, Sir F. ('GSO') *G.H.Q.* Philip Allan and Co. 1920

Fuller, J. F. C. *Memoirs of an Unconventional Soldier* Ivor Nicholson and Watson 1936
 The Decisive Battles of the Western World Eyre & Spottiswoode 1957

Gibbs, Sir P. *The War Dispatches* Anthony Gibb & Phillips 1964

Gilbert, M. *First War Atlas* Weidenfeld & Nicolson 1970

Goodspeed, D. J. *The Road Past Vimy* Macmillan of Canada 1970

Haig, Sir D. *The Private Papers 1914/1919* (Ed. R. Blake) Eyre & Spottiswoode 1952

Jones, H. A. *The War in the Air* (Vol. VI) OUP 1937

Liddell Hart, Sir B. *Foch* Eyre & Spottiswoode 1931
 The War in Outline Faber 1936
 The Tanks Cassell 1959
 Memoirs (Vol. I) Cassell 1965
 Strategy Praeger 1954

Long, G. *MacArthur as Military Commander* Batsford/Van Norstrand 1969

Mackesy, K. (with John H. Batchelor) *A History of the Armoured Fighting Vehicle* Ballantine Books Inc. 1971

Maurice, Sir F. *The Life of General Lord Rawlinson of Trent* Cassell 1928
 The Last Four Months Cassell 1919

Monash, Sir J. *The Australian Victories in France in 1918* Hutchinson 1936 (also Angus & Robertson)

Montgomery, Sir A. *The Story of the Fourth Army* Hodder & Stoughton 1926

Montgomery of Alamein *Memoirs* Collins 1958
 A History of Warfare Collins 1968

Moore, W. *See How they Ran—the British Retreat of 1918* Lee Cooper 1970

Pershing, J. J. *My Experiences in the World War* Hodder & Stoughton 1931

Pitt, B. *1918—The Last Act* Cassell 1962

Repington, C. *The First World War 1914/18* (Vol. II) Constable 1920

Ryan, S. *Pétain the Soldier* Barnes 1969
Sixsmith, E. *British Generalship in the Twentieth Century* Arms and Armour Press 1969
Strong, Sir K. *Men of Intelligence* Cassel-Giniger 1970
Terraine, J. *Douglas Haig: the Educated Soldier* Hutchinson 1963
    Impacts of War 1914 and 1918 Article in *History Today* (January 1966) Hutchinson 1970
Wavell, A. *The Good Soldier* Macmillan 1948
    Les Armées Francaises dans La Grande Guerre (Tome VII) Imprimerie Nationale 1923
    Révue D'Infanterie (Janvier 1938) Charles Lavauzelle et Cie, Paris 1923
Young, P. (with J. P. Lawford) *History of the British Army* Arthur Barker 1970
Privately printed Histories of the East Lancashire and Northamptonshire Regiments
Contemporary private letters and other records
Army Quarterly Index 1920/70, Clowes 1970

Index

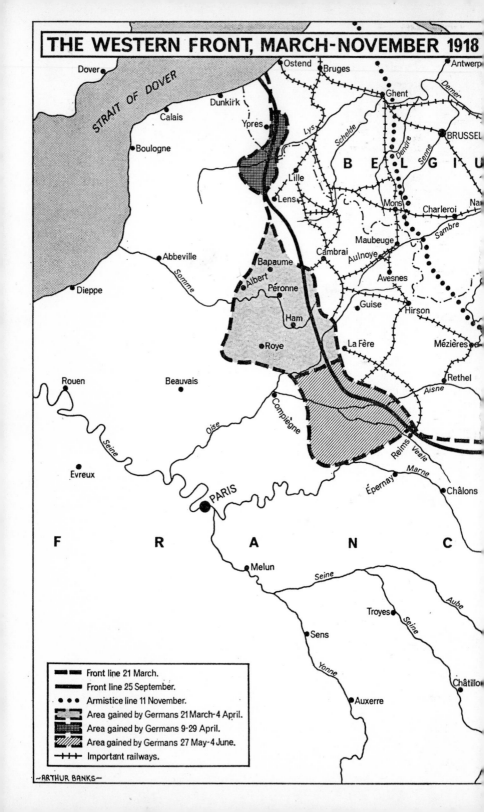

THE WESTERN FRONT, MARCH-NOVEMBER 1918

Dover

STRAIT OF DOVER

Calais

Boulogne

Dunkirk

Ypres

Lille

Lens

Ostend

Bruges

Ghent

Antwerp

Demer

BRUSSEL

B E L G I U

Schelde

Lys

Dendre

Senne

Mons

Charleroi

Nar

Abbeville

Dieppe

Somme

Bapaume

Albert

Péronne

Ham

Roye

Cambrai

Aulnoye

Avesnes

Guise

La Fère

Hirson

Mézières

Maubeuge

Sambre

Rouen

Beauvais

Oise

Compiègne

Seine

Evreux

PARIS

Reims

Aisne

Rethel

Vesle

Épernay

Marne

Châlons

F R A N C

Melun

Seine

Troyes

Sens

Seine

Aube

Yonne

Auxerre

Châtillo

Legend:
- — — — Front line 21 March.
- ——— Front line 25 September.
- • • • Armistice line 11 November.
- Area gained by Germans 21 March-4 April.
- Area gained by Germans 9-29 April.
- Area gained by Germans 27 May-4 June.
- +++ Important railways.

~ARTHUR BANKS~